INFORMATION
and INFORMATION
SYSTEMS

INFORMATION and ____ INFORMATION ____ SYSTEMS

MICHAEL BUCKLAND

PRAEGER

New York
Westport, Connecticut
London

Library of Congress Cataloging-in-Publication Data

Buckland, Michael Keeble.
    Information and information systems / Michael Buckland.
        p. cm.
    Includes bibliographical references and index.
    ISBN 0–275–93851–4 (alk. paper)
    1. Information storage and retrieval systems.   2. Information
technology—Social aspects.   3. Information retrieval.
    4. Libraries—Automation.   I. Title.
    Z699.B83   1991b
    025.04—dc20   90–47541

British Library Cataloguing in Publication Data is available.

A hardcover edition of *Information and Information Systems* is available from
Greenwood Press (New Directions in Information Management, Number 25;
ISBN 0–313–27463–0)

Library of Congress Catalog Card Number: 90–47541
ISBN: 0–275–93851–4

First published in 1991

Praeger Publishers, One Madison Avenue, New York, NY   10010
An imprint of Greenwood Publishing Group, Inc.

Printed in the United States of America

The paper used in this book complies with the
Permanent Paper Standard issued by the National
Information Standards Organization (Z39.48–1984).

10   9   8   7   6   5   4

Contents

Figures and Tables

FIGURES

TABLES

Preface

This book is intended as a general introduction to information systems for anybody whose interests extend beyond the techniques and technology. It is not a manual of practical techniques, nor is it another survey of information technology. It is intended for students and professionals who are interested in the nature of information systems and in how information systems are related to their social context.

One might have thought that, for so important a field, a general introduction would be easily written and redundant. This is not the case. Each different type of information system (online databases, libraries, etc.) has a massive and largely separate literature. Attention is almost always limited to one type of information system, is restricted by technology, usually to computer-based information systems, or is focused on one function, such as retrieval, disregarding the broader context. What is published is overwhelmingly specialized, technical, "how-to" writing with localized terminology and definitions. Writings on theory are usually very narrowly focused on logic, probability, and physical signals. This diversity has been compounded by confusion arising from inadequate recognition that the word *information* is used by different people to denote different things.

Considering the important and pervasive role of information systems in modern society, it is rather surprising how few systematic general introductions to this field have appeared since Paul Otlet's monumental *Traité de documentation* (1934), now little known and rarely read. Good ecumenical approaches are hard to find. Similarly, there has been relatively little interest in constructive comparative study of information systems. Rogalla von Bieberstein's historical and analytical *Archiv, Bibliothek und Museum als Dokumentationsbereiche: Einheit und gegenseitige Abgrenzung* (1975) is one useful example.

The chronic looseness of terminology concerning information and information systems creates an obligation to be explicit about one's own use of terms. Only three different meanings of the term *information* will be used, and I hope that the intended meaning will be clear whenever the distinctions are significant. This book is concerned with information systems: systems that provide information services intended to result in human beings' becoming informed: archives, libraries, online databases, and so on. I exclude information systems that "inform" machines and also genetic and other biological mechanisms because such use of the word *information* seems metaphorical in these examples and less suitable than *control*.

This book originated in 1980 when I sought to clarify for my own benefit the nature of the affinity among different examples of retrieval-based information systems. I hoped to develop a comparative anatomy of species of information systems. The initial result, however, was a fairly detailed analysis of the anatomy of one species only, undertaken as a preliminary case study: *Library Services in Theory and Context* (1983; 2d ed. 1988). The broader, more ambitious goal reemerged in 1988 stimulated by sabbatical leave attached to the University of New South Wales and invigorated by the idea that museums ought to be included in the family of information systems. Museums are not normally viewed as information systems, but they select, collect, store, and retrieve items expected to be informative. They behave like information systems, but to include them in a treatise on such systems would be to challenge some basic orthodoxies of information science. In this and in other ways, I have tended to concentrate on exotic and complex examples because they seemed to me to be not only more interesting but also more useful for the purpose of developing robust ideas about the nature of information systems. Moving from the one species, libraries, to the whole family of species of information systems required me to think more than I had done previously about the basic concepts of information, document, and information processing.

Late in the preparation of the text, I found that some of my ideas and of my approach had been anticipated among the documentalists of continental Europe in the first half of this century, notably in Otlet's *Traité* and Suzanne Briet's *Qu'est-ce que la documentation?* (1951). The ignoring in modern English-language information studies of what had been, internationally, mainstream literature on information retrieval is a remarkable and unfortunate example of intellectual discontinuity.

There is a heavier dependence on examples drawn from library service than had been intended. In part this reflects my experience and the evolution of the book by way of an analysis of libraries. However, since libraries will be generally familiar for all readers, this emphasis may not matter much if the examples are in fact apt.

I am indebted in many directions, especially to Professor W. Boyd Rayward, his colleagues, and their students, and for institutional support, at the University of New South Wales; to Professor Rudolph Z. Domiaty and Frau Christine Stelzer at Graz University of Technology, Austria; to Dr. Doris Florian and the Forschungsgesellschaft Joanneum GesmbH, Graz; to the Austrian Fulbright Commission for a Fulbright Research Scholarship; to John Gathegi and Clifford

Lynch; and, most of all, for the institutional support, library services, and interactions with colleagues and students at the Berkeley campus of the University of California.

Readers expecting a technical how-to book will be disappointed since that is not what was intended. Others will be disappointed that their interests are inadequately or imperfectly addressed or that parts of the vast literatures pertinent to information systems have been neglected. This book is best seen as a fallible, tentative interpretation of the nature of information systems and their relationship to their context.

Part **I**

Introduction

Chapter 1

Information

THE AMBIGUITY OF "INFORMATION"

An exploration of *information* runs into immediate difficulties. Since the notion of information is meaningful only in relation to someone informed, to the reduction of ignorance and of uncertainty, it is ironic that the term *information* is itself ambiguous and used in different ways.[1]

Faced with this variety of meanings, we can at least take a pragmatic approach. We can survey the landscape and see whether one or more particular, distinctive uses of the term *information* seem helpful for our purposes. The definitions may not be fully satisfactory, the boundaries between these uses may be indistinct, and such an approach could not satisfy anyone determined to establish the one correct meaning of *information*. But if the principal useful concepts can be identified, sorted, characterized, and labeled, then some progress might be made. Using this approach, we identify three principal uses of the word *information*:

1. *Information-as-process*. What someone knows is changed when he or she is informed. In this sense, information is "the action of informing . . . ; communication of the knowledge or 'news' of some fact or occurrence; the action of telling or fact of being told of something" (*Oxford English Dictionary* [*OED*] 1989, 7:944).[2]

2. *Information-as-knowledge*. *Information* is also used to denote that which is imparted in information-as-process: the "knowledge communicated concerning some particular fact, subject, or event; that which one is apprised or told; intelligence, news" (*OED* 1989, 7:944). The notion of information as that which reduces uncertainty could be viewed as a special case of information-as-knowledge. Sometimes information increases uncertainty.

3. *Information-as-thing*. The term *information* is also used attributively for objects, such as data and documents, that are referred to as information because

they are regarded as being informative, as "having the quality of imparting knowledge or communicating information; instructive" (*OED* 1989, 7:946).

The key characteristic of knowledge and, therefore, of information-as-knowledge, is that it is intangible. One cannot touch it or measure it in any direct way. Knowledge, belief, and opinion are personal, subjective, and conceptual. Therefore, to communicate them, they have to be expressed, described, or represented in some physical way, as a mark, signal, text, or communication. Any such expression, description, or representation would be information-as-thing. We shall discuss implications of this below.

The distinction between knowledge in the pure sense—denoting what some individual actually knows—and the extended or metaphorical use of knowledge—as in recorded knowledge, knowledge engineering, and knowledge base, to denote a physical representation of what some individual may have known—is of central importance in information studies. Recorded knowledge is knowledge in much the same way that a written biography is a life. The distinction between something, often something intangible, and representations is an essential feature of the study of information and information systems. Unfortunately, careless failure to remember the difference between a word and what it is used to represent is common in the literature and accounts for major problems in the study of information systems (Blair 1990; Swanson 1988).

Some theorists have objected to the attributive use of the term *information* to denote a thing in the third sense noted. Wiener (1961, 155) asserted that "information is information, not material and not energy." Machlup (1983, 642), who restricted information to the context of communication, was dismissive of this third sense of information: "The noun 'information' has essentially two traditional meanings. . . . Any meanings other than (1) the *telling of something* or (2) *that which is being told* are either analogies and metaphors or concoctions resulting from the condoned appropriation of a word that had not been meant by earlier users." Fairthorne (1954, 259) objected scornfully to information as "stuff": "Information is an attribute of the receiver's knowledge and interpretation of the signal, nor of the sender's, nor some omniscient observer's nor of the signal itself."

But language is as it is used, and we can hardly dismiss information-as-thing so long as it is a commonly used meaning of the term *information*. Indeed, languages evolve, and with the expansion of information technology, the practice of referring to communications, databases, books, and the like as information appears to be becoming commoner and, perhaps, a significant source of confusion since symbols and symbol-bearing objects are easily confused with whatever the symbols represent. Further, information-as-thing, by whatever name, is of special interest in relation to information systems because ultimately information systems, including expert systems and information retrieval systems, can deal directly with information *only* in this sense. The development of rules for drawing inferences from stored information is an area of theoretical and practical interest. But these rules operate upon and only upon information-as-thing.

This leads us to two other much-used terms. First, the handling, manipulating, or otherwise deriving new forms of information-as-thing is information processing. Note that one could regard the process of becoming informed as a sort of mental information processing, but to avoid confusion we separate and exclude information-as-process from my use of *information processing*. Second, the means of handling information-as-thing, of information processing, is information technology. Commonly *information technology* is used in a narrow sense to denote computers and associated technology, but, in a more general sense, pen, paper, photography, photocopying, and other devices are also information technology.

The discussion thus far can be summarized in terms of two distinctions: (1) between entities and processes and (2) between intangibles and tangibles. Taken in conjunction, these two distinctions yield four quite different aspects of information and information systems, each of which will be examined more closely in subsequent chapters (see table 1.1).

Our primary concern, however, is not so much information as information systems, artificial arrangements to provide access to information or, better, the combination of users and the artificial system (Davis and Olson 1985, 6). We use the term *information service* to denote the service outcomes—what the user of the information system receives.

One further distinction should be kept in mind throughout this book. In discussion of information processing, information systems, and information technology, a common practice is to restrict use of these terms, often implicitly, to computer-based information processing, computer-based systems, and computer technology. Convenient though this restriction may be in local circumstances, it is inappropriate and subversive in any serious general discussion of information systems and will be avoided in what follows. One might as well tell a milkmaid that she is not milking the cow unless she is using a milking machine.

GOAL

Our goal is to build a better understanding of information systems through the description of their nature. What should be expected of such a description? It is suggested that, to be taken seriously, any general description of the nature of information systems should meet the following requirements:

1. *Information*: The description of information systems should be based on a description of information.

2. *Focus*: A discussion of the nature of information systems should be just that rather than the more usual review of the techniques that can be used in information systems.

3. *Inclusiveness*: The description should be general enough to be able to serve as a description for a wide variety of sorts of information system. The more general, the more inclusive, the better.

Table 1.1
Four Aspects of Information

	INTANGIBLE	TANGIBLE
ENTITY	Information-as-knowledge Knowledge (Chapter 4)	Information-as-thing Data, document, recorded knowledge (Chapters 5 & 6)
PROCESS	Information-as-process Becoming informed (Chapter 11)	Information Processing Data processing, document processing, knowledge engineering (Chapter 12)

4. *Completeness*: For any given information system, the description should be complete in that all parts are, or could be, included.

5. *Structure*: The description should be structural in the sense that it should show how the parts—all parts—are related to each other and to the environment.

6. *Technology*: The description should not be limited to any specific technology, such as computer-based or manual systems. A broad, technology-independent framework is necessary if the scope is not to be artificially narrowed and if the effects of technological change on information systems are to be examined.

7. *Utility*: The goal that would justify the effort is a better understanding of the complexities and difficulties—both conceptual and practical—of information systems and, as a result, better information systems.

It is not claimed that these standards have been met in this book but rather that these are the criteria by which any general introduction to information systems should be judged.

SCOPE

The word "information" and such phrases as "information flow" appear frequently. . . . Often their use is merely metaphorical, or they are convenient labels for an amorphous mass of ill-defined activities and phenomena. . . . Any discipline must define its scope. That is, it must define what matters it will study explicitly. These matters must then be studied and talked about in their own terms. . . . To begin with, the scope must include all those, but only those, phenomena that are essential to the nature of the study. (Fairthorne 1967, 710–11)

The potential scope of an exploration of concepts and contexts of information and of information systems is very extensive indeed. Many disciplines deal with some aspect of information: economics, cybernetics, linguistics, psychology, philosophy, computing, and, of course, the various professions concerned with providing information services.[3]

Our purpose, however, is to be exploratory rather than encyclopedic. We are concerned with the nature and role of formal information systems, especially retrieval-based information systems, and with how they fit in with the rest of the world.

Levels of Information

Information is commonly used in a narrowly limited sense to denote data of a relatively straightforward, instrumental nature: facts and texts of literal significance. This may well be a prudent and practical area on which to concentrate, but it cannot be defended as being the only level at which information-as-process operates. Already by medieval times, a classification, used in relation to religious texts, identified four levels of information:

1. The literal sense of the text.

2. The interpretation of ideas in an allegorical, symbolic sense.

3. A tropological level at which the reader inferred where his or her moral duty lay.

4. Since religious thought can be apocalyptic and visionary, at an anagogic level, the text should inspire profound meditation. (*Encyclopaedia Britannica* 1977, 7:135)

Some texts, such as repair manuals and financial reports, may not often be interpreted above the literal level, and it may be a while before artificial intelligence is effective at the higher levels. But those are not good grounds for restricting information studies to the literal level.

Boundaries and Examples

If information-as-process needs to be viewed broadly, so also does information-as-thing. Clearly attention should not be confined to data coded in machine-readable form, which would exclude printed books. But what about other objects, such as those that museums choose for their collections because they are of significant potential interest as informative objects, as evidence of something or other? It is far from clear that they should be excluded from the category of information-as-thing because they are not texts or numbers. If an archive is an information system, should not a museum, which stores objects because they are informative, also be regarded as an information system? And if a museum, then what about art galleries, assuming that artists seek to convey some message?

It seems unclear where the boundaries should be drawn and where the limits of information and information system may be. Rather than attempt the perilous task of defining these boundaries, declaring that beyond these limits there cannot be information or that a system is not an information system, a more cautious and pragmatic tack will be taken. We shall define by illustration, saying that our scope of interest at least includes such and such examples. Choosing interesting and marginal examples should provide some practical assurance that our coverage is broad, though it may not be fully complete or satisfy purists.

Some traditional and familiar points of departure, such as communications, libraries, and data processing, can be noted. However, when each is included, a variety of additional topics and activities, often not customarily viewed in this way, suggest themselves for inclusion with little by way of logical grounds for excluding them.

Communications, in the sense of interpersonal communications and mass communications, clearly ought to be within our scope. More broadly we should include becoming informed involuntarily, as with fire alarms and compulsory education, and also the political use of information as a tool for personal, corporate, and national goals.

Libraries are a long-established form of information system. If libraries are included, so also should archives and records management, as related examples of document-retrieval services. But if we are concerned with retrieval-based information services generally, we should also consider museums and herbaria, which exist to collect, store, retrieve, and provide access to potentially informative objects. If museums are included, then why not art galleries and botanical gardens? What, one might ask, is an arboretum if not a nonlending tree library?

Electronic data processing, in its various forms, is the subject of a large proportion of the literature on information systems. The use of electronic databases to retrieve information is obviously a candidate for inclusion. However, much of the literature on information technology is not concerned with meaning or with belief and so invites closer scrutiny. If it does not deal with meaning or belief, then why should we concern ourselves with it? In what sense, if any, is it correct to call it *information* technology? Similar questions arise with information processing (electronic data processing) and information theory (the study of the reliability of the transmission of physical signals).

Since information and information handling is pervasive in human activities, an exploration of information systems that did not include the social, economic, and political context and the broad social role of information would be seriously incomplete.

In dealing with this broad spectrum of cognitive, social, and technological activities, we need to remain alert to values: What information might be regarded as good or bad, and in what senses could information systems be regarded as good or bad?

Levels of Information System Complexity

Information systems vary in their complexity. We proceed on the following assumptions with respect to information system complexity.

1. The goal is to be able to describe complex information systems, not just simple ones.

2. Complexity is not merely a matter of the number of components but also of the diversity of sorts of activities involved. On this view, a system that includes behavioral elements (cognitive, economic, political) is presumed to be more complex than even a very complicated mechanical system.

3. Information systems can be sorted into a rough progression of increasing complexity: observation by one party, communication between two parties, and retrieval-based information systems, which can be viewed as indirect communication between parties via some store.

4. Systems that are provided on a noncommercial basis are more complex than, or at least different from, systems that are entirely commercial because of the added political dimension to their provision. A system that combined elements of both commercial and noncommercial provision would be more complex than a pure case of either.

5. Because information systems can be sorted, more or less, by complexity, a theory, description, or explanation of the most complex case should also be able to describe or explain less complex ones. The difference would be that less of the theory would be needed.

On these grounds, we take the description and explanation of the provision and use of retrieval-based systems that inform, provided partly but not only on a noncommercial basis, as the definitive challenge. If that can be achieved, then, we hope, the description and explanation of all simpler cases of information systems will also have been achieved, implicitly or explicitly.

Exclusions

By limiting this book to information and information systems for human beings, we are excluding information within inanimate systems, as in machine control systems, and within or between nonhuman species. Further, since this is intended to be an introductory description of the nature of information and information systems, we shall have little to say about technical details of the processes involved in, for example, cognition, communication, information processing, and information retrieval. Each of these has a large literature.

SOME PROBLEMS AND PARADOXES

In addition to the ambiguity of the term *information* itself and the unclear boundaries of what one might call information science or, more broadly, information studies, there are a number of questions and paradoxes, some of which contributed to the motivation to undertake this exploration. Examples include:

1. Information systems are supposed to inform people, but in practice they are designed to deliver physical stuff, such as books, papers, and signals on glowing screens. All "information systems" deal directly with and only with physical objects such as coded data or documents. Yet receiving delivered documents is not the same as becoming informed, so in what sense do information systems really handle information? Some theorists, insisting that information is some knowledge imparted or a process of imparting knowledge, reject the notion that physical objects can be information. Perhaps information systems are *information* systems only in a sense of information rejected by leading theorists of information.

2. What is and what is not information? Databases in computers and libraries are accepted as information systems, and a significant body of theory has developed around data retrieval and document retrieval systems. But what are some of the less obvious examples of information? For example, in what sense could or should objects in museums be viewed as information? Museums exist to support education and research, and, like archives, libraries, and management information systems, they deal with potentially informative objects. But they do not deal with data or documents, at least not in any ordinary sense of the terms, so the rhetoric associated with computers and libraries does not seem to apply. How should museums be regarded in

this context? If museum objects are regarded as a form of information, what else should also be regarded as information?

3. Is information a commodity? Information has paradoxical properties. If it is useful, it is worth paying for and worth supplying to others. But unlike other commodities, you can share information with others and yet still have as much as you did before. Scarcity is a determinant of price, but since information can be disseminated indefinitely it is not obvious how ordinary notions of scarcity and price apply to information.

4. Processing ordinarily converts old materials into new. Information processing, however, can create new information while leaving the old information intact. How can this be explained?

5. How should retrieval systems be evaluated? The evaluation of retrieval systems remains elusive. Indexes, catalogs, and classification schemes are based on the labeling of objects by attributes found in them or ascribed to them. Effective retrieval might then be the reliability of the system in retrieving the objects that fit the descriptions specified in the inquiry. But this has its limitations in terms of meeting individuals' needs, and so, it has been argued, such systems should be evaluated in terms of the utility of what is retrieved. However, the utility depends on factors extraneous to the retrieval system, notably the state of ignorance at particular times of particular users. It seems unfair to evaluate a system in terms of factors extraneous to it.

6. Is there an optimal size for an information system? One might reasonably have expected that the optimal size would be a topic of central concern in information systems as elsewhere. Some information systems, notably libraries, museums, and computer centers, can be substantial in cost and space requirements. But the literature on the subject is small, of limited helpfulness, and, one suspects, little read. Why?

7. How do information services survive? Some information services, especially noncommercial, publicly funded services, such as libraries and museums, appear to include little feedback from their users. Yet in systems theory, feedback is essential for an organization to adapt and to survive (Pfeffer and Salancik 1978, 43). How then do they not merely survive but are widely regarded as tranquil, crisis-free places?

8. What is information system goodness? How does one know whether an information service is good or bad, improving or degenerating? Can there be a single measure of information system goodness? If so, what is it? If not, why not?

This brief indication of scope and of problems suggests numerous interesting points to be addressed. They are approached in the belief that the principal problem in information science is inadequate understanding of the nature of the issues or, more concisely, inadequate theory. It is not claimed that all issues will be acceptably resolved, but all will at least be addressed. Why should one seek to explore such questions? Because doing so might assist us in three objectives: satisfying our curiosity, developing better curricula for those being educated for these areas, and providing a better basis for the design of future information systems.

PLAN

The remainder of the text is organized in the following manner. In part II we first consider theory, to clarify what sort of description is appropriate (chapter 2), and systems, both systems theory, as a conceptual approach for understanding relationships, and some examples of actual systems to clarify the scope of this inquiry (chapter 3).

We then review the notions of knowledge, information-as-knowledge, and the representation of knowledge (chapter 4). A particular sense of information— information-as-thing—is examined, first in general terms (chapter 5) and then more specifically in information systems (chapter 6). Information technology is discussed (chapter 7).

To complement and to strengthen this introduction to basic information-related concepts, we adopt the notion of access to information as a unifying concept and review different aspects of access to information, which, in effect, constitute a convenient enumeration of the conditions that have to be met if people are to become informed (chapter 8).

In part III we analyze six different sorts of processes involved in the provision and use of information:

1. Inquiries (chapter 9).
2. Information processing (chapter 10).
3. Perceiving and receiving information: observation, communication, and retrieval (chapter 11).
4. Becoming informed (chapter 12).
5. The demand for information services (chapter 13).
6. The providing of information services (chapter 14).

Part IV examines relationships between the concepts and processes identified in the previous parts, starting with the relationships that the processes have with each other and with the environment (chapter 15). The tasks involved in using an information system require expertise. The options available when the user's expertise is inadequate deserve attention, especially the potential role of artificial intelligence systems (chapter 16).

The relationship between information systems and their social context is considered in terms of the social values underlying information systems, the management of information services, and the social impact of improved information handling (chapter 17).

Part V attempts to summarize and to draw some conclusions (chapter 18).

NOTES

1. For a concise and convenient introduction to varieties of meanings of *information* and some related terms, see Braman (1989), Machlup (1983), NATO (1974, 1975, 1983), Schrader (1984), Wellisch (1972), Wersig and Neveling (1975), and Zhang (1988).

2. More specifically "informing" in this sense means "to impart knowledge of some particular fact or occurrence to (a person); to tell (one) of or acquaint (one) with something; to apprise" (*OED* 1989, 7:944)

3. For convenient introductions to several disciplines that deal with aspects of information, see Machlup and Mansfield (1983).

Part **II**

Concepts

Chapter 2

Theory

We now consider what sort of theory would be appropriate when considering information and information systems. A mistaken expectation as to the appropriate sort of theory might lead one to fail to recognize it. Further, if one misunderstood the sort of theory that is appropriate, one might also misjudge the sorts of approaches that would be most likely to be effective to solving conceptual and practical problems. The issue is important given the history of attempts to build theories of information on narrow bases on logic and statistics.[1]

THEORY

Theory is concerned with describing the nature of things. The original meaning of the word *theory*, from which modern uses of the word derive, was a "viewing" or "looking at" (*OED* 1989, 17:902). Hence in general terms, to develop a theory of something is to develop a view, description, or way of looking at it. A better theory would be a better view or description. A good description or way of looking not only depicts something but also explains and fosters understanding of it.

In relation to human activities such as the use of information systems, one finds more specialized definitions. The *Oxford English Dictionary*, for example, offers this:

Theory . . . 4. A scheme or system of ideas or statements held as an explanation or account of a group of facts or phenomena; a hypothesis that has been confirmed or established by observations or experiment, and is propounded or accepted as accounting for the known facts: a statement of what are held to be general law, principles, or causes of something known or observed.

4.b. That department of an art or technical subject which consists in the knowledge or statement of the facts on which it depends, or its principles or methods as distinguished from the *practice* of it. (*OED* 1989, 17:902)

Webster's Third New International Dictionary of the English Language Unabridged (1971, 2371) provides two definitions that seem particularly appropriate:

Theory...3.a.(1) The body of generalizations and principles developed in association with practice in a field of activity (as medicine, music) and forming its content as an intellectual discipline.

3.1.(2) The coherent set of hypothetical, conceptual, and pragmatic principles forming the general frame of reference for a field of inquiry (as for deducing principles, formulating hypotheses, undertaking action).

The first of these four would seem to fit best such phrases as "theory of retrieval-based information systems," "archival theory," and "theory of management information systems," among others.

It should be stressed that we are concerned with theory in the broad sense of a description or explanation of the nature of things, not in the more restricted sense, used in some sciences, of denoting fundamental laws formally stated and falsifiable. This narrow sense is best restricted to those limited areas for which it is appropriate: mathematical-experimental sciences, such as physics, and small pockets within other fields. Unfortunately the high social prestige of the mathematical-experimental sciences in recent decades has led to a tendency to assume that areas and disciplines that are not of this sort are, or ought to be (e.g., Houser and Schrader 1978). Retrieval-based information systems are provided by people to enable other people to become informed. It is not obvious how or why these activities, or scholarship concerning their nature, could or should resemble geometry or physics.

There is a choice of tactics here that Schön (1983, 42–45) summarizes as the "dilemma of 'rigor or relevance.' " Rigorous formal theories can yield results, but the assumptions necessary to sustain rigor lead the results to be divorced from the messiness of reality. Emphasizing faithfulness to reality is likely to be at the expense of academically respectable formal "results." One might adopt a rigorous narrow definition of theory suited to an exact science, in which case the problem is how to use it for an area that is not and may never be exact enough for rigorous theory to have much effective application. Or one takes a more general definition of theory that can be used for an inexact area and hope that the theory can be refined later and made more formal while still subordinated to an emphasis on relevance. We have adopted the latter path. Our approach is deliberately informal and discursive because we seek to ensure that our view is sufficiently broad to be able to include the complicated and messy cases, even if the quest for completeness is at the expense of refinement.

Designating the study of information and of information systems as information *science* may be a good idea for a variety of reasons, but applying the name cannot be expected to change the nature of the field. To set out to review "theory" relating to information systems, limiting oneself to the narrow definition more appropriate to the mathematical-experimental sciences, can be attempted but is predictably, perhaps inevitably, unsatisfying (Boyce and Kraft 1985; Heilprin 1989). A narrow view of theory can be expected to exclude or to miss most of the relevant available theory, of the ''ideas or statements held as an explanation or account of a group of facts or phenomena'' (*OED* 1989, 17:902).

Examples of Theory

Let us explore some examples of notions that would appear to fit the first definition of theory already given.

With respect to *inquiry*, we find, for example, that the higher the level of formal education, the higher the propensity to inquire after specific documents and the lower the propensity to make subject inquiries in a library (Hafter 1979).

The area of *retrieval* (indexing, classification, and the evaluation of retrieval performance) depends heavily on notions of ''aboutness,'' ''relevance,'' ''recall,'' ''precision,'' and ''utility'' and the relationships among them. A prominent theory concerning retrieval is that when searching, there is an inverse relationship between achieving recall (retrieving all relevant material) and achieving precision (retrieving only relevant material). Emphasizing one tends to be at the expense of the other.

The fields of education and cognitive science have developed ideas about *becoming informed*. The idea of cognitive authority helps explain why people believe information that is retrieved for them (Wilson 1977). The demand for information services is sensitive to the accessibility of the service: the less convenient the service is, the less that people will seek to use it (Allen and Gertsberger 1967; Harris 1966; Rosenberg 1967; Swanson 1987).

Various views about the *providing* of information services by the allocation of resources to and within information systems are reflected in the literature on the management of these services. Concepts drawn from welfare economics and public finance, for example, are used to explain and justify the noncommercial nature of public library services (Blake and Perlmutter 1974; Schwuchow 1973; Van House 1983a).

USEFUL THEORY, PROVISIONAL THEORY, BETTER THEORY

So far we have not considered the goodness of theory. The view implicitly adopted throughout can be summarized as follows: Theories are, by definition, mental constructs. They may be expressed or represented in written and graphical form. They may well inspire and guide practical achievements of a concrete form. Yet a theory remains a mental construct. A ''good'' theory is one that matches well our perception of whatever the theory is about. The closer the match, the better the theory is. It is to be remembered that the matching is with our perception of the objects. This explains why a theory can seem good in relation to what is known but then has to be rejected as inadequate when more has become known.

This change from good to inadequate can happen when either of two things happens: (1) another mental construct, another theory, is developed that fits even better the perceptions of the objects regarded as relevant or (2) additional objects are noticed such that the perception of these new objects is incompatible with the original theory. Even if the additional objects have been inaccurately perceived, the theory will cease to be regarded as a "good" one, and efforts to develop a better theory can be expected. Of course, it could happen that the additional objects had been wrongly perceived and that, with a later, revised view of these objects, the original theory might be reaffirmed as being the better one after all. Goodness of theory, then, is a matter of closeness of match between the mental construct and the perception of whatever the theory is about.

A theory can be useful insofar as it serves to assist and guide the development of further understanding (whether called theory or not) or of practical activities. Yet theory should always be regarded as provisional because it is always possible that mental effort might result in a new or revised theory that would match the perceptions of relevant objects even better and because perceptions of relevant objects are likely to change. The perceived relevance of old or new objects may change. Each of these cases means that the theory must now match something different and that the closeness of match—the goodness of theory—must be reassessed. The consequence of all this is that every theory should be regarded as a challenge not only to our mental powers to develop even better theories that might match our perceptions more closely but also to the accuracy and extent of our powers of perception of relevant objects. Even the most attractive theories should be regarded as no more than provisional, temporary improvements:

Neither the rationality of theoretical concepts nor the rationality of practical procedures can be judged definitively, timelessly, or once-for-all. The Practical Reason like the Pure Reason must have an eye not to the Good or the Best, and still less to the Only-Coherent-Conceivable, but rather to the Better; and, the rationality of collective human enterprises being what it is, this means always the Better-for-the-Time-Being. (Toulmin 1972, 371)

IMPROVING THEORY: SCHOLARSHIP AND RESEARCH

Research is concerned with solving problems, practical or conceptual. Within research it is convenient to distinguish between basic research—concerned with increasing understanding—and applied research—concerned with doing something better. The difference is in intent, although these intentions are not mutually exclusive. One may reasonably hope that basic research will not only increase understanding of the nature of something but also lead to better ways of doing some task. Similarly, developing better ways to do something is also likely to increase one's understanding of whatever it is, to develop better theory. Ideally research does both.

In research, as in theory, there is sometimes confusion between research in general and research in the limited area of mathematical-experimental sciences, between scholarship in general and science in particular. There are some characteristics of effective research regardless of the field in which it is applied:

1. Good research is oriented toward problems. The problems can be conceptual (intriguing paradoxes, apparent inconsistencies), or practical (inadequate tools). If a piece of research is not formulated as a problem, then it is less likely to be effective and may not be research at all.

2. Research should be clear, honest, and rigorous in the use of concepts and terms, though clarity is more difficult to achieve in some fields of discourse than in others.

3. It should be creative, based on the need to develop theories and techniques that are "better-for-the-time-being."

4. A crucial characteristic of good scholarship in any field is the active search for contradictory evidence. The quest for data that might refute a hypothesis is widely understood in relation to the formulation of statistical tests. The essence of the scientific method is just this: a two-pronged attack, alternating between conceiving new hypotheses and attempting to refute them. Finding evidence that can be regarded as supporting a theory is all too easy. Less well recognized is that seeking contradictory evidence is a mark of good scholarship in every area: history, law, literary criticism, anthropology, mathematics, information studies.

5. Methods of research need to be appropriate to the problem. Whatever approach is effective is appropriate, regardless of the field or discipline.

Medawar (1967, 87) wrote: "If politics is the art of the possible, research is surely the art of the soluble. Both are immensely practical-minded things." This not only captures the importance of focusing on problems to be solved but also reflects the importance of ingenuity in using whatever research approaches seem likely to work. The exercise of judgment in research, therefore, often consists in determining just how some specific investigation would be more effective (or cost-effective) than another in yielding new understanding (Toulmin 1972, 213). In practice, this judgment is limited by both individual and social constraints.

As with theory, and for the same reasons, there has been a tendency to want to use the scientific method of the mathematical-experimental sciences in all areas. This sometimes has the attributes of folk science in the sense of a body of ideas that is more respected than understood. Pressure to use any particular technique limits the free pursuit of the art of the soluble.

Individuals are limited by their training and their habits. Scholars who are not yet well established are well advised to be cautious in what they undertake and how. Much research is, in practice, minor repetitions and variations of previous work. Free choice among techniques for solving problems is less likely among researchers who had a narrow training, who are past their creative prime, who feel constrained by peer review, or who concentrate on what is fundable.

Immature Science

Ever since the Greeks fell in love with geometry, philosophical thought about the nature of knowledge has been dominated by models derived from mathematics and theoretical physics. . . . [This] has tempted philosophers to concentrate on problems of logical form, to the neglect of questions about rational function and intellectual adaptation . . . in science and philosophy alike, an exclusive preoccupation with logical systematicity has been destructive of both historical understanding and rational criticism. (Toulmin 1972, vii–viii)

This attitude is reflected in the labeling given to areas that do not fit the canon of respectability: "pseudo-science" or, more kindly, "immature and ineffective sciences." The terminology reveals a value judgment. It may be some comfort that most areas of study are in this category. It should be recognized that researchers in "immature and ineffective" fields of inquiry face greater difficulties than do those in mature ones (Ravetz, 1971, chap. 14).

Yet these value-laden labels are liable to miss an important point: poor research in any field can and should be criticized for being unscholarly but cannot always validly be denounced as unscientific. In part this is a problem with the English language. In German (*Wissenschaft*) and French (*science*), a single term is used for all fields of scholarship. In English the term *science* is used only for some areas of scholarship. To confuse the matter further, American use of English tends somewhat to the broader German and French practice, as in "cognitive science," "domestic science," and "library science."

As long as the terminology is value laden, it is likely to be unhelpful. It could be argued that an "immature" field should "grow up" into a mature (mathematical-experimental) science, as has happened with geometry, mathematics, and physics. But some areas of study (especially those that, like the study of information systems, are rooted in human behavior) by their very nature are inherently and incorrigibly immature as an exact science because they are different in kind.

PATHOLOGY OF THEORY

We have noted some difficulties with theory, and the topic deserves more attention. A symptom of difficulty is the enormous contrast between small subfields that lend themselves to quantitative techniques and surrounding areas that do not. This is likely to be compounded by researchers' preference for more tractable, quantitative areas. The scope of this book includes three striking examples.

First, bibliometrics is concerned with the quantitative study of phenomena of documentary discourse, such as authorship, publication, reading, and citing (Hertzel 1987; Narin and Moll 1977). It includes studies of the growth of literature on a given subject, patterns in the distribution of publishing by individual authors

(Lotka's Law), how articles on any subject are dispersed across journals (Bradford's Law of Scattering), the obsolescence of literatures, the epidemiology of ideas, patterns of scholarship, and predicting who will win Nobel prizes. It is an important and interesting field, but the sophistication of the work contrasts greatly with our limited understanding of the phenomena being subjected to manipulation of technical virtuosity. Citation analysis and document usage studies of great complexity are conducted, but little is understood about the causes or consequences of citing or using documents (Brooks 1986, 1987). These latter topics are less easy to investigate, let alone measure or calculate.

Second, similarly extensive work of great sophistication has been done in evaluative studies of retrieval systems (Sparck Jones 1981; Van Rijsbergen 1979). The methodological aspects of these studies are strictly for experts, yet the foundations on which this work is based, mainly comparing the "relevance" of retrieved documents to the queries submitted, are entirely different: ill defined, inconsistently interpreted, and of unclear significance (Swanson 1988; Blair 1990).

Third, sophistication in the optimizing of computer architecture supporting information systems is not matched by comparable sophistication in optimizing the choice of information services to be provided in any given social or organizational context (Hirschheim 1985, 167–85).

UNIQUE, CHARACTERISTIC, AND SHARED THEORY

For historical reasons, the study of information and of information systems is populated (and surrounded) by a variety of established disciplines: computer science, linguistics, logic, librarianship, psychology, and several other fields. The concerns of each of these fields are within or overlap information science. Often they approach the same problems from different perspectives. This situation has hindered the sense of identity of information science, especially when it is assumed that the content of information science must be unique to information science. In practice, a notion may be distinctive to information science only in its specific application—for example, in cost studies. Notions developed outside information science may be incompletely developed, especially in relation to information and information systems, as has been the case with the economic analysis of information services. A notion may develop in some part of information science and then become adopted in other fields also, as in the case of bibliometric analysis. Notions apparently held in common may, on closer investigation, turn out to be misleading or inadequate, as in the case of arguments for introducing fees for service in order to generate feedback in noncommercial situations.

One can view this apparent sharing of theory between fields in two ways. A relatively weak statement would be that there are resemblances between areas of information science and neighboring areas, such that examination of one might be helpful for developing theory concerning the other. This could be called a partial commonality of interest. One might say that since subject classification schemes have some of the characteristics of languages, the study of linguistics might be helpful for those studying classification schemes, and vice versa.

A stronger statement would be that at some level of abstraction, classification schemes are a form of language and that therefore the study of them is, at least in part, an area of linguistics as well as an area of information retrieval studies. In the same way, the study of the use of computers in libraries could be regarded as a specialty within computer science and also as a specialty within librarianship. We could call this a partial coincidence between areas.

Several consequences follow from this overlap, whether it is regarded as coincidence or mere commonality, which appears to be a major feature of any broad definition of information science. It becomes important to relax some of the ingrained attitudes, derived from the territoriality of academic disciplines, which develop in spite of the original meaning of the word *university*. For example, the political processes involved in the allocation of resources to and within information systems would be equally proper as a target of study within information science and within political science. Once developed, a truly persuasive theory could be expected to be regarded as good by the rest of both fields.

If, however, the commonality of interest has not previously been recognized or if the two disciplines have already developed separate technical vocabularies and/or different (provisional) theories, then the development of mutually acceptable theory is likely to be difficult. No discipline or field is ever fully developed, and it could well happen that prevailing theory in one or both fields is insufficiently developed with regard to special features of the area of shared interest.

This overlapping may be a source of academic and political difficulty in the short term, but it should be viewed as a major advantage in the long run for two reasons. First, an irritation can be a beneficial stimulant. Seeking to achieve theory regarded as acceptable by other groups provides a good basis for progress for all concerned. The theories developed by each group provide valid intellectual targets for all groups to question and to improve. Second, there is the practical consideration that the existence of other groups with overlapping interests constitutes a dramatic increase in the talent that could be harnessed to work on the problems.

Many of the bits and pieces of theory concerning information science, that is, the understanding of information and information systems, are in areas of overlap with other fields. But this apparent lack of uniqueness of information science should be seen as a source of strength, not of lack of identity. Perhaps the wisest solution is to view the totality or combination or goal of the interests constituting information science as unique—on reflection, an advantageous situation. One can take pride and interest in something unique and also benefit from the fact that there is so much talent in other areas that can help solve specific problems and build better theory. None of this is to deny the difficulties involved in building better theory in so complex an area as information and the human use of information systems.

We should remember the observation of Aristotle that ''it is the mark of the educated man and a proof of his culture that in every subject he looks for only so much precision as its nature permits'' (Aristotle 1955, 27–28).

NOTE

1. For a fuller treatment of research and theory, see Bunge (1967), Ravetz (1971), and Toulmin (1972).

Chapter 3

Systems

SYSTEMS AND SYSTEMS CONCEPTS

Our concern in this chapter is with the nature of information systems, but these are of little interest or significance, except in relation to their provision and, more especially, their use. Considering information systems in the absence of consideration of the people and purposes involved in their provision and in their use would seem to have little meaning and less benefit. From this perspective it becomes necessary to consider how information systems (and their users) form a system of interacting parts. We should expect that the relationships among these parts will constitute a major part of any adequate description or theory of information systems. We can go further and make some general statements about the nature of such systems in the terminology of systems theory.

Information systems used by human beings are open systems. In other words, the provision and use of information systems are not isolated from the rest of the world. Indeed, as will become clear, they are deeply embedded in and heavily influenced by their social and technical contexts.

An information system used by human beings is also likely to be a complex system, or, in the terminology of systems theory, a large system. A library, for example, may not be very big physically or organizationally. The concept of a library as a set of books that might at some time be inspected by one or more people is quite simple. However, the variety of stages, steps, and interactions that can be involved in learning from materials in a library can be quite complex. By complexity we do not simply mean the amount of technical engineering detail, but rather the diversity of elements and relationships involved. Situations that involve social, economic, political, and cognitive activities are generally very complex.

Another important aspect of systems is their ability to respond to changes, to adapt to their environments, and to maintain sufficient stability to survive. Some

Free to all

I would say this could be interpretted as free to all who would use it.

information systems, especially those that are provided without charge, such as archives and libraries, appear to have contradictory characteristics in this regard. They seem to be weak in the features needed for adaptation and stability: feedback on what is happening is generally weak, incomplete, or lacking; goals may be vague; the services may be criticized for being unresponsive; the managers may have little influence over their environment. Paradoxically such services commonly exhibit the characteristics of systems that are highly adaptive. Archives, libraries, and records centers can have serious problems but rarely crises. They even have a stereotyped public image as being quiet places suitable for the employment of quiet people, and they survive with great stability. We shall return to this paradox.

CONTROLS AND RESPONSES

We have deliberately chosen to view information systems, their users, the provider, and the interactions between them as systems. This approach is adopted not only because it is believed to be helpful for the development of theory but also because an emphasis on the interactions involved as well as on the components seems likely to be useful. How do the parts relate to each other? How might they relate? What actions or relationships might be made more effective or efficient with respect to specific goals or outcomes?

The notion of control is central to the study of systems. *Control*, however, may sometimes seem too strong a word in this context. What is of interest is what responses are made. How do the parts of the system react to problems? How do the responses and interactions of parts combine to form the behavior of the whole? It is the process of response to stimuli that constitutes the means of change and adaptation by internal alteration, by changing relationships, or by influencing the external environment. Responses to opportunities and to threats are of great importance for achieving goals.

What sorts of controls, responses, and processes are at work in information systems? Information processing—the deriving of new forms and representations of existing information—is a process upon which all information systems depend. It is essentially a matter of technique and technology and, as such, provides the technical capability that enables and constrains all else. The literature on information systems is dominated by important practical discussion of information processing. In contrast, we devote relatively little attention to information processing for two reasons. First, an examination of the nature of information systems is intended, not a technical manual. Second, five other distinct sorts of responses characterize information systems and are necessary for even a minimally adequate description of the more complex cases.

1. *Inquiry* can be viewed as the response to wanting to know something, whether from curiosity or from distressing ignorance. Inquiry provides motivation to use information systems and shapes the nature of their use.

2. *Perception*. Information-as-process depends necessarily upon some information-as-thing being perceived. Several possible actions may lead to perception: observation, communication, and retrieval. It may be that something informative happens by chance to be noticed. It may be that information is consciously sought or that someone else was trying to communicate. Communication is the transmitting of information-as-thing (sound, signal, record, document—anything tangible that is regarded as informative) so that it will be perceived. It is hardly communication unless it is perceived. It may be that communication is direct and immediate. It may be that a communication is delayed, indirect, misdirected, or even undirected, in the sense that the intended audience is identified imperfectly or not at all. With information storage and retrieval, the sending of information to storage and its retrieval may have little connection with each other. Much of what is called information science is heavily concentrated on this set of processes and on information processing.

3. *Becoming informed* is the phrase we use to denote the process whereby people's personal knowledge changes in response to information. In terms of the terminology of chapter 1, becoming informed is the information-as-process by which information-as-thing results in the addition of information-as-knowledge.

4. *Demand* for information is a response not only to perceived need (as inquiry is) but also to the perception of an opportunity to do something to meet that need. The scale and nature of demand will vary in response to a variety of stimulating and inhibiting factors.

5. *Provision* of information and of information systems is a response to goals, preferences, and perceptions by those who have resources that can be allocated for that purpose. The actual allocation determines in detail the provision of information services.

At this stage, we merely mention and briefly define these five types of control, or, as we prefer, of response. Each will be examined in more detail in separate chapters in part III, where we shall also consider a process that permeates the information systems and the use of information: information processing. By information processing, we mean the deriving of new information-as-thing.

It will be clear that there are numerous relationships to be considered, including those between and among the principal uses of the term *information*: information-as-knowledge, information-as-process, and information-as-thing. All three are related to knowledge (what somebody knows) or recorded knowledge (information-as-thing, any representation of what somebody once knew). Information-as-knowledge is knowledge that is, or is intended to be, added to someone's knowledge through what we have called information-as-process, following perception of information-as-thing.

These rather abstract relationships mean little except when related to the broader context of human behavior, which provides the motivation, and of the techniques and technology, which provide the technical capability for these activities.

TYPES OF INFORMATION SYSTEMS

Just as the word *information* is used in a variety of ways, so also the term *system* is freely and loosely applied. Almost any arrangement is liable to be called a system. What, then, are we to make of the phrase *information system*?

From the perspective of the person being informed, we can distinguish three sorts of information-receiving situations:

1. *Communication*, in which information is conveyed, intentionally and more or less directly, to the receiver, as in a conversation, a letter, or a lecture, constitutes one class of information-receiving situations.

2. *Retrieval-based information services*, wherein collected and stored information-as-thing is sought and retrieved by the user, represent another sort of information-receiving situation. A retrieval situation is more complex than a communication situation.

3. *Observation*. Information can also be received by other means such as observing an event, conducting an experiment, or contemplating any evidence that has not been communicated or retrieved. We refer to this third class as observation.

We concentrate on retrieval-based information systems rather than observation or communication because retrieval-based information systems involve the additional complexity of selecting, collecting, retrieving, and searching. It is important to try to ensure that theory is capable of describing unusual and complex situations, as well as simpler ones. We assume that theory capable of describing the provision and use of retrieval-based information systems would also be capable of describing the progressively less complex cases of communication and observation. We would not assume the reverse: that a theory adequate for describing observation or communication would also be able to describe or explain retrieval-based information systems.

We approach the description of retrieval-based information systems in the belief that failure to consider these activities as a class has been a significant source of isolation and weakness in the development of theory for particular types of retrieval system: archives, libraries, management information systems, museums, and records management.

Retrieval-based information systems are artifacts. They use technology, such as paper, card, computers, and telecommunications. The prospect is that there will continue to be dramatic change in information systems resulting from the development and adoption of improved information technologies that tend to involve storage and retrieval. This argues for special attention in the development of theory that is broadly applicable to retrieval-based information systems.

Retrieval-based information systems have two foundations: a role—to facilitate access to information—and a mission—to support the mission of whoever funds them. The statement of role stimulates us to ask how *facilitate*, *access*, and *information* should be interpreted in each particular context. Information that forms part of artificial, physical systems must necessarily be some kind of information-as-thing, but that still leaves a lot of choice among data, documents, and other objects. The statement of mission requires a more specific determination of what should be done for each specific system and its particular organizational and social context.

Meanwhile, we face another problem in defining our scope. Human activities are complex, diverse, and interrelated. Hence, attempting to delineate a clear boundary such that information-related activities are within it and other activities are outside it would appear to be difficult—and perhaps not feasible. Our concern, however, is to develop and present a general conceptual framework for considering information systems, and it seems more important, at this stage in the development of theory concerning information and information systems, to worry more about ensuring that a proper diversity of systems is included than where the boundary should be drawn. For these reasons, this exploration will concentrate on some examples of retrieval-based information systems chosen because they represent a challenging diversity of features.

Management Information Systems

Those responsible for managing large and complex organizations depend heavily on information in order to know what is going on, what is changing, and in what direction (Mintzberg 1990). Selected operations are monitored, and the number and names of various objects and events are recorded in management information systems. Davis and Olson (1985, 6) define a management information system as "an integrated, user-machine system for providing information to support operations, management, and decision-making functions in an organization." We use management information systems in the traditional, limited sense of computer-based corporate information systems.

The information-as-thing—the data—in management information systems is predominantly one of five types: date, name, count, code, or identification number (Sprague and McNurlin 1986, 193). Such data tend to have the following characteristics:

1. The data are ordinarily numerical and/or relatively compact, tidy records.
2. The data are internally derived in the sense that the definition of what to collect and the collecting of it is determined and organized by the designers of the management information system in conjunction with their users.
3. Because of the first two characteristics, the data tend to be relatively well defined and suitable for manipulation by computer.
4. Management information systems tend to be most useful for decision makers concerned with relatively short-term operational and tactical decisions that are relatively well defined.

Management information systems illustrate how information systems can blend in with other sorts of systems. The data that are input for the information system are commonly and efficiently derived as a by-product of other functional systems. For example, transaction data from sales records are informative concerning inventory and cash flow, as well as about particular sales transactions. Nevertheless, the characteristics of data in management information systems are not characteristics of all internally derived data or of all corporate information systems, as the next example will show.

Records Management _

Records management is concerned with the (mostly paper-based) documents of an organization, ranging from the official files of individual workers to the massive operational records of the entire organization (Kesner 1988, 5; also Benedon 1969; Maedke, Robek, and Brown 1981; Ricks and Gow 1984; Smith 1986). With exceptions, notably incoming correspondence, the records are mostly internally generated. Hence there is some control over at least the medium and format, which can make for more orderly handling during their life cycle.

Although there may be some control over the physical medium, format, and arrangement of the records, the system designer or system manager has little or no control over the content, over what the texts on the documents represent, as in management information systems. The records, the information-as-thing, tend to be messy in the sense that they may deal with any topic from any perspective and in any form of words.

The limited control, the messiness of the content in terms of what records are about, and the tendency for each document to be unique make it difficult for records managers to deal with what the documents are about. Correspondence may be arranged by correspondent, and in more ambitious systems there may be an index to selected correspondence. In general, however, identification is limited to the primary arrangement in "record series" by function or correspondent and then by date.

Because record management deals with documents that are messy compared with management information system data, and are mainly nonnumerical, the techniques for handling the information resource are different. Management information systems and records management both deal with corporate information, but the difference in the sort of information resource and, therefore, in the techniques used leave little risk of confusion between the two, though they can be expected to converge in the future.

Archives Service

The term *archives* can refer to the archival records themselves, a building where archival records are stored, or an agency responsible for the selection, preservation, documentation, and making available of archival material (Pederson 1987; see also Daniels and Walch 1984). A widely accepted definition is as follows:

Archives are the documents accumulated by a natural process in the course of the conduct of affairs of any kind, public or private, at any date; and preserved thereafter for reference, in their own custody, by the persons responsible for the affairs in question or their successors. (Jenkinson 1948, quoted in Pederson 1987, 4)

The customary distinction between archives and records management is that records management deals with documents used for current operations, whereas archives deal with selected examples of documents that are no longer in current use but are being retained indefinitely for possible future legal or historical purposes.

A feature of archives that distinguishes them from records management is that archivists have even less control over the creation of the material they work with. Archivists can select what they will accept into the archive, but it is not a free choice because they cannot control the sort of material they can choose from, except, perhaps, for some indirect influence through the records managers. So although the appraisal, selection, and discarding of records is a major responsibility of the archivist, the choice is circumscribed.

A characteristic feature of archives, distinguishing true archives from mere collections of correspondence, is the retention of the original order in which they were compiled. This provides a finding order, but, more significant, the chronological sequence and juxtaposition of documents as assembled by specific administrative bodies (the provenance or "fonds") itself adds information that would ordinarily be lost if the documents were rearranged into some order other than by provenance.

In general, each document is unique in itself or in its relationship to other documents. As with records management, the contents—what the documents are about—are untidy and messy.

Library Services

In 1829, Martin Schrettinger provided a concise and durable "concept of the library":

A 'library' is a substantial collection of books, whose arrangement sets each person [who is] thirsty for knowledge in the position to use, without loss of time, any treatise contained in it, according to his needs.[1]

Meijer (1982, 26), in an analysis of the nature of libraries, wrote:

Librarianship is a form of cultural enterprise whose main characteristic is the stimulation of the optimal use of mankind's cultural heritage insofar as it consists of coded thoughts recorded in documents that are and must be held in readiness for use with the ultimate objective of making possible cultural progress (also in the fields of religion and science) in its particular sphere.

Libraries, like archives, do not create their own materials. They select from materials that others, overwhelmingly publishers, create. Archives have been contrasted with libraries by the statement that archives receive while libraries select their materials, but this is merely a matter of degree. Both archivists and librarians select from materials created by others. With both archives and libraries, some material is so important for the goals of the service that there is little option but to acquire it. There is also much material of too little probable future utility to be afforded. In between these extremes is a large area in which the appraisal and selection skills of both are put to test.

The significant differences between libraries and archives appear to be two: one is a difference in the nature of the resource, the other a matter of retrieval technique (see also Blouin 1986).

First, each document in an archive is unique. Even physically identical copies acquire different identities on account of their juxtaposition in relation to other documents—their provenance and original order. In contrast, librarians, insofar as they are concerned with printed books or other mass-produced materials, are ordinarily concerned with selecting one or a few copies of documents that normally exist in editions of thousands of identical copies that are interchangeable. Any copy is ordinarily as informative and as authentic as any other copy. There is an element of interchangeability among different copies of library books that is not present with archival records.

Second, collections get arranged one way or another. The nature of archival resources imposes a form of arrangement: the original order in which they were formed in the course of their life as records. Libraries ordinarily store their documents by subject, by what they are about, using, for example, the Dewey Decimal Classification. Alternatively, for economical storage, library books can be arranged by size and then by the order received (''by running number''), using catalogs and indexes to identify and locate desired items. It is simply a matter of choosing one attribute over another as the basis for arrangement. But the choice derives, at least in part, from the nature of the material and the purpose of the system. Consider the alternatives. To abandon arrangement of archival records by provenance and original order in favor of classifying them by subject or to rearrange library books by provenance would be to diminish the amount of information, of evidence, in the first case and to make both systems more difficult to use.

Library collections include some examples of books that are preserved as examples of bookmaking. The motivation may be aesthetic, but, more generally, such books are preserved so that scholars can examine them as evidence in their quest to understand the history of printing and bookmaking. In these cases, it is not the text that is of interest but the book as a physical object. Collecting books as objects as opposed to books as texts is a significant departure from the normal role of a library. Such a collection is less a library collection than a museum collection of books because the books are being preserved more for their interest as objects than as texts. In these cases, one would not want to transcribe the text and discard the book. This brings us to another kind of information resource: objects as opposed to data and documents.

Museums

Museums are of special interest for information studies because they represent a species of information system with an unusual characteristic: the informative material, the information-as-thing, is neither data nor document but object. The objects may be artifacts or natural. Since addressing exceptional cases is important for developing theories, it is regrettable that the study of museums as information systems has been rather neglected in information science.[2]

That museums should be considered information systems follows from their nature and their purpose. Informative objects are selected, collected, arranged, described, retrieved, displayed, and interpreted so that knowledge may be increased and disseminated. Researchers use museum collections to make new discoveries. Others learn things that they did not know from items in the museum's collections, rather as they do from items in libraries' collections: "the purpose of a museum is to inform and to educate visitors by making objects, with associated interpretive information, available for inspection" (Wright 1983, 111).

Natural history museums, full of skeletons, stuffed pelts, and bodies preserved in fluids, help highlight the question of where the boundaries of information systems might be. Retrieving a digital image from an online encyclopedia or examining a book in a library about, say, an antelope should be informative and would be viewed as an instance of using an information system. So also finding and viewing a stuffed antelope or an antelope skeleton should be informative and viewed as an instance of an information system in action. Ideally, one should have a chance to use multiple media and be in a position to use all of these different forms.

If an antelope skeleton retrieved in a museum can be informative, what about a live antelope retrieved from the wild? Arguably, retrieving a live antelope from the wild does not constitute use of a retrieval-based information system because the informative object (the live antelope) had not been collected and stored for retrieval first—unless, perhaps, it had been preserved as part of a nature reserve. What then of collections assembled in zoos and botanical gardens for educational and scientific purposes? Would that make the zoos and botanical gardens qualify as information systems? If not, then what difference between a museum collection of dead animals and a zoo collection of live ones is relevant to the definition of information systems? We conclude that the boundaries between what is and what is not an information system are not clear and suggest that a system is an information system if it is used as an information system, especially if it has been designed to be used as an information system.

OBJECTIVES OF INFORMATION SYSTEMS

On the purpose of an information system, we quote, as worthy of any sort of information system, the goal that it should:

give sense to its collections, make learning easier, stimulate curiosity, help to avoid pure memorizing which is so detrimental to independent thinking and self-reliance, and fill more and more the harmful gap between formal concepts and intuition, theory and practice.[3]

This was the noble charge given by the Habsburg Archduke Johann (1782–1859) when he established a public institution in Graz in 1811 in order to foster education and industrial competitiveness in Styria. It was called a museum, but the combination of museum, library, and education program intended by Archduke Johann was more advanced than most modern views of a museum.

SUMMARY

In this chapter we have noted the importance of relationships between different components of information systems. In the terms of systems theory, information systems are open and large. They appear to be adaptive, even though sometimes seeming weak in the feedback associated with adaptiveness.

Five responses, or adaptive mechanisms, were noted: inquiry, perceiving (communication, retrieval, and observation), becoming informed, demand for service, and the provision of service. Another important process is information processing.

The variety and scope of what needs to be considered was illustrated by some disparate examples of retrieval-based information systems: management information systems, records management, archives, libraries, and museums.

NOTES

1. "Eine 'Bibliothek' ist eine beträchtliche Sammlung von Büchern, deren Einrichtung jeden Wissbegierigen in den Stand setzt, jede darin enthaltene Abhandlung, ohne unnötigen Zeitverlust, nach seinen Bedürfnissen zu benutzen." M. Schrettinger, *Versuch eines vollständigen Lehrbuchs des Bibliothekswissenschaft oder Anleitung zur vollkommenen Geschäftsführing eines Bibliothekars*, bd. 1. (München: Lindauer, 1829), 11. Quoted in J. Rogalla von Bieberstein, *Archiv, Bibliothek und Museum als Dokumentationsbereiche* (Pullach bei München: Verlag Dokumentation, 1975), 26.

2. This comment is not intended as any criticism of work in taxonomy, museum documentation, or museum theory, nor does it imply that museums have not been studied as information systems. See, for example, Maroevic (1983, 1986).

3. "Versinnlichen, dadurch das Lernen erleichtern, die Wissbegierde reitzen, jenes dem Selbstdenken, und hiermit der Selbstständigkeit so nachtheilige bloss Memoriren, jene schädliche Kluft zwischen dem Begriff und der Praxis mehr und mehr ausfüllen

helfen.'' Excerpt from the *Statuten* of the Joanneum, Graz, December 1, 1811. Reprinted in G. Göth, *Das Joanneum in Gratz* (Graz: Leykam, 1861), 256. See A. L. Schuller, *Erzherzog Johann . . . und was von ihm blieb . . . .* (Graz: Kulturreferat der Steiermärkischen Landesregierung, 1982).

Chapter 4

Knowledge and Information

INFORMATION, KNOWLEDGE, AND BELIEF

Being informed is a state of knowing something. Becoming informed denotes a change in what we know. Becoming informed may commonly include knowing more, but not necessarily. A message may arrive that contradicts rather than confirms what we thought we knew and leaves us in greater uncertainty. We may well feel that the new information leaves us believing that we now know less than before. More to the point, it is not so much that we know less; the ideas that we had held have not disappeared. Rather, our belief in them has diminished.

We take belief to be central to the study of information since we adopt the position that knowledge, and therefore becoming informed, depends on belief. If we did not believe something that had been alleged, then we should not say that we knew it to be the case. We only know that there had been an allegation. If we were unsure of our belief concerning the situation, then we might well say that we did not know what the situation was. If we believed the actual situation to be different from what had been asserted, we should say, more or less cautiously, that we knew that it was not as alleged.

We may know of things in which we did not believe, such as mythological beasts. But this is simply careless phrasing. If we were more careful, we should say of a mythical beast that we know of it and, more specifically, that we believe that it exists as a myth, whether or not we believe that it exists in some actual, nonmythical form.

Even when considering scientific knowledge, it is well to remember that library collections in past times contained plenty of scientific information now no longer believed by scientists on such topics as the orbiting of the earth by the sun (before Galileo), the origin of species (before Darwin), the laws of physics (before Einstein), and much else besides. Presumably some of the newest scientific information will be believed for a while and then, later, no longer believed. That some of what is believed in one century is superseded by different beliefs in a later century is the essence of progress in science as in other areas of scholarship. As Russell (1948, 507) observed, "All human knowledge is uncertain, inexact, and partial."

In brief we take the view that both peoples' knowledge and their opinions are elements of what they believe. We regard a change in what we know as being a change in our beliefs and a change in our beliefs as a change in what we know. More to the point, we view becoming informed as a change in beliefs—either a new belief or a strengthening (or a weakening) in our belief concerning something. Differently stated, it is difficult to see how an individual can be regarded as having become more (or differently) informed if no beliefs have changed. A situation in which a communication resulted in no change in belief would seem to reflect a situation in which the communication was redundant, ineffectual, unintelligible, or disregarded. Such a situation characterizes the absence of a process of becoming informed.[1]

Opinion

We have talked in terms of knowledge as being based on belief, on what we believe we know. It might be tempting to distinguish between knowledge and opinion. One may say, usually disparagingly, that I know something and that if you disagree, that is merely your opinion. There is little doubt that the same processes, by and large, are used both to inform and to influence opinion. Unless we choose to force a distinction, it would seem wisest to regard knowledge and opinion as being at least overlapping and to regard information systems as effecting both. The distinction between knowledge and opinion would seem difficult to sustain, and it does not appear to be a fundamental one for our purposes since both are, at heart, a matter of belief. In the meantime, we can note the use of information services by all sorts of special interest groups as much to change opinions as to spread knowledge, except that they might regard as knowledge what others might consider opinion.

RECORDED KNOWLEDGE; KNOWLEDGE REPRESENTATION

Although we may insist that knowledge is intangible, we can be grateful that knowledge can be represented in various ways: as text, as images, as records, as discourse. The physical representation of ideas, knowledge, beliefs, and opinions can be viewed as a translation or representation from something intangible to something tangible, from knowledge to recorded knowledge. If we chose to be rigorous, we would have to insist that recorded knowledge is not strictly knowledge at all, any more than a drawing of a cat is a cat. Recorded knowledge would be more accurately called a representation of knowledge, an information-as-thing.

Recorded knowledge, like all other representations, can be expected to be more or less imperfect. Even if it were not, people might well misunderstand it and so be able to derive knowledge from it only imperfectly or not at all, as in the case of texts in lost languages. Knowledge inferred from recorded knowledge would not be the old knowledge but new knowledge more or less closely related to the old. Nevertheless, it is of great practical importance that much recorded knowledge is not currently known to any individual but could become so if the record were examined. Making arrangements to enable such recorded knowledge to be read is of ever greater importance. The sum of human knowledge can, in practice, be viewed as being more than the sum of what humans know because recorded knowledge can reasonably be added to that sum (Wilson 1977).

INFORMATION-AS-KNOWLEDGE

The second of the three uses of the term *information* listed in the first chapter was information-as-knowledge, denoting the knowledge imparted in the process of being informed. In this use of the term, information is an increment in knowledge, and, as such, it shares the characteristics of knowledge.

A single act of imparting information, of information-as-process, can have several related but distinguishable sorts of information associated with it. The information-as-knowledge actually imparted by A to B might not be the information-as-knowledge that A had wished to impart, and both may have been different from the information-as-knowledge desired by B.

It is sometimes asserted that information is either "true" or "false," that information should be distinguished from misinformation, or even that information is not information unless it is true for example, "Information can only be derived from data that is [*sic*] accurate, relevant, and unexpected" (Longley and Shain 1989, 260).[2] But, here as elsewhere in life, wishing something to be true does not make it so. What, then, can we say of truth in relation to information?

It is prudent to remember that it used to be "known" and "true" that the sun and planets revolved around the earth. Anyone who could read, or be read to, could have been informed of this by the science books of the day, which are still available in some research libraries. A simple, rather cynical, comment would be that information is true if one believes it to be so. More seriously, beliefs are regarded as true if they are consistent with (and, especially, if entailed by) other prior beliefs held to be true. (For a more refined analysis, see Toulmin 1972.) Ultimately some belief must be held to be true, either as a matter of a priori assertion or from accepted authority, divinely revealed or otherwise, if anything is to be regarded as true.

One may often have cause to question whether one belief held to be true is compatible with another belief also held to be true. Or one might begin to doubt whether one or more of a set of beliefs should still be regarded as true. Again, one may be more inclined to accept information as true if the consequences of its being true are beneficial or, at least, not personally harmful. There is more incentive to question a negative evaluation of one's work by a superior than to challenge astronomers' assertions concerning distant stars. One cannot know everything firsthand. As a practical matter, most information and most knowledge has to be accepted secondhand on someone else's authority (Wilson 1977).

We conclude that the question of whether specific bits of knowledge are true is not central to our concerns. We adopt the position that the process of becoming informed is a matter of the changing of beliefs. Whether these beliefs are held or denied by others and whether they are compatible with some a priori or fundamental assertion need not detain us.

SUMMARY

Knowledge is based on belief. A change of knowledge is a change of belief. The information imparted in the process of information is a change of knowledge, a change in belief. Information in this sense, information-as-knowledge, is a form of knowledge and therefore shares its characteristics and is also intangible. Knowledge, however, can be represented or recorded. This representation is not itself knowledge but an information-as-thing, which can be used to derive new knowledge.

The knowledge actually imparted may not be what the receiver wanted to know or what a supplier of the information intended the receiver to know. Calling something information does not make it true.

NOTES

1. This rather simplified view should suffice for our purposes. For a broader introduction, see Machlup (1980, esp. chapts. 2, 5).

2. The author once listened to a lecture prefaced by the assertion that the speaker was concerned, by definition, only with information that was true. One wanted to ask, at the end of the lecture, how one could know that the statements in the lecture were true in order to ascertain whether one had been informed.

Chapter 5

Information-as-Thing

After the digression on theory, on systems, and on knowledge in the previous chapters we now return to information.[1] In the first chapter, we distinguished three different uses of the word *information*:

1. Information-as-process, the process of becoming informed.
2. Information-as-knowledge, that which is imparted when one becomes informed.
3. Information-as-thing, physical objects such as data and documents that are referred to attributively as information because they are regarded as being informative, as "having the quality of imparting knowledge or communicating information; instructive" (*OED* 1989, 7:946).

A key characteristic of information-as-knowledge is that it is intangible. One cannot touch it or measure it in any direct way. Knowledge, belief, and opinion are personal, subjective, and conceptual. Therefore, to communicate them, they have to be expressed, described, or represented in some physical way—as a signal, text, or communication. Any such expression, description, or representation would be tangible—what we have called information-as-thing. For this reason information-as-thing is of special interest in the study of information systems. It is with information in this sense that information systems deal directly. Libraries deal with books; computer-based information systems handle data in the form of physical bits and bytes; museums deal with a wide variety of objects. The intention may be that users will become informed (information-as-process) and that there will be an imparting of knowledge (information-as-knowledge). But the means provided—what is handled and operated upon, what is stored and retrieved—is physical information (information-as-thing). Knowledge is intangible; recorded knowledge is tangible, is information-as-thing, whether in books or in knowledge databases. "Knowledge-based" expert systems and "knowledge access'' systems are so only indirectly. Directly they are systems based on physical representations of knowledge.

A REVERSE APPROACH: WHAT IS INFORMATIVE?

Instead of the tedious task of reviewing candidate objects and inquiring whether they should be considered examples of information-as-thing, we could reverse the process and ask people to identify the things by or on account of which they came to be informed. People would say that they are informed by a wide variety of things, such as messages, data, documents, objects, events, the view through the window—by any kind of evidence. This point was recognized by Brookes (1979, 14): "In the sciences it has long been recognized that the *primary* source of information is not the literature of the sciences but observation of the relevant natural phenomena. Scientists (and others) find 'sermons in stones and books in the running brooks.' " How might we best sort out these candidates for being regarded as information?[2]

Information as Evidence

One learns from the examination of various sorts of things. In order to learn, texts are read, numbers are tallied, objects and images are inspected, touched, or otherwise perceived. In a significant sense, information is used as evidence in learning, as the basis for understanding. One's knowledge and opinions are affected by what one sees, reads, hears, and experiences. Textbooks and encyclopedias provide material for an introduction; literary texts and commentaries provide sources for the study of language and literature; arrays of statistical data provide input for calculations and inference; statutes and law reports indicate the law; photographs show what people, places, and events looked like; citations and sources are verified; and so on. In each case, it is reasonable to view information-as-thing as evidence, though without implying that what was read, viewed, listened to, or otherwise perceived or observed was necessarily accurate, useful, or even pertinent to the user's purposes. Nor need it be assumed that the user did, or should, believe or agree with what was perceived. *Evidence* is an appropriate term because it denotes something related to understanding, something that, if found and correctly understood, could change one's knowledge or beliefs concerning some matter.

Further, the term *evidence* implies passiveness. Evidence, like information-as-thing, does not do anything actively. Human beings do things with it or to it. They examine it, describe it, and categorize it. They understand, misunderstand, interpret, summarize, or rebut it. They may even try to fake it, alter it, hide it, or destroy it. The essence of evidence is precisely that perception of it can lead to changes in what people believe that they know.

Dictionary definitions of *evidence* include the following: "An appearance from which inferences can be drawn; an indication, mark, sign, token, trace, . . .

Ground for belief; testimony or facts tending to prove or disprove any conclusion. . . . Information, whether in the form of personal testimony, the language of documents, or the production of material objects, that is given in a legal investigation" (*OED* 1989, 4:469). If something cannot be viewed as having the characteristics of evidence, then it is difficult to see how it could be regarded as information-as-thing. If it has value as information concerning something, then it would appear to have value as evidence of something. *Evidence* appears to be close enough to the meaning of information-as-thing to warrant considering its use as a synonym when, for example, describing museum objects as "authentic historic pieces of evidence from nature and society" (Schreiner 1985, 27).

The term *evidence* is much used in law. Much of the concern is with what evidence, what information, can properly be considered in a legal process. It is not sufficient that information may be pertinent. It must also have been discovered and made available in socially approved ways. However, if we set aside the issues of the propriety of the gathering and presentation of evidence and ask what, in law, evidence actually is, we find that it corresponds closely to the way we are using it here. In English law, evidence can include the performing of experiments and the viewing of places and is defined as: "First, the means, apart from argument and inference, whereby the court is informed as to the issues of fact as ascertained by the pleadings; secondly the subject matter of such means" (Buzzard et al. 1976, 6; also Wigmore 1983).

TYPES OF INFORMATION

Pursuing the notion of information as evidence, as things from which one becomes informed, we can examine more specifically what this might include.

Data

Data, as the plural form of the Latin word *datum*, means "things that have been given." It is therefore an apt term for the sort of information-as-thing that has been processed in some way for use. Commonly "data" denotes whatever records are stored in a computer.[3]

Text and Documents

Archives, libraries, and offices are dominated by texts: papers, letters, forms, books, periodicals, manuscripts, and written records of various kinds—on paper, on microform, and in electronic form. The term *document* is normally used to denote texts or, more exactly, text-bearing objects. There seems no reason not to extend the use of *text* and *document* to include images, and even sounds intended to convey some sort of communication—aesthetic, inspirational, or instrumental. In this sense, a table of numbers can be considered as text, as a document, or as data. Text that is to be analyzed statistically could also be regarded as data. There is a tendency to use *data* to denote numerical information and to use *text* to denote natural language in any medium, but it is wise not to assume any firm distinction among data, document, and text.

Objects

The literature on information science concentrates narrowly on data and documents as information resources, but this is contrary to common sense. Other objects are also potentially informative. How much would we know about dinosaurs if no dinosaur fossils had been found?[4] Why do centers of research assemble many sorts of collections of objects if they do not expect students and researchers to learn something from them? Any established university, for example, is likely to have a collection of rocks, a herbarium of preserved plant specimens, a museum containing human artifacts, a variety of fossils, skeletons, and much else besides. The answer is, of course, that objects that are not documents in the normal sense of being texts can nevertheless be information resources—information-as-thing. Objects are collected, stored, retrieved, and examined as information, as a basis for becoming informed. One would have to question the completeness of any view of information, information studies, or information systems that did not extend to objects as well as documents and data. In this we, like Wersig (1979), go further than Machlup (1983, 645), who, like Belkin and Robertson (1976), limited information to what is intentionally told: "Information takes at least two persons: one who tells (by speaking, writing, imprinting, signalling) and one who listens, reads, watches." Similarly Heilprin (1974, 124) stated that "information science is the science of propagation of meaningful human messages." Fox (1983) took an even narrower view, examining information and misinformation exclusively in terms of propositional sentences. Brookes (1974), however, was less restrictive: "I see no reason why what is learned by direct observation of the physical environment should not be regarded as *information* just as that which is learned by observing the marks on a document." Wersig (1979) adopted an even broader view of information as being derived in three ways: (1) "generated internally" by mental effort, (2) "acquired by sheer perception" of phenomena, and (3) "acquired by communication." Our view of information includes Wersig's second and third ways.

What Is a Document?

We started by using a simple classification of information resources: data, document, and object. But difficulties arise if we try to be rigorous. What, for example, is a document? A printed book is a document. A page of handwriting is a document. A diagram is a document. A map is a document. If a map is a document, why should not a three-dimensional contour map also be a document, and, if it is, why should not a globe also be considered a document? It is, after all, a physical description of something. But if a globe is a document, why should one not also consider a model of a ship to be a document? The model is an informative representation of the ship, and the original ship itself, or even a life-size replica, would be even more informative than the model. "The few manuscript remains concerning the three ships that brought the first settlers to Virginia have none of the power to *represent* that experience that the reconstructed ships have" (Washburn 1964). But by now we are rather a long way from customary notions of what a document is.

The meaning of *document* was addressed by bibliographers and documentalists in the Documentation movement concerned with information storage and retrieval problems early in the twentieth century. One solution was to use *document* as a generic term to denote any physical information resource rather than to limit it to text-bearing objects in specific physical media such as paper, papyrus, vellum, or microform. Otlet, Briet, and other documentalists affirmed that (1) documentation (i.e., information storage and retrieval) should be concerned with any potentially informative objects; (2) not all potentially informative objects were documents in the traditional sense of texts on paper; and (3) other informative objects, such as people, products, events, and museum objects generally, should not be excluded (Laisiepen, Lutterbeck, and Meyer-Uhlenried 1980). Even here, however, except for Wersig's contribution (Wersig 1980), the emphasis is, in practice, on forms of communication: data, texts, pictures, inscriptions.

Otlet (1934, 217) stressed the need for the definition of *document* and *documentation* (i.e., information storage and retrieval) to include natural objects, artifacts, objects bearing traces of human activities, objects such as models, designed to represent ideas, and works of art, as well as texts. The term *document* (or *documentary unit*) was used in a specialized sense as a generic term to denote informative physical objects. For example, Pollard (1944) observed that "from a scientific or technological point of view the [museum] object itself is of greater value than a written description of it and from the bibliographical point of view it should be regarded therefore as a document." A French documentalist defined *document* as "any concrete or symbolic indication, preserved or recorded, for reconstructing or for proving a phenomenon, whether physical or mental" (Briet 1951, 7).[5] In this view, objects are not ordinarily documents but become so if they are preserved for informational purposes. A wild antelope would not be a document, but a captured specimen of a newly discovered species that was being studied, described, and exhibited in a zoo for educational and research purposes would not only have become a document but "the catalogued antelope is a primary document and other documents are secondary and derived" (Briet 1951, 8).[6] Perhaps only a dedicated documentalist would think of a antelope as a document. But regarding anything informative as a document is consistent with the origins and early usage of the word, which derived from the Latin verb *docere*, "to teach" or "to inform," with the suffix "-ment" denoting means. Hence *document* originally denoted a means of teaching or informing—whether a lesson, an experience, or a text. Limitation of *document* to text-bearing objects is a later development (*OED* 1989, 4:916; Sagredo and Izquierdo 1983, 173–78). Even among documentalists, however, including three-dimensional objects in information retrieval appears to occur only in theoretical discussions—and not always then (Rogalla von Bieberstein 1975, 12). Meanwhile, the semantic problem remains: What generic term for informative things is wide enough to include, say, museum objects and other scholarly evidence, as well as text-bearing objects? Objecting to the use of *information* or *document* for this purpose does not remove the need for a term.

Most documents in the conventional usage of the word—letters, books, journals—are composed of text. One would include diagrams, maps, pictures, and sound recordings in an extended sense of the term *text*. Perhaps a better term for texts in the general sense of artifacts intended to represent some meaning would be *discourse*. We could also characterize these texts as "representations" of something or other. However, we could hardly regard an antelope or a ship as being discourse, nor are they representations in any ordinary sense. Their value as information or evidence derives from what they signify about themselves individually or, perhaps, what they imply about the class or classes of which they are members. In this sense, they represent something, and, if not a representation, they could be viewed as representative. If an object is not representative of something, then it is not clear how far it can signify anything—that is, be informative.

One might divide objects into artifacts intended to constitute discourse (such as books), artifacts that were not so intended (such as ships), and objects that are not artifacts at all (such as antelopes). None of this prevents any of these from being evidence, from being informative concerning something or other. Nor does it prevent people from making uses different from that which may have been intended. A book may be treated as a doorstop. Illuminated initial letters on medieval manuscripts were intended to be decorative but have become a major source of information concerning medieval dress and implements. A building may be built to function as a house, yet the architect may also have been trying to make a statement.

Events

We also learn from events, but events lend themselves even less than objects do to being collected and stored in information systems for future edification. How different the study of history would be if they could. Events are (or can be) informative phenomena, and so should be included in any complete approach to information studies. In practice we find that evidence of events is used in three different ways:

1. Objects, which can be collected or represented, may exist as evidence associated with events: bloodstains on the carpet, perhaps, or a footprint in the sand.

2. There may well be representations of the event itself: photos, newspaper reports, memoirs. Such documents can be stored and retrieved.

3. Events can also be created or recreated to some extent. In experimental sciences, it is regarded as being of great importance that an experiment—an event—be designed and described in such a way that it can be replicated subsequently by others. Since an event cannot be stored and since descriptions of the results are no more than hearsay evidence, the feasibility of reenacting the experiment so that the validity of the evidence, of the information, can be verified is highly desirable. This adds another element to the full range of information management. If the recreated event is a source of evidence, of information, then it is not unreasonable to regard the laboratory (or other) equipment used to reenact the event as being somehow analogous to the objects and documents that are usually regarded as information sources. In what senses does it matter whether the answer to an inquiry derives from records stored in a database or from reenacting an experiment? What significant difference is there for the user of logarithms between a logarithmic value retrieved from a table of logarithms and a logarithmic value newly calculated as and when needed? The inquirer might be wise to compare the two but would surely regard both as information. Indeed it would be a logical development of current trends in the use of information technology to expect a blurring of the distinction between the retrieval of the results of old analyses and the presentation of the results of fresh analyses conducted as needed. (Sprague and McNurlin 1986, 194)

To include objects and events, as well as data and documents, as species of information is to adopt a broader view than is common. However, if we are to define information in terms of the potential for the process of informing, as evidence, there would seem no adequate ground for restricting what is included to processed data and documents as some would prefer, for example, by defining information as "data processed and assembled into a meaningful form" (Meadows et al. 1987). Perhaps the assumption is that without processing, the data might not be intelligible and so not informative, but there are two difficulties with such a restricted definition outside of electronic data processing. First, it leaves unanswered the question of what to call other informative things, such as fossils, footprints, and screams of terror. Second, it adds the additional question of how much processing and/or assembling is needed for data to be called information. In addition to these two specific difficulties, there is the more general criterion that, all things being equal, a simpler solution is to be preferred to a more complicated one. Therefore we retain the simpler view of information-as-thing as being tantamount to physical evidence: whatever thing one might learn from (cf. Orna and Pettit 1980, 3; Bearman 1989).

WHEN IS INFORMATION NOT INFORMATION?

The assumption is sometimes encountered that information is not information unless it is true. This implies that one has to determine whether apparent information is true before knowing whether one has been informed and by what authority truth is established. But even if we dismiss the argument that untrue information is not information, we could still ask, What could not be information? Since being evidence, being information, is a quality attributed to things, we may well ask what limits there might be to what could or could not be information. The question has to be rephrased as, "What things could not be regarded as informative?" We have already noted that a great variety of things can be regarded as informative, so the range is clearly very large.

We might say that objects of which nobody is aware cannot be information while hastening to add that they might well become so as and when someone does become aware of them. It is not uncommon to infer that some sort of evidence, of which we are not aware, ought to or might exist and, if found, would be of particular importance as evidence, as when detectives search, more or less systematically, for clues.

Determining what might be informative is a difficult task. Trees, for example, provide wood—as lumber for building and as firewood for heating. One does not normally think of trees as information, but trees are informative in at least two ways. Obviously, as examples of trees, they are informative about trees. Less obviously, differences in the thickness of tree rings are caused by, and so are evidence of, variations in the weather. Patterns reflecting a specific cycle of years constitute valuable information for archaeologists seeking to date old beams (Ottaway 1983). But if lumber and firewood can be information, one hesitates to state categorically of any object that it could not, in any circumstances, be information or evidence. We conclude that *we are unable to say confidently of anything that it could not be information.*

This leads to an unhelpful conclusion: if anything is, or might be, informative, then everything is, or might well be, information. In that case, calling something information does little or nothing to define it. If everything is information, then being information is nothing special.

Being Information Is Situational

Information-as-process is situational. Therefore, evidence involved in information-as-process is situational also. Hence, whether any particular object, document, data, or event is going to be informative depends on the circumstances, just as the relevance of a document or a fact is situational depending on the inquiry and the expertise of the inquirer (Wilson 1973). It follows from this that the capability of being informative, the essential characteristic of information-as-thing, must also be situational. We may say of some object or document that in such-and-such a combination of circumstances, in such-and-such a situation, it would be informative; it would be information; it would be information-as-thing. But we could in principle say that of any object or document. One just has to be imaginative enough in surmising the situation in which it could be informative. And if one can describe everything in this way, we are little further forward in identifying what is or is not information-as-thing.

It is a matter of individual judgment, of opinion, whether some particular thing would be pertinent and, if so, whether the probability of its being used as evidence would be significant, and, if so, whether its use as evidence could be important. (The issue might be trivial, or, even if important, this particular evidence might be redundant, unreliable, or otherwise problematic.) And, if so, whether the importance of the issue, the importance of the evidence, and the probability of its being used, in combination, warrant the preservation of this particular evidence. If all of these are viewed positively, then one would regard the thing (event, object, text, or document) as likely to be useful information and presumably take steps to preserve it or, at least, a representation of it.

Information by Consensus

We have shown that the virtue of being information-as-thing is situational and that determining that any thing is likely to be useful information depends on a compounding of subjective judgments. Progress beyond an anarchy of individual opinions concerning what is or is not reasonably treated as information depends on agreement or on at least some degree of consensus. We can use a historical example to illustrate this point. It used to be considered important to know whether a woman was a witch. One source of evidence was trial by water. The unfortunate woman would be put in a pond. If she floated, she was a witch; if she sank, she was not. This event, the outcome of the experiment, was, by consensus, the information-as-thing needed for the identification of a witch. Nowadays it would be denied, by consensus, that the exact same event constituted the information that it had previously been accepted by consensus as being.

Where there is a consensus of judgment, the consensus is sometimes so strong that the status of objects, especially documents, being information is unquestioned, as with telephone directories, airline timetables, and textbooks. In these cases, arguments are only over niceties such as accuracy, currency, completeness, and cost. As a practical matter, some consensus is needed to agree on what to collect and store in retrieval-based information systems, in archives, databases, libraries, museums, and office files. But because these decisions are based on a compounding of different judgments, it is not surprising that there should be disagreement. Nevertheless, it is on this basis that data are collected into databases, librarians select books, and museums collect objects. It is a very reasonable prediction that copies of the San Francisco telephone directory will be informative, though there is no guarantee that each and every copy will necessarily be used.

Information-as-thing, then, is meaningful in two senses. First, at quite specific situations and points in time, an object or event may actually be informative; that is, it will constitute evidence that is used in a way that affects someone's belief. Second, since the use of evidence is imperfectly predictable, the term *information* is commonly and reasonably used to denote some population of objects to which some significant probability of being usefully informative in the future has been attributed.

COPIES OF INFORMATION AND REPRESENTATIONS

Copies: Type and Token

In the provision of access to information by means of formal information systems, the question of whether two pieces of information are the same (or, at least, equivalent) is important. When copies are identical, one would speak formally of types and tokens. Examples that are not the same as each other are referred to as different *types*; identical copies are referred to as different *tokens*. If only one example exists, then one would say that there is only one token of that type.

The creation of identical, equally authentic copies is the result of particular technologies of mass production, such as printing. If you want to reread a particular book (type), you would want to read some copy (token) of it, but you would not insist of rereading the exact same copy as before. Similarly, if you had read a book on some subject and wanted to know more, you would ordinarily move on to reading a copy of another different title (different type) in preference to reading a different copy (different token) of the same title.

This feature of equally acceptable copies is sometimes (but not always) found in other examples of information systems. Some sorts of museum objects are mass produced, such as telephones. With telephones as with printed books, one example is as acceptable as any other from the same production run. There is, however, a major qualification. In archival practice, as in museums, two physically identical documents may be regarded as different if they have a different provenance or have some special relationship to other items in the collection, making them different by association.

In electronic databases, the situation is a little less clear. One can have copies of two sorts: there can be temporary, virtual copies displayed on a screen, or one can make copies of a longer-lasting form on paper or other storage medium. These copies might not, from some engineering error, be quite the same as the original. However, it is ordinarily assumed that either the copy is authentic or that errors will be so marked as to be self-evident. There may be difficulty in knowing whether the copy is a copy of the latest, official version of the database, but that is a different issue. With handwritten texts, one should expect each example to be at least slightly different, even if it purports to be a copy. The person making a copy is likely to omit, add, and/or change parts of the text. A significant feature of medieval studies is the necessity of examining closely all copies of related manuscripts not only to identify the differences but also to infer which might be the more correct version where they do differ.

In general, then, the prevalence of identical, equally informative, equally authoritative copies is unusual except among printed materials in libraries. More common is the case where copies are not altogether identical, though they may be equally acceptable for some purposes.

Interpretations and Summaries of Evidence

Much of the information in information systems has been processed by being coded, interpreted, summarized, or otherwise derived from earlier information. Books are a good example. Virtually all of the books in any collection are based, at least in part, on earlier evidence, both texts and other forms of information. Scholarship is permeated with descriptions and summaries or, as we prefer to call them, representations. Progress in information technology facilitates the deriving of new representations, new information-as-thing. Representations have important characteristics:

1. Every representation can be expected to be more or less incomplete in some regard. A photograph does not indicate movement and may not depict the color. Even a color photograph will generally show colors imperfectly and will fade with time. A written narrative will reflect the viewpoint of the writer and the limitations of the language. Films and photographs usually show only one perspective; something of the original is always lost. There is always some distortion, even if only through incompleteness.

2. Representations are made for convenience, which in this context tends to mean easier to store, to retrieve, or to understand.

3. Because of the quest for convenience, representations are normally a shift from event or object to text, from one text to another text, or from objects and texts to data. Exceptions to this, such as from object to object or from document back to object (physical replicas and models), can also be found (Schlebecker 1977).

4. Additional details related to the object but not evident from it might be added to the representation, either to inform or to misinform.

5. Representation can be iterated indefinitely. There can be representations of representations of representations . . .

Materials at the forefront of most fields of scholarship are difficult or unintelligible for most nonspecialists because the concepts and specialized terminology are not understood. Hence summaries, introductions, and explanations are useful. The resources and presentation match the competencies of the users. (Museums vary greatly in their attention to this point.) People tend to adapt to what is provided. A summary is, by definition, an incomplete representation. However, the evidence needs to be sufficiently detailed for the sorts of inquiries for which the service is provided. These two requirements are potentially in conflict, the first argues for simple explanations and the second against simplification.

Progress in information technology continually permits improvements in our ability to make physical descriptions, examples of information-as-thing. Photographs improve on drawings; digital images improve on photographs. The voice of nineteenth-century singer Jenny Lind was described by Queen Victoria as "a most exquisite, powerful and really quite peculiar voice, so round, so soft and flexible" (Sadie 1980, 10:865). Although this description is better than none, we could learn much more from a phonograph recording.

Reproductions of works of art and of museum artifacts may suffice for some purposes and have the advantages that they can provide much increased physical access without wear and tear on the originals. Yet they will always be deficient in some ways as representations of the original, although, as in the case of works of art and museum objects, even experts cannot always identify which is an original and which is a copy (Mills and Mansfield 1979).

SUMMARY

Information-as-thing deserves careful examination, partly because it is the only form of information with which information systems can deal directly. People are informed not only by intentional communications but by a wide variety of objects and events. Being "informative" is situational, and it would be rash to state of any thing that it could not be informative, hence information, in some conceivable situation. Varieties of information-as-thing vary in their physical characteristics and so are not equally suited for storage and retrieval. There is, however, considerable scope for using representations instead.

NOTES

1. This chapter is based on M. K. Buckland, "Information as Thing." *Journal of the American Society for Information Science* (forthcoming).

2. Note that we are restricting our attention to physical things and physical events. Some people would say that some of their knowledge comes from paraphysical sources, notably from divine inspiration. Others would deny any such nonphysical source of information. To the extent that it occurs, information science would have to be incomplete if such sources were excluded. Not knowing what to say on the subject, we merely note it as a possible area of unusual interest within information studies.

3. See Machlup 1983, 646–49 for a discussion of the use and misuse of the term *data*.

4. Cf. Orna and Pettit (1980, 9), writing about museums: "In the first stage, the objects themselves are the only repository of information."

5. "Tout indice concret ou symbolique, conservé ou enregistré, aux fins de représenter ou de prouver un phénomène ou physique ou intellectuel." S. Briet, *Qu'est-ce que la documentation?* (Paris: Editions Documentaires Industrielles et Techniques, 1951), 7.

6. "L'antilope cataloguée est un document initial et les autres documents sont seconds ou dérivés" (Briet 1951, 8).

Chapter 6

Information in Information Systems

Bearing in mind that information-as-thing is the one and only form of information with which information systems can deal directly, we now focus our attention on some aspects of information *in* information systems.

COLLECTING INFORMATION

To a large extent retrieval-based information systems are collections. People tend to think of archives, libraries, museums, records centers, and databases as collections. The assembling of materials for use in information systems is often a very large investment in labor, space, and other expenditure and so warrants careful attention.[1]

Fundamental to consideration of collections is the distinction between substance (information-as-thing) and arrangement (collection management). This distinction is easily overlooked given the ambiguity of *collection*, which as a common noun denotes something physical (assembled materials) and as a verbal noun denotes a process (collecting). In the terminology of computing, we are concerned not simply with files but also with file organization, with logistics, with how individual files should be arranged, where files should be located, and when and where additional copies of files should be deployed. File organization (collection management) is of major importance for all retrieval-based information systems. The optimal solution is highly situational, depending on many factors: the number and sizes of files; the frequency, urgency, and nature of use of each file; the feasibility of using extra copies, summaries, or other substitutes; the costs and capacities of different forms of physical storage; the speed and costs of transporting files; and the standards of service to be provided. A change in any of these factors is liable to make any given arrangement cease to be optimal.

Although collecting is ordinarily a first stage or precondition for retrieval, physical collocation in the normal sense is not strictly necessary. Some objects, such as people and buildings, do not lend themselves to being collected. In some cases, such as archaeological and cultural objects, moving something from its context may significantly diminish its value as information. Physically moving objects may be unnecessary so long as their location is known. They can still be cataloged, described, located, and learned from. In effect, they constitute a "virtual" or "distributed" collection. Familiar examples of retrieval from virtual collections include catalogs of paintings of particular artists, directories of consultants, and tourists' guidebooks to historic monuments. One might also create some description or representation of them: a film, a photograph, some measurements, a directory, or a written description. What one then collects is a document describing or representing the person, building, or other object.

Note that file organization is not directly concerned with the substance or meaning of the contents of a file. The relationship is, at most, indirect. The substantial content of the file is likely to affect the manner in which the file is used, which in turn is a factor in determining optimal file organization. There is little cause for confusion between files (stuff) and file organization (deployment).

We are not directly concerned here with the materials that are or might be collected. Nor are we concerned with the definition of specific collection development policies, with the practice of selecting, or with techniques for evaluating individual collections. These technical concerns are important, are highly situational, and have had much written concerning them. Instead we are interested in roles of collecting per se in the provision of information systems. It is, at root, a logistical exercise to improve service. Why is it done? We distinguish four roles:

1. *Preservation role*: Any data, documents, or objects that are not collected and preserved are likely to be lost, unavailable now and in the future. It is difficult to predict what might be of interest to someone in the future. When in doubt, it is prudent to preserve nonrenewable resources.

2. *Dispensing role*: A quite different reason for collections is the need to provide convenient physical access to copies. Different species of information system vary greatly in the relative importance of the dispensing role. The making of additional copies for ease of access, as opposed to preservation and security purposes, is relatively limited in archives and management information systems compared with libraries where the dispensing role accounts for most of libraries' budgets and space needs. If someone asks to see a book, it is not entirely satisfactory for the librarian to answer that a copy is preserved in the British Library in London. The need is for a copy here and now. Printed books, unlike corporate management data or archival records, are created in multiple, equally authentic copies. Yet, being on paper, a localized medium, the printed book as a medium both allows and requires duplicative local collections for effective information service. Desired material not held in one's local library collection is made available only with delay and inconvenience for the would-be reader

and effort for the librarian. Consequently, other things being equal, the greater the amount of material that is made available locally, the better the service is (Buckland and Hindle 1976).

3. *Identifying role*: Where collected items can be scanned directly, the arrangement of materials on shelves also permits the collection to play an identifying (or "bibliographic") role in the sense of being a tool for the identification of what materials exist. If the material is arranged by subject, for example, users seeking to identify material on a given subject, as in a bookshop or a museum, can and do seek out the appropriate section and examine the display to identify suitable material, whether or not a bibliography, catalog, index, or other guide is also provided. In this sense the array of items that can be viewed is performing an identifying or bibliographic role analogous to that of a catalog and quite different from the dispensing and preserving roles.

4. *Symbolic role*: The three functional roles noted above seem insufficient, even taken together, to explain collecting behavior adequately. Collections also have a symbolic role. Large collections, particularly of special materials, bring status and prestige whether the materials are used or not. The symbolic value of collections and of buildings to house them is particularly marked in the case of museums and, to a lesser but still substantial extent, in libraries (Sherman 1989).

Complexity and the Relationships between Roles

In a simple situation, the three functional roles are tightly connected. Imagine a single, small, uncataloged collection of a few documents in an isolated situation. What has been preserved *is* what is available, and what is available can easily be identified but only by examining them as they are arranged.

Increasing the size or complexity of an information system leads to specialization of functions. As complexity is added, these three roles diverge and become less tightly coupled.

As soon as two or more collections of materials become available, the archival role of any single collection ceases to determine what is available. The user of one collection can extend its resources by drawing on the resources held in other collections. Cooperative collection development becomes a formalization of this opportunity for increasing service through specialization in preservation activities and thereby extending the overall capacity to serve. The relationship between types and tokens (e.g., titles and copies), within or across collections, defines the extent of the preservation role. For any given total number of holdings, if there are many tokens of each type (copies of each title), the preservation task is relatively small. If all items are of different types, with only one copy of each, then the task is more severe.

Even a few items become easier to use if they are arranged in a systematic manner. As the amount of material, the quantity of use, and the sophistication of service increase, the limitations of depending solely on examination of the items themselves for identifying become more serious. The traditional response is to augment the shelf arrangement by systems of additional, symbolic shelf arrangements using surrogates for the items themselves: index entries arranged in various ways. The use of multiple index entries for each item has some significant advantages. A rather extreme development of this augmentation of the bibliographic role of shelved materials is to depend entirely on catalog records for this purpose, as can be seen in mail-order catalogs and research libraries with closed access. Users have to use the catalog to obtain an item if they are ever to see it.

As one considers two or more collections, the utility of a single collection as a guide to what exists diminishes, depending on the relationship between types and tokens across collections. If each collection were identical, any one collection would be a guide to all that is available. As the collections become more disparate, with less overlap, each (and the catalog of each collection) would become less effective as a guide to what exists. The traditional response is a consolidated listing of surrogates, a union catalog.

As these examples indicate, a given collection could play a dispensing role without an archival role or without an identifying role if there has been enough specialization in the broader context of which it is a part.

Dimensions of Collecting

The development of collections has several dimensions. The most basic is whether to establish a collection and where—and whether to discontinue or move it. Individuals are differentially affected by the location of information collections, especially because the geographical location not only affects ease of use but also because organizational control is often affected by location. The decentralization or recentralization of corporate data centers or of branch libraries can be a sensitive issue (Seals 1986; Sprague and McNurlin 1986).

Collecting information is also highly sensitive to the physical attributes of the medium of the material concerned. The advent of electronic media in information systems traditionally based on paper and physical objects—archives, libraries, museums, records management—is beginning to have radical consequences for collecting practices, as well as modes of service.

Attributes and Arrangement

When more than a very few items have been assembled, some systematic arrangement facilitates retrieval. Generally only a one-dimensional array of objects is practical. Practice varies according to the attribute of the object selected to be the basis for arrangement. Archives are arranged by administrative provenance and the original order of assembling (Daniels and Walch 1984); libraries usually arrange their collections by subject matter (Hyman 1982); the arrangement of data in computer-based systems (file organization) varies considerably according to the situation, and it is the interface rather than the file organization that becomes important for the user.

HISTORICAL CHARACTER OF INFORMATION IN INFORMATION SYSTEMS

Historical Features of Information

All communications and every information-as-thing is historical in that each is the product of a particular time. For many purposes, such as daily conversation, this does not matter. Our words, although expressed at a specific point in time, are heard so quickly that the delay is imperceptible and unimportant.

Documents and other evidence might have been slow in the making and might have been stored for a considerable time before being retrieved. A letter or newspaper from a distant place may reflect the situation as it had been at the time of writing, but does it reflect the situation now? Is the financial report downloaded from the corporate database still as up to date as the central version? Is the central database overdue for updating? For this reason, the use of retrieval-based information systems is necessarily and unavoidably a historical activity, and the historical nature of information is a central feature of information services, even though not always recognized as such.

Setting aside the special cases of deliberate and accidental misrepresentation, the most that can be said of the representations (data, text, images) in information systems is that they record what was alleged to be accurate at some past time. It is usually assumed that the records are still accurate at the time of retrieval. Two points are fundamental to these representations. First, they are only representations. They describe and should not be confused with what they describe. A statement that the moon is made of green cheese does not cause the moon to be made of green cheese. Second, even if the description were accurate at some time, it does not follow that the accuracy will continue. Even an accurate statement that, on a given day, the exchange rate for the U.S. dollar was 13.90 Austrian Schillings does not constitute reliable evidence that the exchange rate is now 13.90.

For the conscious study of the past, the historical nature of records seems self-evident. What is easily overlooked is that all use of retrieval-based information systems is necessarily historical. Records are descriptions of how something is supposed to be. In accounting information systems, the records describe how income and expenditures were supposed to be at the time the record was made or, more conveniently, for some earlier time since it is inconvenient to try to keep absolutely up to date. Weather stations record the temperature and other climatic conditions at particular points in time. A will records the maker's intentions at the particular date with respect to the disposition of property. Even if one consults such records promptly, one cannot know with certainty that the financial situation indicated in the accounts, the temperature at the weather station, or the desired disposition of property is still as described. Indeed, change within hours is to be expected in the first two cases. One may choose to assume that there have been no significant changes but that is different from knowing that there have been none. One cannot ascertain from the inspection of data whether what is represented was originally or is still, at the time of inspection, an accurate reflection of whatever is represented.

It is, of course, more sensible to regard records as documenting something at the time the record was made. Even here, the evidence is not entirely certain. It may since have been discovered that there had been an arithmetical error in the accounting, a malfunction in the weather station equipment, or a mistyping in the will.

The importance of this historical aspect will depend on the changeability of what is described. The information may not be volatile enough for the lapse of time to be a matter of concern. The longitude and latitude of the city of Berkeley does not vary, but the availability of specific houses for sale does. One can therefore use an old gazetteer to ascertain geographical coordinates with more confidence than one can use an old list of houses for sale when seeking to buy a house.

For some special purposes, the convenient administrative fiction is used that the recorded description is deemed to be accurate unless it can be proved incorrect. This is to be expected when referring to retrievable data is substantially more convenient than ascertaining the actual state of affairs. The description, or, more precisely, the most recent retrieved description, is officially true. This is assumed of airline seat reservations and of house ownership. Proving that official records are in error may be a substantial task.

In the humanities, the range of uses for which evidence is needed is extensive. Most obviously, this includes biographical data of all kinds: age, attitudes, activities. Further, there are literatures of many genres that reflect the human experience. A proper understanding of the social and cultural contexts that are distant in time or place is important for the proper comprehension of the human experience in those times and places. The range of circumstances in which people need to use records to reconstruct the past or to explain what followed is very large: stage-set design, restoration of houses, appreciation of past literature, and so on.

In scientific studies, essential features are the statement of hypotheses and the replicability of experiments. Hypotheses cannot remain known candidates for testing unless they are recorded. Experiments cannot be replicated unless an adequate description is presented. These descriptions have to be stored for future, critical examination if scholarship is to cumulate. Without this ''archive'' or ''corpus'' denoting the ''body'' of science, the cumulative development of science through the scientific method would not be possible.

The same is true with objects that are not records. A museum object is regarded as informative about the situation whence it derives, just as a document is. It is possible for both objects and records to be misleading. They might be unrecognized fakes, might have been misidentified or misleadingly described, and, even if neither a fake nor wrongly attributed, might still be misleadingly untypical. Of course, the situation from which it derives is likely to have changed in the meantime.

The time aspect of retrieval-based information systems adds a problem with respect to the selection of materials. It is not simply a matter of choosing to acquire evidence that is useful now but the much more difficult challenge of choosing what would be useful now or in the future.

Communication through Time

The significance of the lapse of time as a characteristic of retrieval was noted explicitly by Mooers (1951) in a paper that is said to contain the first use of the term *information retrieval*. Mooers described information retrieval as "communication through time."

This image of information retrieval as communication through time is in keeping with the lack of a direct link between the source of the message and the recipient. One can imagine messages (data, documents) as having hooks (tags, labels, or descriptors) attached to them and then being placed in some timeless void where they remain until an inquiry in the form of one or more hooks reaches into the same void and pulls back any messages with one or more hooks coinciding with those of the inquiry.

But as one starts to work around the edges of this definition, it becomes a little frayed. In some situations, the resources are not merely passively stored but are reported more or less promptly to those who are interested or are assumed to be interested. Examples can be seen in periodic reports generated by management information systems and in selective dissemination of information (SDI) services. This could be regarded as preemptive information retrieval, but the notion of a standing order would appear more apt. There is some delay, even if attempts are made to minimize it. Even with prompt online processing, the indirectness and the sequential, discontinuous, two-stage nature of the process (storage, then retrieval) still remains and still takes time even though it may not be very much.

In information retrieval, the indirectness or discontinuity of communication permits and, indeed, ensures delay over and above the time required for communication itself. The simplest conclusion would seem to be that although information retrieval can properly be regarded as communication through time, it is not the only form of communication in which time is significant. Delay, one would conclude, is an attribute of all communication and of all uses of information-as-thing but is particularly marked in retrieval-based information systems.

Indirectness

By the "indirectness" of information retrieval systems, we refer to the characteristic that designers and operators can only guess who will seek what information or when it will be sought. Not only does one not know who will seek to use it, one does not know when or how, or why. This point should not be taken too literally. One must have some general sense, possibly vague or unreliable, as to what sorts of people and what sorts of inquiries they are likely to bring, else one would not know what to collect or what sort of access to provide to it. This foreknowledge will vary. The designer of a management information system may be able to negotiate some quite explicit agreement as to what sorts of inquiries particular potential users say they will make. Libraries and museums may be created to serve identified educational and research programs for specified groups. Recent experience in providing service will provide a basis for predicting service needs in the near future. Experience elsewhere in similar situations may be a useful guide. There is, therefore, some basis to knowing at least generally what to expect.

Nevertheless, not knowing precisely or completely who will ask what question or why or how is a very important characteristic of retrieval-based information systems. It is not known what perspectives or vocabulary users will bring or the extent of their expertise. To some degree, this lack of prior knowledge is shared by other communication systems. In general, one is unable to predict, or later to ascertain, who heard a radio broadcast, read a particular issue of a newspaper, or how much they understood, or how beneficial the message was to them.

In retrieval-based situations, however, there is a further complication: it is the user, with or without someone else acting as a mediator, who defines what information should be retrieved and takes action to retrieve it. The vocabulary of each would-be user is inevitably somewhat different from that of the designer of the information system, since no two persons' vocabularies and knowledge are exactly the same. There could be substantial difference if the designer (a category in which we include the indexer for present purposes) is distant in time, education, and culture from the eventual would-be user.

It is this indirectness that permits, indeed requires, description by the user of what is wanted. This in turn makes the representation of the inquiries and representations (indexes, abstracts, classification, etc.) of the contents so important.

We conclude that:

1. Information retrieval involves communication through time, although not all communication through time involves information retrieval.

2. Information retrieval is necessarily indirect communication.

3. Both the delay and the indirectness are liable to exacerbate difficulties caused by the problems of definability.

TYPE OF SYSTEM BY TYPE OF INFORMATION

We now review the characteristics of the information that is handled in the five types of information service given as examples in chapter 3, looking at the characteristics of the information collected in them (cf. Sprague and McNurlin 1986, 189–99). We use three features:

1. *Source*: Was the material created (MIS), received from inside the organization (archives), received from outside (libraries, museums), or a combination (records management)?
2. *Form*: Is the material primarily composed of coded data (numbers, names, dates, as in MIS), text (archives, libraries, records management), or objects (museums)?
3. *Uniqueness*: Are the materials unique (archives, records management, museums) or copies (libraries, MIS)?

These characteristics, somewhat simplified, are displayed in table 6.1. The pattern in the table suggests a number of tentative and speculative comments:

1. Each of the five types of service emerges as different from the other four. These are genuinely different types of information system.

2. Degrees of affinity are indicated. First, management information systems have the least affinity with the others; only one aspect out of three (source) is shared with any of the others, and that only partially with records management. Second, museums are unique in that their information is in the form of objects, not text or coded data. Museums are similar to libraries in that their information is externally derived but differ in that their information tends to be unique. They resemble archives in the uniqueness of the information but differ in that their material is not internally derived. Third, strategic planning depends heavily on knowledge of developments in the environment and especially on the actions of others. Such information is primarily received from the outside and, most commonly, as texts. Hence management information systems based on internally derived data have an inherently limited basis for building strategic decision support systems in any situation in which knowledge of the environment is important. Evolving a management information system in this direction would make it more similar to a library in that it would become dependent on information derived from the external environment (Pieptea and Anderson 1987).

3. The "Source" column suggests further interpretation. Other things being equal, those who create information resources (MIS, records management) should have a relatively clear understanding of what the material signifies. Material that is internally generated (records management, archives) should be more easily understood by the providers of service than if the material has been received from outside (libraries, museums). To the extent that this is true, there is some kind of rough progression from top to bottom of table 6.1 in terms of increasing effort and expertise required of the providers of service to explain their information resources. With management information systems, what the data mean should be known because the providers of the service were involved in defining them. The status and content of internally generated material should tend to be more familiar than externally generated material. Even in scholarly museums, items whose identity and significance may be only vaguely known to the staff

Table 6.1
Information Systems and Characteristics of Information

Information System	Characteristics of Information		
	Source	Form	Uniqueness
MIS	Created	Code	Copies
Records Management	Created (and received from inside)	Text	Unique
Archives	Received from inside	Text	Unique
Libraries	Received from outside	Text	Copies
Museums	Received from outside	Objects	Unique (mostly)

are held and even exhibited. The situations are not equal in the demands made on the providers to be able to explain what they are providing.

4. The "Form" column also suggests further interpretation, this time in terms of the expertise required of the user to become informed. The numbers in management information systems have been defined before being collected so there ought to be little ambiguity about them. Texts, designed to be read, are likely to be to some degree self-explanatory. Objects are simply objects; a viewer's understanding of what they are and what significance they have depends entirely on the beliefs and expertise brought by the viewer. In this sense the "Form" column also represents some sort of rough progression; as one moves from top to bottom, there would seem to be some sort of tendency for the expertise demanded of the user to increase and the need for explanation and interpretation by staff increases.

5. In considering the "Uniqueness" column, however, the issue seems to be more one of technology. On the face of it, dealing with identical copies would appear to be a distinguishing feature of libraries. But libraries would not be dealing with truly identical copies if printing and photocopying had not been invented. Manuscript materials in library collections before printing were not exactly alike; errors of transcription and improvements were made as scribes did their copying. The move toward electronic texts may move the situation back in the direction of the manuscript era where there could be a multiplicity of copies that are not necessarily quite the same and the relationships between them and their authenticity become unclear. Perhaps this important distinguishing characteristic of libraries is a temporary one, based on a particular information technology, printing, characterized by mass production. The extent to which management information systems can be said to be based on providing copies derives from the use of computers.

The preceding discussion has been superficial and speculative but can at least serve as a reminder that the things that can be stored for retrieval in actual or virtual collections vary in significant ways. Buildings, films, printed books, and coded data impose different constraints on the tasks associated with information retrieval systems: selection, collection, storage, representation, identification, location, and physical access. Put simply, a museum, an archive, a library of printed books, an online bibliographic database, and a corporate management information system of numeric data can all validly be regarded as species of information retrieval system. But differences in their attributes, including their physical form, affect how the collected items can be handled (Buckland 1988b).

Purpose

The intrinsic interest of photos, books, fossils, paintings, statistical compilations, and so forth is enormous. However, this interest needs to be balanced against the purposes of the information system. In general, the purpose of an archive, library, museum, or, indeed, any other information system is seen as answering the inquiries that arise, but these systems can also be designed to arouse curiosity.

An information system is both a resource for inquiry and a vehicle for seeking to inform those people who might not inquire. Either way, an information system is purposive. Depending on one's values, one may agree or disagree with any given purpose, but information services are based on *some* purpose, however partisan, frivolous, altruistic, or ineffectual. A characteristic of effective information systems management is the continual effort to make information resources more conveniently available in a manner that corresponds to the local use of evidence.

SUMMARY

In this chapter we have concentrated on aspects of information-as-thing that appear important for information systems.

Information retrieval involves communication through time, although not all communication through time is information retrieval. All use of retrieval-based information systems is necessarily a historical activity.

Information retrieval involves communication that is necessarily indirect. Both the delay and the indirectness are liable to exacerbate difficulties caused by the problems of identification and definability. Because communication is indirect in retrieval-based information systems, the user has no choice but to search for what is wanted.

The potential range of informative material is truly enormous in extent and variety, and much of what is held in collections summarizes or explains other evidence. This is both understandable and desirable: not all evidence is equally intelligible or convenient; not all inquiries are equally complex; not all inquirers are equally motivated or bring equal personal knowledge or cognitive skills. It is therefore important that information systems either include material at various levels of explanation or be adept at explaining it. There would be limited benefit in having *Aesop's Fables* in the original classical Greek in a primary school library, in a management information system containing inadequately explained data, or museum exhibits that are not labeled.

Information systems vary greatly with respect to the source of their information (from inside or outside their organization), the form of their information (data, documents, objects), and the extent to which they deal with unique material or copies. Comparison on these points provides some basis for noting similarities and differences among MIS, archives, records management, libraries, and museums.

Information services are concerned with knowledge, facts, and beliefs, but as a practical matter, information systems deal with vast quantities of physical objects (including representations of knowledge, facts, and beliefs) using various forms of information technology. Hence information technology and changes in information technology are of great importance for information systems.

NOTE

1. This section draws on M. K. Buckland, "The Roles of Collections and the Scope of Collection Development," *Journal of Documentation* 45 (1989): 213–26.

Chapter 7

Information Technology

DEFINITION

Technology is used for handling physical processes. As such, it is of extraordinary importance for dealing with information-as-thing: data, texts, objects, and events.[1] *Information technology*, like *information system* and *information processing*, is commonly used in a restricted sense to denote electronic computing and communications technology. However, we define *information technology* as any technology used in handling information. There seems no logical basis for defining it otherwise. Information technology thus includes pen, paper, card, microfilm, and any other nonelectronic as well as electronic information technologies.

Information services are concerned with knowledge, facts, and beliefs (for a good discussion, see Bergen 1984). Frederick Kilgour (1978, 12–19) defined the purpose of a library as being "to actively participate in the evolution of those profoundly human creations: beauty, faith, justice, and knowledge." As a practical matter, however, information systems, libraries not excluded, deal with physical objects, with information-as-thing, with representations of knowledge, facts, and beliefs. Information systems deal with data, texts, and objects, with millions of these objects on endless miles of shelving, in untold filing cabinets, and on innumerable magnetic and optical devices with enormous data storage capacities. It is reasonable to expect, therefore, that any significant change in the nature or characteristics of the technology for handling the representations of knowledge, facts, and beliefs could have profound effects on information systems and information services.

We use *technique* to denote a way of doing something and *technology* to denote a physical resource that can serve as a tool for accomplishing something. Any given technique will make more or less use of different technologies. Any changes in means for handling physical objects are likely to be of extraordinary interest to those concerned with information systems, for good practical reasons.

Each tool, each technology, has its capabilities and its limitations. Improvements in technology bring changes (usually increases) in capabilities and changes (usually, but not necessarily, reductions) in limitations. In other words, the effect of improvements in technology will be to change—generally to reduce—practical constraints. We would say of some new technology that it is an improved technology only if its capabilities and limitations were preferable for our purposes. If they were not preferable, we would not regard it as an improved technology. In general terms, improved technology has the effect of diminishing technical constraints and in this sense has a liberating effect.

Our concepts and understanding are based on what we know and are familiar with. Much, though not all, information technology in this century has been relatively stable until the recent adoption of electronic digital computers. Much information handling has been firmly based on the technology of paper and of card. Small improvements are relatively easy to grasp: large changes are not. The implications of any radical change in technology are unlikely to be understood or appreciated for a long time, except, perhaps, by a few visionaries who are able to concentrate on key underlying principles—visions may or may not prove accurate, for example: "Fifteen years from now there will be a chip in your telephone receiver with more computer power than all the technology the Department of Defense can buy today. All the written knowledge of the world will be one of the items found in every schoolchild's pocket" (Reingold 1985, 16).

There is a massive literature on how computer technology could, should, or might be used in information systems, and the information systems management literature is rather dominated by technological issues (Sprague and McNurlin 1986). The adoption of new technology involves practical difficulties and false starts when attempts are made to implement it. The capabilities and limitations may have been misjudged. Much can go wrong, for example, when introducing computer systems (Hirschheim 1985, 248–49; Salmon 1975, chap. 9).

Considering a new technology and its possible applications is not easy. It is difficult not to think of a new technology in relation to prevailing implementations of current technology. But the implementations of the current technology are necessarily based on its capabilities and limitations, which are different from those of the new technology and necessarily result in a constrained and distorted interpretation of what is ideally needed. One would like to be able to consider new technology in relation to first principles, to a theoretical definition of what would constitute ideal information service. As a general rule, the more radical the change, the greater is the need to go back to first principles with respect to what the underlying objectives are. (It may very well be wise to implement technological changes in a gradual manner, but that is a matter of tactics rather than of principle or strategy.) Unfortunately, thinking in abstract terms about practical matters is not only difficult but also remote from our experience. A prudent approach is threefold: (1) to study the potential application of new technology to current activities; (2) to take a fresh and critical look at the capabilities and limitations of the older information technology in relation to our goals; and (3) to use the change of technologies as an opportunity to improve our theory, our understanding of the nature of what we seek to do.

COMPARING INFORMATION TECHNOLOGIES

Both the nature of the limitations of traditional, paper-based information systems and some consequences of the introduction of computer-based technology can be briefly illustrated by reviewing some of the capabilities of each. Ideas that are expressed in terms of only one technology are necessarily limited. Any one technology is better understood if compared with others (Nass and Mason 1990).

Characteristics of Materials on Paper

Archives, libraries, office procedures, and records management evolved to provide access to resources on paper. The technology of paper has characteristics that are so familiar that they tend to be overlooked.

1. No special equipment is needed to read them.

2. They are strictly localized: The reader must read a document on paper where that document is. The reader must go to the document, or the document must be physically transported to the reader. Possibly another copy can be acquired or made, but each copy would still have to be where its reader is. Obvious though this may seem, it is a massive constraint on paper-based information systems since the use of the material is, in practice, highly sensitive to locations. A document at hand is used more than a book elsewhere, let alone at a distant collection. For example, even when book funds are inadequate, selective duplication of library materials in different libraries on the same campus or in the same public library system is generally needed, and there is at least mild contention over the locating of unduplicated material of interest to two or more groups at different locations. The size of locally held collections is itself taken as a measure of the worth of a library. The "architecture" of paper-based information is dominated by the localized nature of paper as a medium. For the users, local is beautiful. Remote, centralized storage may be efficient but is a significant degradation of service for the users, more so with paper than with electronic data.

3. Paper, like a telescope, is unsuited for simultaneous viewing by two or more people. Either another copy must be found (or made) for additional readers or users must take turns.

4. Materials on paper are treated as a capital, public good. They are acquired and made available without charge. They are bought at a one-time cost as an investment, the cost is not passed on to the reader, and, until the copy becomes

worn out, there is no additional cost (other than circulation and reshelving workloan) involved in its' being read by one more person. If demand exceeds supply, three options exist: rationing use by limiting loan privileges, increasing supply by adding another copy, or lowering the standard of service by letting additional would-be readers wait (Buckland 1975). This traditional library model of financing an information service is not the only option, but, for paper-based systems, the alternatives are more difficult to implement because of the nature of paper as an information technology.

5. Paper materials are not easy to revise or update, except for minor corrections to individual copies. Devices such as errata slips are not very effective. It may be more effective to replace the entire document. But after the copies of an edition have been distributed, who would know where they all are to replace them or to make the corrections?

Characteristics of Microforms

Texts have been microphotographed from the earliest days of photography. In addition to documentary uses of photography, the systematic use of micro-formed documents developed gradually after microfiche was standardized by Otlet around 1906. Microfilm came into substantial use in the 1930s, used by banks to record used checks (Johnson 1932) and by libraries to copy newspapers. The use of microforms was greatly extended by the dissemination of technical reports on microfiche by the U.S. government and with the adoption of computer output on microform (COM).[2]

Microfilm and other microforms represented a significant departure from paper materials yet differ on only one of the characteristics noted above: special equipment is needed to read them. This adds a requirement to maintain a new sort of equipment: microform readers and printers. Microforms are therefore even more localized than paper materials. Not only must the would-be reader and the microform be in the same place, there must also be a usable machine to read it in that place. Microforms are even less suitable for correction or revision than paper documents. Nevertheless, the low cost of acquiring, distributing, and storing copies of microforms makes them a reasonable choice for some sorts of information work, such as distributing catalogs and preserving old newspapers, in spite of their unappealing form and attributes.

Characteristics of Electronic Documents and Databases

Electronic documents and databases have tended to differ from paper not, like microforms, on just one of the characteristics of paper-based materials but on all five.

1. As with microforms, special equipment is required to read them—equipment that is substantially more complex, more expensive, more useful, and more obsolescent than microform readers. Not only is the equipment used to provide

access to information in databases more elaborate than is that of microforms, but the equipment has other novel features. A microfilm reader displays an image of a record and does little else, except, maybe, produce a copy. Computers used in conjunction with databases not only allow retrieval of copies of records but also a great deal of manipulation: records can be reorganized, reformatted, and combined with other machine-readable text; records can be edited and stored again in revised form; and numerical data, such as census tables, can be retrieved and subjected to statistical manipulation. A census table on paper or microform would have to be transcribed by hand into machine-readable form. The equipment used to gain access to databases is, in general, usable for other purposes also. A personal computer can be used for word processing, electronic mail, statistical analysis, and manipulation of personal data, as well as accessing databases. Moreover, there should be a convenient linking of each of these functions such that data could flow conveniently between them.

2. Usage of a database is not inherently localized. For example, thousands of people all over the world use the databases made available through the DIALOG service, but few of these people have ever been to Palo Alto, California, where the databases reside. There is a strong trend for at least professional workers, managers, and students to have personal computers that enable them to access records from their laboratories and homes and when traveling as an alternative to using their office workstations. Data can be copied from remote databases. Just as it does not matter where a paper document came from so long as it comes in a timely and reliable manner, so also it does not matter to an online searcher where the data on the screen have come from so long as they too come in a timely and reliable manner. (There could well be cost differences, but that is a separate issue.) Vickery and Vickery (1987, 323–24) observe:

The logic of print on paper is local availability through multiple outlets of multiple copies of a particular document. Printing entails a multiplicity of local booksellers and libraries. The logic of the new information technology is quite different—it is that of multiple access via telecommunications networks to a single copy of a document remotely held in machine-readable form. Neither logic is implemented in pure form—local book supplies are supplemented by interlending networks . . . and local forms of electronic store are becoming available.

3. Further, given suitable equipment, users of databases can, in effect, make simultaneous use of the same database, whereas it is not practical to make simultaneous use of the same book. Contention for the same book is a major source of frustration for library users.

4. The use of databases has, in general, not been budgeted as a capital, public good. Typically databases—telecommunications, computer charges, and other elements—have been provided on a pay-as-you-use fee basis. These expenses— real, monetary charges—are commonly passed on to the users as a recharge. With paper and microform documents, charging by the amount of use is not

Table 7.1
Characteristics of Information Technologies

	PAPER	MICROFORM	DATABASE
1. Equipment required?	NO	YES	YES
2. Remotely accessible?	NO	NO	YES
3. Simultaneous use?	NO	NO	YES
4. Usage measurable?	NO	NO	YES
5. Revisable?	NO	NO	YES

feasible. With computer-based records, however, this constraint is removed. It is technically quite easy to determine usage-based charges. Whether one chooses usage-based charges, usage-insensitive subscription fees, or provision of uncharged access as a public good or administrative overhead is a matter of management policy and depends on what one is trying to accomplish. The technology allows the choice.

5. Electronic processing is designed to support convenient correction, revision, and updating.

Table 7.1 provides a simplified summary of these characteristics of records on paper, in microform, and in machine-readable form.

The rise of nonlocalized media and versions in nonlocalized media of localized originals has substantial implications for collection development. Remote access to an electronic version of a text or a digitized image of a museum object will sometimes be an acceptable, even preferred, alternative to inspection of the original. How will this affect collection development?

To be satisfactory, solutions using electronic documents would have to address the four roles of collections:

1. The preserving role would require techniques appropriate for the medium.

2. The dispensing role would have greater flexibility in implementation. Since electronic documents, unlike paper, microform, and museum objects, are not inherently localized, there is more scope for acceptable trade-offs between local storage and remote access.

3. The identifying role would benefit from the possibility of combining the versatility of online indexes with the benefit of immediate access to the electronic text or image and with the advantage of browsing in more dimensions than a single sequence that rows of items on shelves permits.

4. The symbolic role should not be neglected and will presumably take on some new form or be sublimated.

INFORMATION TECHNOLOGY AND THE USE OF
INFORMATION SERVICES

The process of becoming informed involves a combination of mental effort and technological process. Circumstances vary greatly, but, as one example, we can envisage a professional, a manager, or a scholar who might read a document and then produce a summary, rebuttal, or commentary, perhaps in a different language. As another example, numbers might be copied into a calculator and statistical summaries generated automatically. The former case is largely mental labor, yet a variety of mechanical aids might prove useful. Paper, pencil, and cards are traditional aids; a dictionary, perhaps, or photocopies of the originals; a word processor might be helpful in the preparation of the summary or in preparing a concordance or other mechanical analysis of the text. The technology used to assist in these processes is information technology. The use of, for example, calculating machines to massage numerical data to calculate statistical summaries is as much a process of creating a representation as is taking a photograph.

Historically, retrieval-based information services, such as archives, libraries, and records centers, have been more directly concerned with handling representations than with their creation. Inasmuch as computer centers and laboratories provide the equipment to create events and to convert one set of evidence into another, they can also be involved in the creation of new information. The emphasis rather than the overall goal differs. Perhaps it is characteristic of the new information technology that the boundaries between creating, retrieving, and using information are dissolving and that, in the future, information systems will support all three in a more unified manner.

Information technology can be expected to continue to make progress in supplying more powerful and cheaper tools. For this reason alone, one should expect that there will be more and more options available (U.S. Congress 1986). Meanwhile, texts, images, and sounds are increasingly available in digitized form. The more these materials are available in machine-readable form, the more scope there is to use information technology to aid in the reading, copying, excerpting, analyzing, inferring, and adding to the resources.

The continuing increase in the power and economy of computing, data storage, and telecommunications means that we can worry less about efficiency and more about the purposes of information systems.

SUMMARY

Information system users are concerned with the search for intangibles, notably knowledge and entertainment. Nevertheless, the situation is dominated in practice by the sheer mass and complexity of physical objects needed to support these concerns. Different technologies have different capabilities and limitations, and therefore technological change alters the constraints on effective information service. Specifically, new technology enables improvements in the physical storage and handling of records. However, the fact that a record has been stored in some place does not mean that you know that it exists, that you could find it if you wanted it, that you could understand what it signified if you found it, that you should believe it if you understood it, that it is not contradicted by some other record, or that just those who should have access to it do have access to it. Therefore, paradoxically, we may expect that the liberating power of the new technology will (and should) induce renewed attention to these traditional non-technological concerns of information service.

Planning and statements of mission and objectives are understandably influenced by what is known to be technically feasible. Improvements in technology reduce constraints on what is feasible. A natural consequence is that ideas, plans, and policies tend to reflect obsolescent understanding of the possibilities.

NOTES

1. This chapter draws on M. K. Buckland, "Library Materials: Paper, Microform, Database." *College and Research Libraries* 49(1978): 117–22.

2. Convenient introductions can be found in *ALA World Encyclopedia of Library and Information Sciences*, 2d ed. (Chicago: American Library Association, 1986), s.v. "Micrographics," 548–52, and *Encyclopedia of Library and Information Science* (New York: Dekker, 1976), v. 18, s.v. "Microform," 76–99, and "Microform Publication," 99–114.

Chapter 8

Access to Information

In the previous chapter, we identified five examples, or types, of retrieval-based information service: archives, libraries, management information systems, museums, and records management. In this chapter, we look at the range of concerns or functions that need to be included by considering what is necessary for access to information.

Each individual information service has its own special focus with respect to mission, groups to be served, sorts of material to be collected, and techniques employed. Nevertheless, access emerges as a recurrent theme.

The term *access* is frequently used in relation to quite different bits and pieces of information service. Indexes provide subject access to collections; censorship impedes access to materials; new telecommunications technologies permit remote access; fee-based information services are differentially accessible because not everyone can afford the cost; most library collections are open access, meaning that users can go directly to the shelves; most museum shelves are closed access in that only staff can get to and handle the collections; some services are inaccessible to the wheelchair bound; and most books are effectively inaccessible to people with limited reading skills. Occasionally two or more different sorts of access are considered at the same time. For example, the *Lacy Report* covered several aspects of access, including changes in information technology, libel, censorship, illiteracy, preservation, and the future of libraries (American Library Association 1986). Yet each of these senses of access is related. Each refers to one or more aspects of providing means of access to information, of enabling users to accede either to a source of information or, in a fuller sense, to knowledge, to understanding.

Access can be regarded as a unifying concept for the whole field, and we shall use it in this way. In this chapter, we start with the assumption that all of the provision and use of retrieval-based information services is concerned with access to information, and we proceed to categorize, in top-down fashion, the different aspects of access.

SIX ASPECTS OF ACCESS

We have defined access as the means to enable an inquirer to learn from—to become informed by—a source pertinent to an inquiry, to accede to the evidence that results in acquiring the knowledge desired.

It may not always be possible to provide access. No pertinent source may exist for some inquiries; with some obscure inquiries, the source may exist, but understanding it might be beyond anybody's expertise, as with fragments of lost languages.

In simpler cases, one or more suitable, intelligible, credible sources exist, and the problem of access reduces to bringing a source and the inquirer together. However, six types of barrier have to be overcome if access to information is to be achieved:

1. *Identification*: A suitable source needs to be identified. This indicative access is the realm of bibliography, documentation, classification, indexing, and information retrieval. Commonly one thinks of this in terms of finding pertinent data or documents about the topic of the inquiry, but, more generally, the retrieval system may need to be responsive to requests for retrieval on any of several attributes, often, but not necessarily, what they are about. (This is usually at least a two-stage process: deciding where to look ("channel-selection") as well as identifying a specific book, record, or other source.)

2. *Availability*: The inquirer needs to be able to inspect the source or a copy of it. This physical access, or document delivery, is a matter of logistics and technology. If a source that has been identified cannot be located and made physically available in an acceptable fashion, then another source needs to be identified and made available.

3. *Price to the user*: We use *price* to denote what the would-be user must expend to use the service. The price may include, but is not restricted to, money. "The real price of everything, what everything really costs to the man who wants to acquire it, is the toil and trouble of acquiring it" (Smith 1976, Bk. 1, chap. 5, para. 2). The "real price" includes time, effort, and discomfort ("I was too embarrassed to ask . . . "), as well as money. In particular, price includes the effort of learning to use difficult, user-unfriendly systems (Culnan 1985). The price must be acceptable to the inquirer. To the extent to which it is not, price is a barrier to access.

4. *Cost to the provider*. Not all expenditure of money and effort is borne by the inquirer, least of all in archive and library services, which are traditionally free, in the sense that monetary charges are not usually made. In this context we use the term *cost* to denote what has to be expended by the providers of service. To the extent that the sponsors or providers of service may incur expenditure of effort, money, space, or inconvenience, the arrangement would

have be acceptable to or, at least, not incompatible with their view of their role, mission, and values. Meeting the need may encroach on values of a social, cultural, or political nature. The detailed profile of any information service is largely defined by the allocation of resources, and this allocation is based on the resources and social values of those who allocate.

Providing access to appropriate evidence might in some cases be regarded as an unacceptable challenge to these values: to national security, to private or corporate vested interest, or to social values, as in the case of indecent or irreligious materials (*Library Trends* 1986, 3–183). These nonmonetary values have a long history of restricting access in a manner similar in nature to restrictions caused by financial shortages. "How strange it is that for most liberal thinkers—academics as well as statesmen—knowledge is almost always 'good' and worthy of wide diffusion, although history is full of attempts by governors—political, moral, and religious leaders, and well-meaning parents—to discourage the spread of 'dangerous' or 'unwholesome' knowledge" (Machlup 1980, 12).

5. *Understanding: Cognitive access.* Once physical access to a suitable source has been achieved, another condition for successful access is that the inquirer has sufficient expertise to understand it. If not, then some combination of two remedies is possible: explanation and education. Explanation would involve additional interpretation of the source—a translation, perhaps, if the existing source is in a foreign language or an explanation by someone with more expertise, either on an informal basis or by the creation of a new summary that is easier to understand. Education is another solution in that the inquirer may be able to acquire more expertise, for example, by consulting a dictionary, an encyclopedia, or someone who has the requisite expertise, and may then be able to understand the book.

There is one further aspect involved in "acceding to knowledge," which has not traditionally been thought of as having to do with access yet plays the same kind of role in practice as the other aspects and so can reasonably be included in the discussion of access: acceptability.

6. *Acceptability.* *Acceptability* denotes two related issues: First, inquirers may be reluctant to accept a particular source as credible, regarding it with suspicion as having inadequate "cognitive authority" (Wilson, 1983). Second, the inquirer may be unwilling to accept the evidence of the source because it is unwelcome in what it signifies and conflicts with other beliefs, a matter of cognitive dissonance (Festinger 1957; Greenwald and Ronis 1978).

Including credibility as a criterion for becoming informed can be questioned. Arguably you *are* informed *of* something that you might regard as unbelievable, as, at best, a curious error. Your beliefs are, in a sense, added to rather than changed. You "know of" something rather than "knowing that" something is the case. You may understand something, but if you do not accept its validity, you are hardly informed by it. Everyone will agree that some sources should be denied credibility. The problem is in deciding which.

ACCESS AND THE AMBIGUITY OF "INFORMATION SYSTEM"

There is an ambiguity in the meaning of *information system* that can be clarified in terms of these six aspects of access. In a common, and limited, sense, the phrase *information system* is used to denote systems that retrieve potentially informative things: data, documents, objects, information-as-thing. We could make this usage clearer by using the phrase *information-supplying system*, and for this limited sort of information system, the notions of identification, availability, price to the user, and cost to the provider constitute a useful categorization of the conditions that must be met for success.

Alternatively, we may wish to adopt a broader view of information systems whereby we are explicitly concerned with becoming informed, to information-as-knowledge, not merely access to information-as-thing. We could use the phrase *systems that inform* for this more ambitious sense of information system (Shaw and Culkin 1987). For this more extended task, the additional requirements for cognitive access and acceptability constitute a necessary expansion of the conditions for success. Each one of these six dimensions constitutes a type of barrier to access; each one must be satisfied if access is to be affected.

Our view of the nature and scope of information systems will depend on whether, as in this book, we choose to be concerned with systems that inform or, as is commonly the case, only with information-supplying systems. This choice will also define what range of research is perceived to be relevant and the content of professional education for information systems specialists.

SUMMARY

The variety of ways in which the term *access* has been used is symptomatic of the complexity of retrieval-based information services. The notion of access can provide a helpful unifying concept for the field as a whole as long as access is viewed in a broad, multidimensional way.

The very diverse nature of the different aspects of access means that quite different sorts of actions are needed to remedy difficulties on each. For example, the remedy may be technical (better retrieval systems for identification, better delivery for availability); additional time, effort, or money (price); an increase in resources or a change in social and political values (cost); instructional (remedying inadequate expertise for identifying materials or for understanding them when they are made available); or altered attitudes (acceptability).

Part **III**

Processes

Chapter 9

Inquiries

In part II we examined some important concepts and the use of the term *information* in relation to information systems. Part III contains six chapters, each examining one of the six different sorts of process associated with the provision and use of information systems. A major part of the agenda is to seek completeness by exploring complex as well as simple cases. For the relatively complicated case when a retrieval-based information system is provided and used, each of the six quite different sorts of process is needed: inquiry; information processing; perceiving, receiving, and retrieving; becoming informed; providing a service; and demand for service.

The first of these six process-oriented chapters is concerned with inquiries—with the motivation to become informed. The motivation to choose to use some particular information system is a separate matter (addressed in chapter 13).

MOTIVATION TO KNOW

We are concerned here with the motivation to know and, in particular, with inquiries as the driving force for the use of information systems.

What Do People Want or Need to Know?

What an individual may want or need to know is clearly extensive. It would include not only the narrowly technical and professional needs upon which formal information systems have concentrated but also social knowledge and, indeed, anything the absence of which would cause the individual to feel lacking. The range of things that an individual might want or need to know appears to be boundless, limited in practice by that individual's awareness, curiosity, and stamina.[1]

Felt needs would be heavily influenced by three factors:

1. The individual's personal values and motivation. This is turn could be roughly and imperfectly sorted into subcategories such as information needed to cope ("survival information"), information needed to succeed, information needed to become well regarded, and information wanted for idiosyncratic curiosity and for entertainment.

2. The information needed would be highly situational (Wilson 1973). What one needs to know varies from one social, geographical, and professional context to another. Each social, geographical, and professional situation has its own particular values and frames of reference both linguistically (how things are described) and cognitively (how things are learned).

3. Both of the other factors are largely defined by cultural influences and social pressures: standards of acceptable behavior and life-style, criteria for being well regarded and successful, personal goals in relation to one's situation. Even curiosity and entertainment (for example, in the choice of hobbies) are affected by social trends and fashions.[2]

We concentrate here on what people feel the need to find out ("distressing ignorance"). There are additional things that some people believe that others ought to know in their own or society's best interests ("harmful ignorance") (Wilson 1977) and also changes in knowledge and beliefs that others may wish to effect for reasons altruistic or otherwise. Hirsch's *Cultural Literacy: What Every American Needs to Know* (1987) is an example of prescribing some of what other people should know, as, indeed, is most discussion of educational curricula. Influencing what people in other countries know is an important aspect of any national foreign policy (Hausrath 1981; Price 1982; Stephens 1955).

Inquiries and the Use of Information Systems

The conventional view of information is that it is needed and used for instrumental purposes. Researchers have even tried to measure the value of information or the amount of information in terms of its instrumental impact on decisions. But information systems are not always and only used to obtain obviously instrumental information. College libraries, for example, are extensively used as study halls, as places where one may use seats and tables to work with materials that are not library materials. Parents can and do take small children to public libraries so their children can borrow books. One motivation, possibly a dominant one, may be that the reading of the books would foster the children's reading skills.

Many information systems are provided by special interest groups, by corporations, and by governments as an important part of their strategy for achieving their objectives. Specialized agencies such as the U.S. Information Agency, the British Council, industrial marketing boards, and Christian Science reading rooms are expected not simply to inform but also to influence opinions. This situation becomes a lot more understandable and reasonable if knowledge is viewed as being composed by beliefs. Changing beliefs can be expected to change assumptions and thereby attitudes, consumer behavior, and political actions. In a different direction, the recreational reading of escapist literature hardly involves information in the rather limited customary usage of the word.

How, then, are we to view these quite diverse activities if we are to consider them in relation to ordinary notions of information and information system? It cannot be denied that these varied activities are associated with the use of information systems within our scope of interest, especially libraries and museums. We suggest that information—the process of becoming informed—should be interpreted in a very broad sense. Commonly in writings about information, a narrow, utilitarian perspective is adopted: one uses an information service because one needs "facts" in order to do something (to make a decision concerning what to do, say, write, or believe). Verifying a reference, checking an airline schedule, looking up a physical constant, discovering someone else's line of argument, ascertaining the exact wording of a text, and finding instructions on how to build a wall are examples of the use of information systems in the traditional, instrumental sense. These sorts of activities fit conventional views of information systems very well.

One can speak in general terms of the individual's desire for knowledge, a positive way of describing what we are concerned with. However, at risk of sounding negative, we suggest that the nature of the situation is easily and more effectively understood if this description is inverted and the use of information services is viewed in terms of the reduction of distressing ignorance.

It is not obvious that either the desire for knowledge or the reduction of distressing ignorance can adequately account for all of the uses of information systems. We can note that this addresses the motivation rather than the consequences of using information systems. We can stretch the motivation to include idle curiosity. The boundary between belief and aesthetic feelings is a blurred one. We should not assume that motivation to know is entirely separate and independent of other motivations. In brief, although inquiries can be explicit, clear, and instrumental in nature, there seems no grounds for proceeding on the basis that all inquiries are so tidy or, indeed, that there is any clear demarcation between the desire to inquire and, for example, aesthetic desires.

For these and similar reasons it would seem wise to follow Pratt (1982) in arguing that the traditional practice of restricting information (as a process) to practical, utilitarian purposes is simply too narrow (cf. Shera 1972, 115–25). Instead one should take a broader, more fundamental view of informing to include the receipt of signals for a variety of purposes: functional, aesthetic, intellectual.

We can see the difference between the limited utilitarian view and the broader view by considering the use of a music recording. On the utilitarian view, a musicologist who listened to the recording in order to ascertain how the player had interpreted or adapted the composer's score would have been said to have been informed, but someone who had simply chosen to listen to the music for enjoyment, relaxation, and inspiration would not be said to have been informed but only entertained. On a broader view of information, one would argue that audible signals were received by both individuals and that these signals "informed'' their brains in some way. The experience of one may have been mainly aesthetic in nature, and the motivation of the other may have been narrowly utilitarian. More realistically, the experiences of both were likely to have been both aesthetic and utilitarian, albeit in differing proportions. On a broad view, both were examples of being informed. Instead of arguing that some uses of information are instrumental and others are not, we prefer the view that all uses of information are more or less instrumental. Some uses are instrumental in a more direct and utilitarian way than others. There is a continuum.

This broader definition of information has advantages. First, it is based on information as a physiological and psychological process rather than on the vagaries of motivation for the process or on possible, expected consequences of the process. It is a simpler, more general definition and is highly compatible with biological and systems concepts. Second, it enables one to treat a broad spectrum of information systems as part of a varied but continuous whole without having to demarcate by using unsatisfactory distinctions between such terms as *educational*, *recreational*, *utilitarian*, *instrumental*, and the like in order to define information as in Waples et al. (1940, 13). Further, it enables one to recognize that an act of information can have various effects—inspirational, recreational, utilitarian, educational—singly or in combination, expected or unexpected.

This broad definition is hospitable to the inclusion of recreational reading, the use of information systems to influence opinions, and parents' use of books to foster reading skills in their children. As for more eccentric uses (for example, those who use museum galleries and library reading rooms as places to escape from the weather), one can observe that means can become ends and be glad that human beings are versatile enough to find uses for institutions over and beyond those for which they were intended.

ORIGINS AND CHARACTERISTICS OF INQUIRIES

We now consider the characteristics of inquiries. For our purposes, we merely need to assume that inquiries originate. It is not essential to understand how and why they arise. However, it does seem plausible to view inquiries as being in response to distressing ignorance. We are all enormously ignorant in the sense that there is a great deal that we do not know. Some things we are unacquainted with. Some things we do not understand. One only has to look at a computer tape library, peruse an encyclopedia, contemplate a library, or watch a crowd, composed as it is hundreds of individuals each with his or her own public and private lives, to realize how little of human knowledge each of us possesses. Yet each example represents only a very small selection from the totality of human knowledge known or recorded. Beyond that, there are so many things that are not yet known.

In a very important sense, this colossal individual ignorance does not matter. People can and do live pleasant, happy, satisfying lives unaware of the characteristics of the moons that circle Jupiter, ignorant of the early history of the

Danube basin, and unable to tell anyone the chemical formula for common salt. The assumption that ignorance is bliss is less dependable than the certainty that everyone is more or less in ignorance, whether or not also in a state of bliss.

Ignorance becomes important only to the extent to which it becomes distressing or harmful. We use the term *distressing* to denote occasions when an individual is not only conscious of ignorance but also feels a desire to acquire knowledge in order to reduce the ignorance and, thereby, the distress. Such ignorance may be a gap in personal knowledge. For example, one may want to fly from San Francisco to New York but not know the times of the flights. In this case, not knowing the time of the flights makes it difficult to make detailed arrangements for the journey, a distressing situation. There are two possible solutions: one can inquire, in which case the knowledge acquired fills the gap and removes the ignorance, or one can decide not to travel after all, in which case the ignorance remains, but since the intention of traveling has been removed, the ignorance ceases to be distressing and is therefore no longer of concern.

There are also less clearly motivated examples of distressing ignorance. One might, for example, like to know something of the history and culture of Austria. It is not that one's life, employment, or physical well-being would be spoiled for lack of such knowledge but rather that there is a curiosity, a desire to know. Unlike the need to know about flights to New York, there may be no urgency, and the degree of distress may be very mild. Nevertheless, in one's personal system of values, a positive value has been assigned to that missing knowledge, and so the lack of it has become distressing in some way. Becoming informed is a means of achieving a goal. Using an information system is instrumental for that purpose.

Ignorance is not necessarily a gap in our knowledge. We may have acquired conflicting knowledge, as when we hear two apparently irreconcilable accounts of the same event. This constitutes ignorance in the sense that we do not know what to believe. We might decide that we do not care, but, if we do care, then the incongruence or dissonance becomes another case of distressing ignorance. We define inquiries as attempts to acquire knowledge, to change our beliefs, or to make sense (Belkin, Oddy, and Brooks 1982; Dervin and Nilan 1986; Neill 1987; Swigger 1985).

Some authors, notably Wilson (1977), have written in terms of "harmful ignorance." We prefer "distressing ignorance" for inquiries that originate from an individual on the grounds that the inquiries would not originate unless the individual felt some sort of distress, even if only in the form of curiosity. One might argue that anything distressing is, by definition, harmful, but that requires a particular definition of harmful and also interferes with the use of the term *harmful* for situations in which the individual is unaware of and therefore undistressed by genuinely dangerous ignorance. For example, if the public were unaware that the water supply had become infected by dangerous germs, the people using the water supply would be in genuinely harmful ignorance. Yet as long as they remain unaware of the danger, they would not be distressed. The supplier of the water, however, if aware of the problem, would know that the consumers were in harmful ignorance and that they ought to be informed so that they could boil the water or take other precautionary measures. *Harmful ignorance* seems a particularly useful term to use in relation to those who diagnose information needs for others.

From Ignorance to Inquiry

Given that one is conscious of distressing ignorance, there are several possible courses of action

1. The distress rather than the inquiry might be eliminated. One might decide not to travel to New York or lose interest in the history and culture of Austria.
2. One might seek to remove the ignorance by mental effort alone. Perhaps by searching one's memory, the desired knowledge might be found. Perhaps by mental effort, one might conclude that two apparently conflicting accounts of the same matter can be reconciled.
3. One might inquire of others. One might ask a friend, telephone an office, look in a book, interrogate a database, or visit a library. This raises new questions: What determines where the inquiry is directed? What happens as a result of the inquiry?

Types of Inquiry

It would be convenient and elegant if one could separate cleanly an inquiry as a pure reflection of an individual's need and a search statement phrased in terms of some particular source of information. If they existed separately, one could concentrate on the former as part of this discussion of inquiries and defer consideration of the latter for the next chapter on perceiving, receiving, and retrieving. Such a separation is unrealistic, however, because people tend to express their inquiries in a manner influenced by the sources they use.

Markey, refining an earlier analysis by Taylor, suggests that inquiries can be considered in four stages:

1. The actual ("visceral") but unexpressed need for information.
2. The conscious within-brain description of the need (the "conscious" need).
3. The formal statement of the need (the "formalized" need).
4. The question as presented to the information system (the "compromised" need). (Markey 1981; see also Jahoda 1977; Vickery and Vickery 1987, chap. 7)

REPRESENTATION OF THE INQUIRY

We have referred to "the question as presented to the information system (the 'compromised' need)." If you want to ask a question of a person, you have to express it in such a way that the person can understand it, sometimes difficult when traveling in foreign countries.

More generally, inquiries have to be expressed in terms that information systems can handle. Collections of informative things—whether data, documents, or other objects—are arranged by one or more attributes. Each attribute is expressed (represented) in some more or less formalized way. In an art museum, paintings are ordinarily arranged by school—in effect by a combination of style, time period, and place of origin—and not, for example, by alphabetical order of artists' names. Finding a particular painting or type of painting is facilitated if you know the school or time and place of origin.

Books on economics are usually grouped by a sign reading "Economics" in a book shop but by a sign reading "330" in a library using the Dewey Decimal Classification. For an inquiry in an online bibliographic retrieval system, one usually has to represent the inquiry in terms of the keywords used to index the documents in the database. For an inquiry concerning teaching methods in Austrian universities between the two world wars, one might try the following combination—

HIGHER EDUCATION or UNIVERSITIES
and TEACHING METHODS
and AUSTRIA

—possible with a specification of the historical period.

In the stylized conventions of subject headings in a library card catalog, one would represent the same inquiry as a single, complex, multiconcept subject heading composed according to specific rules not only to represent the specific topic but also to be filed and findable at one predictable point: AUSTRIA, *Higher education*, 1918–1939.

Alternatively one could represent the same inquiry in terms of the artificial notation of the library's classification scheme and then search the shelves or a classified subject catalog under, for example, 378.1709436 in the Dewey Decimal Classification.

Unless one can represent the inquiry in a search statement expressed in the terms of the information system, only a combination of chance and tedious sequential searching will allow one to find out whether pertinent material is there.

Source as Surrogate for Inquiry

Not only do inquiries tend to be compromised by expression in the terms expected to be effective in dealing with an information source, there is also a tendency to express inquiries by asking not for what is actually wanted but for an information source thought likely to contain what is wanted. Suppose that we had an inquiry and wanted to ask other people in case they know what we want to know. We could simply ask people as we happened to meet them.

Probably, however, we should adopt an indirect approach: (1) seek to identify the name of someone who might have the requisite knowledge, (2) try to find that person, and then (3) ask that person.

At stage 2, we would be seeking a person not because that person is wanted as an individual but as a source of the knowledge desired. If we discovered, at any stage, that that person did not have the requisite knowledge or was unintelligible, then our interest in him or her would end. In other words, the interest in the person is solely as a source of the desired knowledge. The person, in a sense, represents the desired knowledge. This is an indirect approach in that, at stage 2, we would be asking directly for the person as an indirect means to become informed.

This indirect approach is likely to be preferred if we are shy about publicizing our particular distressing ignorance; if we suspected that the people most conveniently at hand were unlikely to know the answer to our question or even to understand it; and/or if it were particularly difficult to describe what it was that we wanted to know. In each of these cases, the indirect approach would be preferable in the sense that less discomfort and/or less effort would be involved. Similarly, it is commonly easier to ask for a book than to define the knowledge desired, especially since what is sought may well be in a book with a wider coverage. For example, "Where is the *Encyclopedia Britannica*?" may suffice for an elementary inquiry concerning the Coptic church. "Where is this year's state budget?" should enable one to discover the size of a particular state agency's budget allocation. "May I use the San Francisco telephone directory?" is certainly simpler than asking for a particular individual's telephone number.

We infer from these examples that when a book (or other source) is sought, commonly the name of the source is being used as a surrogate definition of the knowledge actually being sought (Jahoda 1977, 87). It may not be the only source. It may not even contain what is desired.

This tendency to specify not the objectives of the inquiry but rather the presumed address of the answer to the inquiry appears to be common in the use of retrieval-based information systems. It also underlines the importance of maintaining the distinction between an inquiry and a search or, in Markey's terminology, between different stages of need.

URGENCY AND IMPORTANCE

An inquiry may be expressed as a statement of need; the expression of that need may well be influenced, or even replaced, by the terminology or address of a presumed source. Two more characteristics are needed to complete the categorization of inquiries (and searches):

1. The perceived importance of the inquiry, reflecting the degree of distress felt, will determine how much effort the individual is willing to exert and the point at which he or she will decide to abandon the search. In effect, the importance, in conjunction

with the perception of probable effort, determines whether (and how far) a search derived from an inquiry will be pursued.

2. The urgency attributed to an inquiry will determine when it is pursued. Less important but more urgent inquiries may be attended to before other more important but less urgent inquiries. The urgency of a given inquiry (and its importance) can be expected to vary over time.

SUMMARY

What an individual needs to know is extensive and includes not only the narrowly technical and professional information on which formal information systems have concentrated but also information concerned with social and personal interests. Information needs are situational and cultural.

Distressing ignorance is when one feels the need to correct some gap or anomaly in one's knowledge. Possible solutions include thought, losing interest, and inquiry. Inquiries, however, need to be expressed in terms that the potential source of information—whether a person or a retrieval-based information system—can handle. Representing the inquiry as a question or search statement is of great importance and is yet another example of the importance of representation in information systems. Inquiries and their fates depend also on their perceived importance and their perceived urgency.

NOTES

1. For a convenient summary of studies of information needs and users see Dervin and Nilan (1986).

2. For a good example see Barber's (1980) analysis of the social, cultural, and religious influences behind the popular interest in "natural history" in nineteenth-century Britain.

Chapter 10

Perceiving, Receiving, and Retrieving

DEFINITION AND STRUCTURE

In the previous chapter, we considered the sorts of inquiries that may arise and how inquiries have to be compromised to be expressed when using an information system. In the next chapter, we discuss how people become informed when they receive or perceive information. In this chapter, we examine how people come to receive information, through observation, communication, and retrieval.

The Receiving of Information

The notion of information is meaningful only in relation to someone becoming informed (Otten 1975). The receiving of information, the sensing of some information-as-thing, is a necessary condition for becoming informed. The receiving of information has traditionally been seen as the last part of the more general process of communication, but that view is incomplete. Since information can result from observation, communication is not a necessary condition for information.

What sorts of ways of receiving information are there? The threefold typology used in chapter 3, resembling that of Wersig (1979), offers a useful approach:

1. *Observation*: The receiving of information is necessarily the receiving of some information-as-thing. The receiving of any information-as-thing depends on its being sensed: seen, heard, smelled, tasted, or felt. As a general term for this sensing or receiving, we use *observation*. We now proceed to isolate two special cases of observation.

2. *Communication*: In a physical sense, all observation could be seen as involving communication in that rays, sounds, smells, and vibrations emanating from what is observed constitute the physical means by which anything is observed. However, we limit use of *communication* to the subset of observations that involve intentional

communication. Observing that a police officer is signaling one to stop would be classified as communication; seeing a traffic accident or a sunset would not. On this basis, observed communications are a special case of observation.

3. *Retrieval*: Another special case of observation is when the information-as-thing has been collected and stored so that the would-be receiver can select and retrieve what is to be observed. Commonly, but not necessarily, retrieved materials are stored communications.

The relationship between communication and retrieval is ambivalent. A conventional view would be that information retrieval is a special case of communication because the objects stored and retrieved are ordinarily things intended as communications, such as financial records, correspondence, and scholarly literature. But some sorts of stored and retrieved objects, especially museum objects, such as fossils and artifacts, are not communications in any normal sense.

In terms of the natural theology of the eighteenth and early nineteenth centuries, natural objects would have been regarded as signs from the Creator. Also one might argue that an object would not have been collected for retrieval unless it was regarded as potentially informative, which implies a sense of intending communication in the future. But these are both less than communication in the usual sense.

Here as elsewhere in human behavior, it is easier to identify examples of different types than it is to draw clear boundaries or develop mutually exclusive categories. A detective's noticing a suspicious footprint in the sand at the scene of a crime would ordinarily be regarded as an observation but if the footprint had been made deliberately as a misleading clue, it would be a communication.

Three forms of communication can be identified. Direct communication occurs when a message is communicated directly from the source to the recipient, as in face-to-face conversation. Indirect communication has two parts. Store-and-forward communication occurs when the signal is stored somewhere and then forwarded on to the recipient, as in the case of a letter, which may be stored and forwarded a number of times before being delivered to the recipient. Store-and-retrieve communication occurs when the signal is stored somewhere so that the recipient can choose to retrieve it, as is usually the case with electronic mail (Vervest 1985).

Forms of communication also vary with respect to the sender's control over who receives the signal. As we move from direct communication, through store-and-forward, to store-and-retrieve modes, the sender has progressively less control, both with respect to whether the intended recipient does in fact receive it and whether other unintended recipients receive it instead or in addition. The sender may not care very much who, if anyone, receives the message and who does not. The message may be, "For the record" or "To whom it may concern." The message may be very private to one particular individual ("For your eyes only'') and so be a candidate for cryptography, or it could be intended for as many people as possible.

Communication has to do with the transmission of messages by an originator to a recipient. Within communication, retrieval-based information services can be seen as constituting a special class in which the fate of the message is lost to the communicator and is controlled successively by the provider of the retrieval-based system, who decides which messages will be stored and how they will be retrieved, and the users, who determine which of the retrievable messages will be received and which will be read. However, the relationship between communication and information retrieval is not clear-cut. There are problems with viewing retrieved information as a special case of communication. One is that the boundary is unclear. Consider the case of a weather report in a newspaper. The distribution of newspapers is a traditional example of mass communication, but if one went to a newspaper office or a library in order to look for an old newspaper to ascertain what the weather was in, say, Sydney on November 23, 1941, it would be regarded as a classic example of information retrieval. What, then, if one went to the library to examine the weather report in today's newspaper? That would also generally be regarded as information retrieval, only the date of the document is different. And what if, instead of the library, one stopped at the newspaper shop and retrieved a copy of today's paper to examine the weather report? The user, the document, the action, and the intent are the same; only the location is different. Would the fact that the document had been stored in one pile in one place rather than another pile in another place make the difference between what is and is not information retrieval? If not, then what if the same person reduced the effort of traveling to the library or newspaper shop and had the paper delivered? Would this be different from having had the library deliver a copy of the 1941 newspaper? And would examining the weather report in the daily paper be significantly different from turning on the television at a particular time to catch the weather forecast? More generally, if it is information retrieval to visit the library to see, more vaguely, what was in the paper on November 23, 1941, how does seeing what is in today's paper in the library differ, or in a copy from the newspaper shop, or in a copy in one's home, or whatever is on television? But by this time, we have moved all the way from a traditional view of information retrieval to a traditional view of mass communications.

A second problem is semantic. Retrieving and examining a document from a library collection concerning, say, a platypus, and learning from the document would normally be regarded as a typical example of information retrieval in the sense of retrieving a communication. But retrieving the skeleton or a preserved specimen of a platypus from the collections of a natural history museum might be equally or even more informative. The fact that the latter is an object and not a document may be of little or no significance to the receiver. Both cases are a matter of becoming informed as a result of retrieving an informative something from a collection assembled for this purpose. There seems no good reason to deny that the retrieval of the dead platypus is an information retrieval system in action. But one does not ordinarily speak of being communicated to by a dead animal.

We draw two conclusions from these difficulties. First, the study of communication is important for, but is not coextensive with, the study of information. Second, human activities tend not to fall into tidy clear-cut categories. It is often more practical for our purposes to identify clear-cut, unambiguous examples and to use them as a basis for discussion without worrying initially about marginal cases or where the boundary is between one type and another. Perhaps more refined definitions and clearer boundaries will be developed in the future.

The Receiver's Perspective

Just as the sender may have imperfect control over who, if anyone, receives a communication, so also the options and roles of the receiver vary considerably. Looking at this matter from the receiver's point of view, it is convenient to work backward from the end point for this chapter (and the starting point for the next), which is physical access to information: hearing, seeing, or otherwise being in a position to sense some kind of evidence.

1. *Sensing information.* The simplest case of receiving information occurs when the recipient plays a passive role, involuntarily sensing some evidence that was not sought. Being awakened by a fire alarm, smelling smoke, or overhearing the neighbor's radio are good examples. More complex cases arise when information is actively sought and when arrangements are developed to make this possible. The range of activities in acquiring information can be viewed, albeit crudely, as stages of increasing complexity.

2. *Asking for information,* as when one asks someone what time it is or for directions to one's destination, adds an active role for the would-be receiver of information. One is asking a source for a message. It is a minimal role but characteristic of informal information systems.

3. *Searching for and retrieving information,* as in a database or a library, requires a more systematic approach. It places a greater onus on the would-be user to identify, locate, and retrieve. Rather than asking a source for a message, one is searching for a message itself. This pattern is typical of the use of formal information systems.

4. In order to retrieve, it will usually be necessary for somebody, possibly the receiver, to have *collected and arranged* the objects expected to be informative and any indexes to them.

5. It may be necessary for someone, possibly the receiver, to *create, recreate, or transform* information in order for it to be stored and retrievable in a usable form.

Not all of these actions are needed in all cases. Successful development and implementation of a formal, computer-based database for personal use would generally require one to be concerned with all five. Providing a typical library or museum service necessitates the first four. Using a typical library, museum, or database will involve the first three. Casual, informal inquiry, as in asking a friend, would use the first two. Sensing is indispensable in all cases—a necessary condition for all cases of becoming informed and the only requirement for receiving information in a passive or involuntary way. In the simplest of cases, there is a receiver but no communicator, at least no conscious sender. One may merely happen to notice an event or a fossil in a rock. By and large, these categories represent a progression of increasingly active roles and increasing effort for the person perceiving the information, although some or all of the searching, retrieving, and creation may well be performed by others.

The perceived (and the actual) effort involved can be expected to vary greatly in individual circumstances. It may sometimes be easier (and more reliable) in some circumstances to perform a simple experiment (e.g., does this substance burn?) than to ask others or to seek the answer in formal information sources. One would be recreating the knowledge by generating new information rather than by identifying and locating old evidence, old information-as-thing. If one were stranded on a deserted, library-less island and needed to light a fire, experimentation would clearly be the practical approach. Perceptions of probable effort are personal and situational.

FOUR BASIC DIFFICULTIES IN RETRIEVAL

There are four different problems of information retrieval systems, which become increasingly serious as more complex retrieval tasks are undertaken yet receive relatively little attention in the literature.[1]

1. *Scale*: The very same needle that is so hard to find in the proverbial haystack would be easy to find a pincushion. Online bibliographic databases and online library catalogs with large databases currently retrieve hundreds or even thousands of references when usually only one, a few, or any one of a few are wanted. Identification techniques suitable for small collections can be expected to become less satisfactory when used on large collections.

2. *Multiple attributes*: Retrieval would be much simpler if people were only ever interested in one attribute of the items stored. In a commercial business, a manager might want arrangements of sales transactions by the name of the item sold, by date of transaction, by customer, and by sales area. In botanic collections, whether databases, herbaria, books, or gardens, one might want to arrange the items by taxonomy, by habitat, and by appearance. The Australian Botanic Garden in Canberra, for example, arranges its plants in up to four sequences, each based on a different attribute: taxonomy, habitat, preferred soil type, and aesthetic appearance. But multiple arrangements of multiple copies of objects rapidly become uneconomical and impractical. Instead of using additional copies of the objects themselves, the usual solution is to create representations as surrogates or substitutes for the original. Representations are more or less imperfect as substitutes for the original object, but their use can nevertheless be

advantageous. A library catalog card is an excellent example of an economical surrogate, but it can serve as a surrogate for a book only to a very limited extent since it does not contain the text.

Using surrogates instead of originals involves a trade-off between (1) the benefit of the convenience of being able to use them to create additional arrangements based on other attributes and to add related evidence not in the original and (2) the disadvantages of their cost and of their being imperfect replicas, usable for only limited purposes. Disadvantages stemming from their imperfections as representations may be circumvented when they contain a reference to the address of a more complete representation and/or the original object being represented.

In the case of library catalog cards, it is customary for each of the different sets of surrogates (cards filed by author, cards filed by title, and cards filed by subject heading) to contain the same information ("unit entry") and for all to have the address ("call number") of the cataloged document. Sometimes surrogates arranged by different attributes will be of differing degrees of completeness. In museum documentation systems, there is likely to be one set of surrogates arranged by accession number with a relatively complete description of the object ("item index") and much briefer sets of surrogates arranged by other attributes ("feature index"). The latter are, in effect, an index to the former as well as to the object documented (Orna and Pettit 1980). In computer-based systems, the links to more complete surrogates and to the original, if also stored in the computer, can be made transparent to the user, thereby achieving the appearance of numerous arrangements of the objects by different attributes.

Future interests cannot be fully foreseen, and there can be unlimited aspects of the collection about which inquiries might be made.

3. *Variation of language*: It is a characteristic of language that there are unlimited different ways of describing anything. It cannot be assumed that different individuals will use the same representation to denote anything or that the same representations will have the same significance for different individuals or for the same individual at different times.[2]

4. *Definability*: Not everything is equally easy to define. A numbered seat of an identified airline flight is relatively straightforward. Describing an elephant is less easy, though an elephant is easily recognized. Heat is less easy to identify but can be sensed and measured. Abstract social concepts and human feelings can be difficult to define unambiguously and to distinguish from related concepts and feelings. Areas of knowledge vary greatly in the extent to which they can be represented unambiguously. Varying degrees of vagueness or blurredness appear to be more or less inherent in knowledge. This seems to be a conceptual rather than a linguistic problem, though it has consequences in language, representation, and retrieval: "vagueness or blurredness has no positive aspect and is a conceptual rather than a linguistic disease, hence it is rather more difficult to cure" (Bunge 1967, 97–98; also Buckland 1988c, 94–96; Daft, Lengel, and Trevino 1987). Fugman's Axiom of Definability states that "the compilation of

information relevant to a topic can be delegated only to the extent to which an inquirer can define the topic in terms of concepts and concept relations'' (Fugman 1985). Not only the searcher but also the indexer must deal with problems of definition. It is also necessary for the indexer to achieve the same level of definability in the designation of the attributes when they are arranged in a retrieval system.

TYPES OF RETRIEVAL

Retrieval has been usefully defined by Belkin and Croft (1987, 109), who limit their attention to texts, as "the means for identifying, retrieving, and/or ranking texts (or text surrogates or portions of texts), in a collection of texts, that might be relevant to a given query (or useful for resolving a particular problem). In particular, retrieval techniques address the issue of comparing a representation of a query with representations of texts for the same purpose."

We distinguish four types of retrieval:

1. *Physical retrieval*: Delivery of what has been identified and located is an important engineering problem but need not detain us here.

2. *Locating*: We know the identity of what we want. Where is it? This is a matter of using a directory to find the address of a particular item. Routine use of a telephone directory to find the telephone number or address of an acquaintance is an example of locating. So-called known-item searching is of this type.

3. *Identification*: More difficult are cases where we first have to identify what there is that we may wish to locate and to obtain. Identification has to do with determining which, if any, items in the collection match acceptably the attributes specified in a search: "Any demographic data concerning Bulgaria?" "What books were written in English by Fritz Machlup?" This is essentially a matter of fitting the description (Wilson 1968). The challenge is to describe something you do not know that may not exist.

4. *Identification by subject matter*: We distinguish this special case of identification because of its importance in information systems: What is the document about? Documents are of interest primarily as recorded knowledge, so there is a choice. Instead of seeking to identify a particular document for itself, one might instead want to identify items pertinent to a particular piece of knowledge—or ignorance—but this cannot be done directly. Knowledge is intangible and so cannot be retrieved mechanically; it can, however, be represented ("recorded knowledge"). Hence, what knowledge is represented is an attribute of a text. More simply, we want to know what a text is about. Subject indexing and subject classification are tools to permit the identification of documents about some topic. In practice, subject indexers, being mindful of the purpose of their information system and of the interests of those to be served, may choose to represent some portion or aspect of the recorded knowledge that they believe their users would or should wish to have imparted. In our terminology, they might well be less interested in simply representing the knowledge than in representing some knowledge to be imparted, some intended information-as-knowl-

edge. Similarly inquiries are likely to be for representations of some knowledge that the inquirer seeks to have imparted (information-as-knowledge).

Although we have distinguished identification by subject matter as a special case of identification, the distinction is not always clear-cut in practice. Identification, locating, and physical retrieval are different in kind, though they are often combined in practice.[3]

Multiple and Repetitive Searches

Searching and retrieval can be repetitive in two senses. First, inquiry may be iterative and interactive in the sense that the asking of one question and seeing the response is likely to lead to the asking of another, repeatedly until one is satisfied or gives up. Second, storage and retrieval systems may be embedded within one another, as can be illustrated by considering the use of a library. One user may treat the subject arrangement of the documents on the shelves as a retrieval mechanism by going to the section designated for books on the subject of interest. A second user might approach the library catalog and use the bibliographic data on the catalog entry to verify a bibliographic citation and consider it sufficient to depend on the catalog record instead of inspecting the actual document. A third user might do exactly the same as the second user but use the data on the catalog records not as a goal but merely as directions for finding a document on the shelves. A fourth user might go to the librarian and express an inquiry verbally. The librarian, acting as a retrieval system, would endeavor to convert the inquiry into the terms of the library system and deliver the data required—whether a document or mention of specific data from within a document.

When a document is found, further retrieval mechanisms, such as an index or table of contents, may be used to identify more specifically what is wanted. Dictionaries, concordances, bibliographies, and encyclopedias—all examples of retrieval mechanisms—may well be used independently or in conjunction with other means of searching. It is clear that many examples of retrieval systems exist in libraries and that they can be used independently or sequentially.

BASES FOR RETRIEVAL

Retrieval can draw on three bases:

1. The actual physical attributes of the item—what Blair (1990) calls the "brute facts." Examples include words on the title page or in the text and citations of other items.

2. Description of the document itself and its context: authorship, publication, and relationships with other documents.

3. Description of the content—what the document is about. Where the intent is to retrieve (a representation of) knowledge, a special problem arises: retrieval cannot be based

on an intangible specification but must depend on the matching of representations of intangibles.

These three bases for retrieval are different, but that does not mean that they are unrelated. For example, the title of a document is clearly a physical part of the document, and it can be used for identifying a particular document. However, a title may also have been chosen by the author as a more-or-less summary representation of the knowledge represented either in the whole (e.g., *Economics: An Introduction*), in parts of it (e.g., *Einstein's Socks, the TMT Factor, and Other Connaught Circus Fribblings*), or not in any recognizable sense (e.g., *Ubik*). Therefore, words of the title (and words in the text) are more or less usable as economical, but not very reliable, alternatives to descriptions of contents.

The description of items can be expressed in two ways: items can be labeled (inscribed, marked), or they can be placed in some relationship to others (ordered, parked) (Fairthorne 1961).

Systems of labeling (''indexing languages'') vary with respect to:

- Notation, varying from artificial classification schemes using numbers or other codes (e.g., library classification schemes) to (relatively) natural language (e.g., subject headings).
- Vocabulary control, the recognition of synonyms and near synonyms.
- Structure, relating broader, narrower, and other related terms.
- Fineness of detail.
- Coordination: Complex description built up of multiple simpler concepts may be pre-coordinated at the indexing stage (as in library subject headings (AUSTRIA, *Higher Education*, 1918–1939) and classification schemes (378.170936) or postcoordinated later at the time of searching, as is common with online, Boolean, retrieval systems.

RELEVANCE AND RETRIEVAL EFFECTIVENESS

The traditional approach to evaluation of the retrieval performance, especially identification by subject, is to compare actual retrieval results with what the results should ideally have been. After each search, the outcome is expressed in terms of four categories created by the following two criteria: (1) retrieved (identified as fitting the description) or not and (2) relevant (actually fitting the description) or not. The resulting matrix is shown in table 10.1.

Two criteria of retrieval success are calculated for the results of each search.

1. *Recall*: What proportion of all relevant items were actually retrieved? This would be $x/(x + v)$ in table 10.1 and is a measure of the completeness of retrieval.
2. *Precision*: What proportion of retrieved items were relevant?: $x/(x + u)$ in table 10.1. This is a measure of the purity of retrieval.

Table 10.1
Retrieval Matrix

	RELEVANT	NOT RELEVANT
RETRIEVED	x	u
NOT RETRIEVED	v	y

A persistent finding is that in operational retrieval systems, there tends to be a trade-off: improving recall tends to involve diminished precision, and vice-versa. Sometimes complete recall is wanted. More often the need is for any one item that fits the description or for the few that fit best.

A second persistent finding is that all retrieval systems are imperfect, often seeming comparably imperfect, yet retrieving different sets of relevant items (Pao and Worthen 1989). This suggests that the use of multiple retrieval systems—using indexes, word searching, citation searching, and classification systems—could be a better strategy than trying to perfect any one system.

Once one gets away from small collections of data and straightforward cases of identification, two practical problems of measurement become important. First, since relevance, like the quality of being information, is situational and subjectively perceived, there is no objective way to assess it. Little consensus is found in distinguishing between x and u and, even if there were, second, it is impractical to identify all of unretrieved relevant items v. In consequence, formal retrieval evaluation tests based on the measurement of x, u, and v exhibit considerable formal rigor built on nonrigorous foundations (Swanson 1988; Blair 1990).

An additional problem has been the varying and commonly imprecise use of the terms *relevant* and *relevance* to denote actual or supposed relationships of inquiries, data, and users. As with *information*, it would seem wise to use these terms only in a vague general sense or with explicit definitions whenever used in a specific sense or else to substitute more precise terms whenever an exact meaning is needed (Buckland 1983).

The basic relationships in retrieval are the matching of the representation of the inquiry with the representations of what is stored and the relationship between the inquirer's intent and the outcome.

Alternatives to *relevant* and *relevance* for denoting relationships include the following:

1. *Pertinence*, or topicality, as a matter of consensus of subjective judgment, of the match between any two representations of knowledge, whether of information need, information-as-knowledge, or of recorded knowledge.

2. *Responsiveness*: The performance of the retrieval system in retrieving all and only those items that are characterized by the attributes specified or implied by the representation of the inquiry.

3. *Beneficiality*, also a matter of subjective judgment in the sense that the item retrieved by the system is considered useful by the user. Beneficiality is also situational, depending on the varying needs, particular values, and ever-changing knowledge of different and changing users. Pertinence is used as a predictor in identifying what would be beneficial.

CONCLUSION

In this chapter we have been concerned with the receiving of information—directly as information-as-thing, indirectly as information-as-knowledge. Receiving information is the central concept in information studies. Not all information results from intentional communication.

The ways of receiving information can be sorted into three groups: the general class of observation and the special cases of communication and retrieval. However, although distinct examples can be usefully identified, the boundaries between them are not clear.

From the receiver's point of view, one can start with involuntary receipt of information and work backward to include progressively more complex cases: merely receiving; asking; searching and retrieving it; assembling material that could be retrieved; and creating evidence, either for immediate use or to be stored for subsequent retrieval.

Retrieval contains three functions: identifying, locating, and physically retrieving. Identifying depends heavily on the processes of representation, drawing on three elements: the physical features of the items, descriptions of the items, and descriptions of what the items represent.

Relevance is widely, if often vaguely and inconsistently, used to denote relationships in retrieval. Pertinence, responsiveness, and beneficiality are three useful relationships.

Some semantic problems in information retrieval are inherent in the nature of the field. Others represent a remediable lack of care and rigor. Greater care in the use of words, more attention to theory in the sense of the description of the nature of things, and an insistence on using the most accurate and specific terminology would all help.

The term *information retrieval* itself deserves special attention. It is commonly used in an inexact, generic way to describe specific systems, which could be and should be more precisely defined as, for example, text retrieval, bibliographic data retrieval, numerical data retrieval, pattern retrieval, and so on.

NOTES

1. For a general introduction to information retrieval, see J. E. Rowley, *Organizing Knowledge: An Introduction to Information Retrieval* (Aldershot, England: Gower, 1987); L. M. Chan, *Cataloging and Classification: An Introduction* (New York: McGraw-Hill, 1981); R. Hagler and P. Simmons, *The Bibliographic Record and Information Technology* (Chicago: American Library Association, 1982); B. S. Wynar, *Introduction to Cataloging and Classification*, 7th ed., ed. A. Taylor (Littleton, Colo.: Libraries Unlimited, 1985). For information retrieval theory and testing, see G. Salton and M. J. McGill, *Introduction to Modern Information Retrieval* (New York: McGraw-Hill, 1983); *Information Retrieval Experiment*, ed. K. Sparck Jones (London: Butterworths, 1981); *Information Retrieval Research*, ed. R. N. Oddy et al. (London: Butterworths, 1981). For a convenient review of retrieval techniques, see N. J. Belkin and W. B. Croft, "Retrieval Techniques," *Annual Review of Information Science and Technology* 22(1987):109–45. For a detailed treatment of indexing and classification systems as "documentary languages," see W. J. Hutchins, *Languages of Indexing and Classification: A Linguistic Study of Structures and Functions* (Stevenage, England: Peter Peregrinus, 1975); also D. C. Blair, *Language and*

Representation in Information Retrieval (Amsterdam: Elsevier Science Publishers, 1990). For museums, see E. Orna and C. Pettit, *Information Handling in Museums* (New York: Saur, 1980), and R. B. Light, D. A. Roberts, and J. D. Stewart, eds., *Museum Documentation Systems: Developments and Applications* (London: Butterworths, 1986).

2. For a discussion of this "unlimited semiosis" see Blair (1990) and Markey (1984).

3. This categorization develops and refines an earlier approach in which all retrieval searches were categorized in terms of both information specificity (the degree to which the information was specified within type 4) and also document specificity (the degree to which the document was specified within type 3, excluding type 4). Locating (type 2) was regarded as the limiting extreme case of document specificity in which there was no uncertainty concerning the identity of the document (Buckland 1979).

A traditional practice in librarianship is to divide searches into known-item searches and subject searches. Although useful, this categorization is incomplete or misleading. A known-item search is a matter of locating something (our retrieval type 2). A subject search would be identification by subject (our type 4). The known item–subject search categorization does not allow for identification based on the fitting of the descriptions using any other attributes within type 3 (e.g., authorship, language, date). These are either excluded or loosely included under subject searches.

A distinction between data retrieval and document retrieval is found in the information retrieval literature (e.g., Blair 1984, 1990; van Rijsbergen, 1979). The assumptions are that data retrieval yields the information desired, whereas document retrieval (more accurately, reference retrieval) yields references to what is expected to be the information desired; and that data retrieval involves locating (our retrieval type 2), whereas document retrieval involves identification (our type 3) and, especially, identification by subject (our type 4). Since these assumptions are often valid, the data retrieval–document retrieval distinction can be useful. However, the first assumption is misleading since document retrieval systems also function as data retrieval systems when what the searcher wants is the reference (data), not the document referred to. A system capable of only data retrieval is therefore a limited case within the more general category of data-and-document retrieval systems. The second assumption is often invalid since both locating searches for documents and identification searches for data are common (Buckland 1988c, 85–87). There are also problems of definition; a data set can be considered as a document and vice versa.

Chapter 11

Becoming Informed:
Information-as-Process

BECOMING INFORMED

Having considered the receiving of information, we now look at the use made of what is received. It is a quite different sort of process. There are enormous literatures on this topic, notably in cognitive science, education, and psychology. We limit ourselves to commenting briefly on a few aspects relevant to information systems.

To have been informed is to be in a state of knowing something. Becoming informed denotes a change in what we know. It may commonly, but not necessarily include knowing more. News may arrive that contradicts rather than confirms what we knew and leaves us in greater doubt. We may well feel that the new information leaves us knowing less than before. More to the point, it is not so much that we know less but that we now know differently. The ideas that we had held have not disappeared, but our belief in them has changed.

The process of informing requires someone susceptible to being informed; otherwise the informing cannot take place. It also requires some prior expertise on the part of the individual who might become informed. A book that is understandable can be informative. But what of a book in a dead language that nobody can understand, or a book lost on a desert island, or, more commonly, a book in the hands of a reader who lacks the expertise to understand it? Most people would probably learn very little from even the best encyclopedia if it were written in an unfamiliar foreign language. In none of these cases can it be said that much informing is likely, and if there is no informing, how can the book be regarded as informative? The answer is twofold. First, certain conditions have to be met for the process of informing to take place; the informative object has to be found and physically accessible, for example. Second, it would be more accurate to describe examples of information-as-thing not as informative objects but as potentially informative objects, recognizing that they are not

Figure 11.1
The Process of Becoming Informed

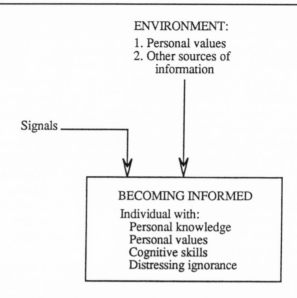

ENVIRONMENT:
1. Personal values
2. Other sources of
   information

Signals

BECOMING INFORMED

Individual with:
  Personal knowledge
  Personal values
  Cognitive skills
  Distressing ignorance

informative in all circumstances. Whether information-as-process occurs depends substantially on factors external to the "informative object," such as whether the reader can understand it.

In brief, whether information-as-thing (an object) is associated with information-as-process (someone becoming informed) is situational. Signals, data, information-as-thing, may, when perceived by somebody with appropriate prior knowledge and suitable cognitive skills, contribute to a change or increase in that person's knowledge. Here we are concerned with the process of becoming informed. We view this as a two-stage process in (figure 11.1). The first stage is the physiological perception of the signals. Can they be seen or heard? The second stage is the cognitive process of becoming informed. For this, other factors are involved, notably prior knowledge and cognitive skills. In the case of a book one might ask:

• Can the person read—as opposed to merely see—the text?
• Is the text in a language that the reader can understand?
• Are the concepts and terminology comprehended by the reader?

If any one or more of these three conditions are not met, then it is unlikely that the individual would become informed.

Some of the paradoxes of becoming informed can be readily explained once variations in the reader's prior knowledge and cognitive skills are taken into account. For example, one book can be simultaneously highly informative and not at all informative on the same subject area. A textbook would be uninformative for an expert who is already familiar with what is in it, very informative for a reader with some knowledge of the subject, and uninformative for a novice who could not understand it. A brief note or inscription might be highly informative to the expert who has the necessary background knowledge and cognitive skills to understand its significance but not to the beginner who does not.

The situation is similar in the case of allegories and other sorts of allusions. The expert reader, one with substantial relevant prior knowledge or insight, will get more out of the text than will someone without such knowledge, who would probably not even notice the symbolism and allusions.

The vexing problems of choice of criteria for the evaluation of retrieval systems results in part from this aspect of information-as-process. Retrieval can be performed more or less effectively but only in terms of attributes assigned to or derived from the retrievable objects. What can be done, therefore, is retrieval with respect to chosen attributes, "fitting the description." However, the ultimate goal is to be informative. But the extent to which a document is informative depends largely on the reader and therefore on factors external to the objects retrieved or to the retrieval system.

What results is a troublesome paradox: information systems exist so that users may become beneficially informed, yet information systems cannot simply be evaluated on their ability to inform beneficially because becoming informed depends, in part, on factors that are situational and external to the information system. We shall return to this paradox.

INFORMATION AND THE CHANGING OF WHAT IS KNOWN

What can be said about changes in knowledge? What causes lead to a change in what one knows? Our answer is that knowledge changes as a result of some combination of two elements: thought and evidence. Reflection, thinking, cogitation—whatever one may wish to call the working of the mind—can lead to new beliefs. One might believe that, for example, propositions A and B are incompatible. After further thought, however, one might conclude that one or both are unbelievable, that there may be some additional evidence as yet unknown to one, that one does not adequately understand the situation, or that they are compatible after all. Evidence might come in the form of an experiment, event, communication, record, or some physical clue.

The relationship of the three factors—thought, evidence, and belief—is crucial. No amount of evidence will change belief without any thought at all. At least some thought is a necessary condition for becoming informed. Beliefs change through thought alone in the sense that new evidence is not necessary for beliefs to change. One might reach the conclusion that since A and B are believed, C should also be believed. It may simply be a matter of reflecting on the consistencies and consequences of one's existing beliefs.

Credibility and Acceptability of Information

Why should anybody believe the information they receive? This basic question has been remarkably neglected in the literature of information systems, perhaps because it is not an engineering question and also because it is an awkward issue to address.

The credibility or acceptability of information can be viewed as having two aspects. The first is that those receiving information may be reluctant to accept a particular source as credible, regarding it as having insufficient "cognitive authority." Depending on second-hand knowledge is unavoidable, at least to some extent, since we cannot possibly know everything ourselves at first hand. But it is unwise to trust everything that others could pass on to us, especially things that we may not fully understand or are unable to verify. Just as being information or evidence is a status attributed to something perceived as being informative, so also the authority of the source of the information itself is a quality ascribed to the source. Sources cannot unilaterally assert authority. Authority has to be given to them and can be taken away (Wilson 1983).

Confidence in information can be increased in several ways—for example, coming from or being endorsed by a trusted source, confirming the results of earlier experience, or consistency with other evidence.

The second aspect is that confidence is more likely if the recipient wants to believe the information. Commonly the recipient does not want to believe what is received, quite apart from the authority of the source. Unwelcome news is likely to be ignored. It may conflict with cherished beliefs, a matter of cognitive dissonance (Festinger 1957; Greenwald and Ronis 1978).

Everyone will agree in principle that not all information should be believed. The problem is in determining which.

A CASE STUDY

A case study can be used to illustrate and to summarize many of the points that have been made so far in this and preceding chapters. In the second century before Christ, Hieron II, king of Syracuse, a city-state in ancient Greece, suspected that his new crown had not been made of pure gold as it should have been and that some less expensive silver might have been substituted, so he posed the problem to his adviser, Archimedes:

Archimedes was puzzled till one day, as he was stepping into a bath and observed the water running over [the side], it occurred to him that the excess of bulk occasioned by the introduction of alloy could be measured by putting the crown and an equal weight of gold separately into a vessel filled with water, and observing the differences in overflow. [Silver, being lighter and, therefore, bulkier than gold, would displace more water]. He was so overjoyed when this happy thought struck him that he ran home without his clothes shouting "eureka, eureka" ("I have found it, I have found it"). (*Encyclopaedia Britannica* 1910, 2:368)

In the terminology of previous chapters, King Hieron had felt a sense of distressing ignorance concerning the purity of the crown. He communicated an inquiry to Archimedes. Archimedes shared his king's concern, as well as his ignorance. They might have decided that they did not care, in which case there would no longer have been any sense of distress. However, Archimedes resolved the problem by the perceiving and understanding of pertinent evidence: the informative event of the overflowing bathwater and the spilled water as an informative object, both within our broad definition of information-as-thing. The water's being information was situational. It takes unusual imagination and extraordinary circumstances for spilled bathwater to be regarded as useful information. Archimedes' thinking, combined with his perceiving of pertinent information, enabled him to derive the knowledge that was needed to resolve the distressing ignorance. He will then have used a message (information-as-thing) to communicate this information-as-knowledge to King Hieron. Because he was aware of the background, Hieron would probably have recognized the significance of Archimedes' exclamation, "Eureka!" In contrast, startled bystanders in the street, even if more intelligent than King Hieron, would have found Archimedes' behavior and "Eureka!" unintelligible unless they were very well informed about the background to the situation. We know of these events only because we can become informed by reading (perceiving) and understanding a written text (information-as-thing) that is a representation of the event.

MISINFORMATION, HARM, AND DISTRESS

Misinformation

Let us consider the case of misinformation wherein one's knowledge is changed to include "facts" (or rather beliefs) that are false. In simple cases, this is fairly straightforward. If the flight to New York is scheduled to leave San Francisco airport at 9:27 A.M. but the travel agent states that it is scheduled to leave at 9:27 P.M., one has been falsely informed.

If one probes more deeply into the question of truth and falsehood, one gets into difficult philosophical issues, which we prefer to leave to others. We simply note that one can be misinformed (intentionally or otherwise) and that even information believed to be correct at the time may well be regarded as misinformation at some later time—or vice versa.

Harm and Distress

Misinformation is generally associated with harm and distress. One may be distressed or harmed (or both) by missing a flight to New York because one was misinformed about the time of departure. However, although misinformation is commonly distressing and harmful, truth is different from benefit. It can happen that one is distressed by information generally accepted as correct, as when learning that there is not a single "real" Santa Claus. One can even be harmed by correct information. An example of this is implicit in the assertion that publishing reliable predictions of earthquakes would cause more disruption than not publishing them. (Misinformation and lack of information are not the same, but the difference does not appear important for our purposes.)

On the other hand, it can conceivably happen, even if only exceptionally, that misinformation is beneficial. This would have been the case had the plane to New York, missed through misinformation, crashed.

Our intention here is merely to assert that knowledge is not necessarily always beneficial and that ignorance and misinformation are not always harmful or distressing. Yet in so arguing we are necessarily asserting social values since *beneficial* and *harmful* imply some standard of value.

LIMITATIONS IN HELPFULNESS

Some limitations in the range of help provided by information systems should be noted.

Incompleteness

All information systems are more or less incomplete with respect to the information stored and the means of access to it. They are more or less appropriate for any given inquiry.

Historical Features of Retrieved Objects

Every information-as-thing and all communications are historical in that each is the product of a particular time. For many purposes, such as daily conversation, this does not matter. Our words, although expressed a specific time, are heard so quickly that the delay is imperceptible and unimportant. Documents and other evidence might have been slow in the making, might be slow in being received, and might have been stored for a considerable time before being retrieved. For this reason, the use of retrieval-based information systems is necessarily and unavoidably a historical pastime. Whether the age of the evidence matters depends on the circumstances. One might want to know what last week's weather forecast was instead of today's.

The data derived from information systems tend to be the reporting of the latest version that happens to have been stored in the system. This means that all information systems are in practice more or less unsuited for the answering of questions the answers to which are highly volatile (Crowley and Childers 1971).

Help with Some Sorts of Access Only

In chapter 8 we noted that six different sorts of access barriers need to be overcome for anyone to become informed through a retrieval-based information system. In practice, information services tend to concentrate rather heavily on some access problems more than on others.

Indicative access—the identification of what is available—is a major feature of retrieval-based information systems. Libraries emphasize this aspect and have the untypical advantage that since the material they store is largely duplicative of what other libraries and booksellers handle, they can take advantage of shared economies in cataloging and indexing. The location ("holdings") data are unique to each library, but the identification ("bibliographic") data are not and can be acquired economically from published bibliographies and cooperative databases. Archives, records management systems, and museums, dealing with material that is mainly or entirely unique, have no such option and must struggle to develop their own systems to the extent that they can afford. Other databases need a data dictionary but rarely have the messy complexity and virtually unlimited variety of topics characteristic of archives, libraries, and museums.

Physical access is also a generally accepted feature. Archives, libraries, museums, and records centers provide physical access to material within their collections. Libraries ordinarily will also obtain material not in their collections by purchasing it or getting it on interlibrary loan. Physical access in the form of an image on the glowing screen or a printout is a basic assumption of computer-based information systems, and, usually, in principle, this will be accessible from wherever the user's workstation may be located. Physical access, then, is another accepted function.

In contrast, there is rarely significant help with cognitive access or acceptability. Individual archivists or museum staff are invaluable for their assistance to visitors who ask for help in understanding the collections. Libraries may supply supporting materials such as dictionaries and encyclopedias, but understanding the books in the library is generally regarded as the users' responsibility. As to whether the information retrieved should be believed, that is an issue about which most information professionals tend to be reticent.

SUMMARY

Physically receiving a text or other information does not guarantee that the recipient becomes informed. Two major barriers to access have to be overcome:

1. *Cognitive access*: The recipient must have sufficient expertise to understand or, at least, misunderstand the information. Either leads to a change in knowledge.

2. *Acceptability*: The recipient must be willing to accept the information, believing it to be true and not rejecting it as awkward. One would know of the rejected assertion but that is not the same.

Information is in general regarded as beneficial and misinformation as detrimental, but it can be the other way around. In practice, information systems have systemic limitations: all are more or less incomplete, all information in them is more or less historical, and indicative access and physical access are emphasized over cognitive access and acceptability.

Chapter **12**

Information Processing and Representation

DEFINITION

In the first three chapters of part III, we have examined inquiries, perceiving, and becoming informed. We noted that inquiries have to be represented in an appropriate language. Use of a formal information retrieval system requires expression of the inquiry in the retrieval language of the system. A problem in the mind is intangible. It might be resolved just by thinking about it. Additional information-as-knowledge, also intangible, may be helpful, but information-as-knowledge can be derived from an information system only if an inquiry is posed in a tangible form and a tangible outcome, some information-as-thing, such as a message or a retrieved record (text, image, or set of data) is yielded and perceived. Becoming informed results in new knowledge, which in turn cannot be shared except by means of some tangible expression such as a communicated message or a text of recorded knowledge.

The making of tangible representations of the intangible is of central importance for information systems. We include in our use of *representation* the deriving of new tangible representations (information-as-thing) from existing representations by any combination of human and artificial means. We use the term *representation* broadly to denote all forms of this process. We limit the use of *information processing* to denote the deriving by machine of new tangible forms (new information-as-thing) from existing tangible forms (existing information-as-thing).

Taking processing to mean the changing of something into something else, we are concerned with a transition from information in one state into another state. Since we are, or could be, concerned with two sorts of information, tangible and intangible, four permutations are imaginable (table 12.1):

1. From intangible to intangible would be processing knowledge into new knowledge directly, not via paper or computer but simply by thinking about it. In this case the

Table 12.1
Transformations of Information

FROM:	TO:	INTANGIBLE	TANGIBLE
INTANGIBLE		1. Thinking	3. Expressing
TANGIBLE		2. Perceiving	4. Information processing

thought process, if successful, results in new information-as-knowledge. We agree with Wersig (1979) that this kind of information process could well be called "human information processing." But there are other well-established terms, such as *thinking* and *reasoning*, so we will follow convention and restrict our use of *information processing* to the derivation of new information-as-thing.

2. From tangible to intangible would be the process of deriving knowledge from recorded knowledge or other "information-as-thing." Perceiving leads to "becoming informed" ("information-as-process").

3. The transformation from intangible knowledge to tangible information, as when someone represents his or her knowledge as a text. Since artificial machines cannot deal directly with intangible knowledge, only with physical representations, this option is available only to humans.

4. Transforming existing tangible information to new tangible information would be the process of deriving new "information-as-thing" from existing "information-as-thing." This is the customary usage of *information processing*, reflected in the following definition of information processing: "The derivation of 'information objects' from other 'information objects' by the execution of algorithms" (*Dictionary of Computing* 1986, 182).

The nature of information processing by machine and by humans is shown in figure 12.1

Physical Things and Information-as-Thing

Information has a significant characteristic: it gets used but does not get used up. When you cook, you derive new cooked food from the original raw ingredients. The ingredients are used up or transformed in the process. Information processing is different. After new information has been derived from the old, the original information is ordinarily still available. If you change money from one currency into another, you can spend the new but not also the old. But if you translate a book from one language to another, you can still enjoy the original text as well as the new. If you derive wood from a forest, those trees are lost to the forest. But if you derive an average from a statistical sample, the sample remains. Others can recalculate the average from the same sample as often as they wish. The sample will still be there.

This is not to say that information cannot be lost, changed, or destroyed. Clearly it can. We may want to destroy the old evidence so that no one else can see it. Magnetic recordings can be erased, and books can be burned.[1] Sometimes the goal is to change physical evidence, to alter the old, as when fraudulently altering a check or passport. However, information processing itself is ordinarily a matter of deriving new forms of information without affecting the old. New information may very well affect how we view the old and what we believe about it, but that is a different issue.

We are concerned here with the processing of information, which signifies that we are concerned with the processing of physical things only to the extent

Figure 12.1
Information Processing

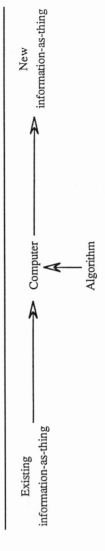

(a) Information processing by computer

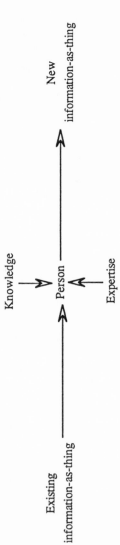

(b) Human information processing

that these things are regarded as information, as evidence. On this basis, transcribing or translating the text of a book into another language is a form of information processing.

Information can be limited or reduced in various ways.

First, an individual's knowledge may fade from poor memory and it dies when the individual dies, though we may hope that important knowledge has been communicated to others or expressed as recorded knowledge.

Second, the physical object (the "physical evidence") regarded as information can be lost or destroyed. This does not in itself mean that any knowledge is lost. There may be another copy; you may still remember a code word even if you lose the piece of paper it had been written on; a new record could still be made. Problems arise when the only physical medium bearing the recorded knowledge is lost, no living person remembers it, and it is difficult or impossible to reconstruct.

Third, the loss of the physical object may well reduce the credibility of some piece of knowledge. Skeptics may want to see the record in black and white before they are willing to believe it. For this reason people create and forge documents.

Fourth, we may, for whatever reason, cease to regard some physical object as being information. Maybe we begin to suspect it is fraudulent or decide that we had misunderstood it.

Fifth, since objects are information if they are regarded as being informative, we can multiply indefinitely the number of physical phenomena that we decide to regard as information. Arguments arise when there is a lack of consensus concerning the significance of some phenomenon such as a cryptic message or an ominous event.

The quality of being information-as-thing is attributed to physical objects. Records bear marks. Meaning may be ascribed to the marks. It is convenient but metaphorical to speak of records or marks as "containing" meaning.

The Measurement of Information

The physical attributes of what is regarded as information-as-thing can be measured in various ways: computer records are counted in bits and bytes; books are reckoned in volumes and in meters of filled shelves; manuscripts are measured in numbers of standard-sized boxes and in cubic feet. Exotic versions of these physical measures encountered in the literature include "multiples of the Library of Congress" for quantity and "Bibles per square inch" for density. Rhetoric about the information explosion sometimes purports to describe an increase in knowledge, but the figures used derive from increases in the physical quantity of information-as-thing, which is not the same at all. Fifty copies of the Bible occupy more space than one but do not contain more knowledge. Five different introductory texts on economics probably record more knowledge than one but not five times as much. In any case, since knowledge is intangible, it is not susceptible to counting. For this reason, the idea of measuring units of knowledge or of information-as-knowledge ("informons"?) is misguided in principle, though we might be able to infer indirectly and imperfectly what an individual knows by setting tests.

There is the specialized use of the word *information* in relation to quantitative measures of signaling performance in information theory, but that is a technical usage unrelated to meaning or knowledge and so outside our scope. (See Bar-Hillel 1964, 275–97, and Fairthorne 1967.)

Physical properties of examples of information-as-thing are easily measured; information-as-knowledge is not measurable and apparently could not be.

ACTIVITIES OF REPRESENTATION

We can illustrate the range of information processing by noting some examples.

The simplest examples of information processing constitute a relatively closed system. Transcription of a text or set of data to create a copy is a particularly simple form of information processing. Transliteration from one character set to another is also relatively straightforward, especially when there is a one-to-one equivalence. Telecommunication is essentially transcription from one copy to another but with the new copy being delivered at a distance. The technology may be very complex, but the goal is simple: transcription to a distant place with minimal alteration. Ordinarily these simpler forms of transmission are to increase convenience of physical and/or cognitive access. Cryptography, in contrast, is transcription designed to minimize cognitive access.

One stage more complex than transcription is processing to make clearer the evidence that is present but insufficiently clear. Examples include image enhancement of pictures and simple statistical analysis of numerical data. Computing an average does not affect what the average is but makes clear what would otherwise be difficult to perceive. Even so it could be argued that descriptions, including statistical analyses, generally add something, even if only an assumption that an average or a particular distribution is meaningful in relation to the data.

Processes of summarizing or condensing information are frequently used in information systems. Common examples are statistical summaries of numerical data (average, mean, type of distribution, standard deviation), summaries and abstracts of text, and copies of images. Small, in these cases, may not mean beautiful or as informative but more convenient.

Additional complexity occurs when instead of transliteration, text is translated into a different language. This is more difficult because it is no longer a matter of substituting equivalent characters. The nature of language is such that a literal translation is not always possible. Literal translation of some recorded knowledge into a foreign language would not, in general, be quite the same as the result of expressing the same knowledge directly into the second language. A statement that is the literal equivalent is not necessary comparable in what it signifies.

Words, concepts, and mental perspectives differ between cultures and therefore between languages.

With translations we are dealing with examples that are much less closed. In the case of transcription, transliteration, and telecommunications, we prefer the processing of the information to be closed in that the intrusion of extraneous elements into the processing should be avoided or minimized. But closed systems are unnatural, existing only in academic imaginations and artificial, abstract designs. In real worlds, all systems are more or less leaky, more or less open. Unwanted elements intrude when, for example, errors arise in transcription, transliteration, or telecommunication. The errors may be human or mechanical, but the effect is the same. A major feature of telecommunications in practice is the struggle to minimize the amount of extraneous interference (noise) that reduces the purity of transmission. With translation between languages, cultural as well as linguistic differences prevent effective literal translation. External elements may need to be incorporated during information processing in order to achieve a translation that is comparable in its effect.

Wanted intrusions occur when, for example, additional information, inferences, or references adds to the information and increases the intelligibility of the information. A summary can be more helpful if it refers to similar things. Description of any sort ordinarily benefits by the addition of some comparison. The remaining examples of information processing activities all reflect the more natural situation of open systems in that the processing of the information involves the introduction or use of material from outside the information being processed.

Almost all explanation is aided by some redundancy in the information, such that if it is not fully understood initially, the additional, redundant elements may make it so. Further, discourse using forms and terms familiar to the recipient, by adding helpful images, concepts, and terms not in the original, is likely to be useful. In this sense explanation is a form of translation—not between languages but within one language. The literature on communication and on rhetoric has much to say on these matters.

One step beyond explanation is what we might call development, wherein not only is the information explained but developed and expanded. A translation might also include explanatory notes. A new edition should be better developed than the old one. A new book on some topic ought to be better than previous ones. Documents ordinarily derive or build on earlier ones, not only incorporating old ideas and explaining them but also, one hopes, adding new ideas. Both author and readers hope for an improvement on what had been written before.

Scholarship as Information Processing

Changes and increases in knowledge are documented by the generation of representations, by the deriving of new information. Insofar as an increase in knowledge draws on existing physical evidence, it draws on information-as-thing.

The goal of every discipline is to create better understanding. To be generally effective, knowledge has to be documented; it has to be represented. Documented scholarship needs to be continuously reexamined, reappraised, and reinterpreted. Successful scholarship involves the reassessment of old evidence and the creation of new evidence. In this sense, scholarship is a form of information processing. So is the creation of educational materials.

Returning for a moment to the four permutations of tangible and intangible information, it seems clear that deriving one information-as-thing from another information-as-thing should form the basis of our view of information processing. However, *information processing* is an unfortunate phrase because the activity is better viewed as derivation rather than processing since the essential feature is the derivation of new forms, not the changing of the old. Further, the brief discussion of information processing, especially of explanation and of development, makes it clear that newly derived information commonly incorporates new elements. Therefore, it would seem prudent not to exclude from our view of information processing the derivation of information-as-thing from intangible knowledge.

INTERPRETATIONS AND SUMMARIES OF EVIDENCE

The material assembled in information systems, most obviously in archives, databases, and library collections, is hardly raw data but typically material that has already been processed and refined. This is to be expected. For most inquiries, the original objects are not what would be most helpful. It would not be sensible to refer every individual with a question about Mark Twain to the Mark Twain archives. That would be unhelpful for the inquirer and physically bad for the archives. Almost always a book about Mark Twain, which may well have been based on material in the archive, would be sufficient and more practical for all concerned. The book about Mark Twain could well have drawn on and condensed information from other sources and explain or interpret the relevant ideas and evidence. These processes of interpretation and summarizing are central to understanding both the nature and the use of information systems.

We use the term *interpretation* in a broad sense, not just as a matter of translation from one language to another but in the sense of explaining: "to explain the meaning of, to elucidate, unfold, show the purport of; to translate into intelligible or familiar terms" (*Chambers's* 1959, 555).

In the case of foreign literatures, both interpretation and summarizing can be seen. The original writing is not always the first choice. Suppose, for example, that there were an interest in Swahili literature. In North America, an English translation is likely to be the preferred choice, or a book about Swahili writings, perhaps containing abridged texts or translated excerpts, or even an encyclopedia article. Yet each of these options, while progressively more convenient, also contains progressively less of the original evidence. Something is always lost in translation or in summarizing.

The notion of summarizing or reducing evidence can be illustrated using examples from the sciences. In statistical studies, the goal is usually to reduce large amounts of data into progressively smaller summaries; large quantities of numbers can be aggregated into summary tables. Tendencies and patterns in the data can be briefly expressed as, for example, a curve or formula representing the relationship between two variables. Useful though this simplification and diminution in physical size can be, some of the evidence is necessarily lost in the process of reduction. The objective of statistical techniques is to maximize the physical reduction in size while minimizing the loss of evidence. Similarly, in chemistry an important goal is to analyze some material or process in order to describe it by a succinct formal statement, such as a chemical formula.

In biology one can illustrate this process of reduction—this trade-off between convenience and loss of evidence. Suppose that one were interested in woodpeckers. Some aspects of woodpeckers, such as woodpecker behavior, can be learned only from live woodpeckers, preferably woodpeckers in the wild. For other purposes, a dead woodpecker would suffice. Studying live woodpeckers, however, is less convenient than studying dead ones, which can be housed and handled more easily. Similarly, more can be learned from a film of a woodpecker than from a still photograph, but the latter is easier to make, to handle, and to examine. A set of measurements of woodpeckers is even easier to handle, but much less can be learned from measurements than from photos, films, or actual woodpeckers.

Reproductions, even photographs of works of art and replicas of museum objects, cannot reflect all the evidence of the originals. However, they may well suffice for many purposes and have two striking advantages: they can be made much more widely available and can be used without wear and tear of the originals.

We have used the term *summarizing* with some hesitation. There is no question that the summarizing, condensing, and interpreting of evidence pervades recorded knowledge. In the case of statistical studies, "summarizing" is an apt description of the process of making evidence more convenient and, indeed, more understandable. In literary and historical studies, however, where words rather than numbers are the principal basis for description, the commentaries intended to make the original more understandable can easily be larger than the original. (Consider, for example, the relative sizes of some originals such as the Bible or the works of Shakespeare with the corpus of writings about the Bible or Shakespeare.) Further, commentaries are more likely to complement the original (and each other) than to serve as a substitute. In the humanities, interpretation and summarizing are likely to constitute an expansion.

Information processing, the deriving of new representations, has a special significance in relation to retrieval-based information systems:

1. Where events and objects cannot be collected and stored for retrieval, representations of them can, in general, be made and used in their place.

2. Where multiple arrangements by different attributes are desirable, representations, whether copies or summaries, can be made to serve as surrogates for the original.

3. Retrieval itself depends on matching a representation of an inquiry against either original objects or, more usually, representations of the original objects.

Indexes, abstracts, physical and mathematical models, classification schemes, statistical summaries, and catalog entries are all examples of representations of objects.

The importance of information processing, in a broad sense, is enormous, as can be seen by considering what would be lost if it did not occur. Without information processing, retrieval-based information systems could not exist, informative objects could not be copied, communicated, translated, summarized, explained, or developed, personal knowledge could not become recorded knowledge, and personal knowledge could not be communicated to others, since the creation of messages is a form of deriving information-as-thing.

Education, scholarship, debate, political process, technological development—and, therefore, information systems—are permeated with these processes of interpreting and summarizing. Articles and books summarize, cite, refute, and build upon earlier work. This is especially noticeable in the scholarly literature where the growth of material has created the need for abstracting and indexing services, for guides and reviews. Encyclopedias, handbooks, and textbooks, all examples of summarizing and interpretation, perform a useful role.

INFORMATION PROCESSING BY MACHINE

We have been examining information processing in a broad sense and turn to a narrower sense: information processing by machine. Mechanized information processing depends on the physical representation of information-as-thing in machine-readable form. Two sorts of information can be represented very successfully for machines. First, explicitly defined quantities, including zero, can be represented in several ways, including the sliding of rods, as in a slide rule, and the turning of wheels, as was used in analog computers. However, the dominant method is digital, as used in modern computers, using binary codes expressed by the presence or absence of physical holes or magnetic charges. Second, logical statements can also be expressed mechanically, notably by switches (relays, gates, transistors) in electric circuits.

As a result there appears to be no limit in principle to the capability of information processing machines to derive new information from old as long as the matter being processed can be handled in the form of logic and quantities, including probabilities. Other matters of a qualitative nature can be handled only to the extent to which they can be approximated in quantitative and logical terms, including calculation and simulation. Expert systems, for example, depend on expert human judgment being represented in the form of logical if-then rules. In general, activities that are not fundamentally quantitative or logical can benefit from mechanized information processing to the extent to which quantitative or logical approximations can be devised, even if these approximations are ultimately inappropriate. There are two excellent examples of such approximations in subject searching in mechanized information retrieval systems: the use of Boolean logic and the use of automatic full-text searching are unsatisfactory in theory and very useful in practice. Ingenuity in design and improvements in technology will lead to better approximations and greater utility, even though theoretical objections remain.

SUMMARY

Limiting use of the term *information processing* to electronic data processing and the use of algorithms may be sensible in the context of computing but not for any general view of information and information systems. Information processing is the derivation of new informative objects, new information-as-thing, usually but not exclusively from earlier information—whether events, objects, discourse, or knowledge. Information processing activities include copying, transliterating, telecommunications, translation, summarizing, explaining, and developing informative objects.

Information processing, in the sense of deriving new representations from old ones, has great significance in relation to retrieval-based information systems. The derivation of representations, such as photos, descriptions, and statistical summaries, enables the storage of at least a version of what might not otherwise be storable. Representations, whether copies or summaries, allow multiple arrangements and multiple means of access to the original and to multiple copies of the original. Representations can be multiplied to permit physical access in many places.

Of special interest is the extent to which human activities, notably education, scholarship, political processes, and technology, are permeated with the use of representations of knowledge and informative objects derived from them.

NOTE

1. One might argue that burning a book in order to destroy the text should be regarded as a flagrant form of information processing but that, in contrast, burning a book because one needed warmth and was indifferent to text should not be regarded as information processing. A rejoinder might be that the book burned as fuel did nevertheless involve the destruction of a text that might well be regarded, at least by somebody, as information and so would, in addition to being a form of heating, also be a form of information processing. Suppose instead that a log of wood had been used as fuel. Logs are an accepted form of fuel, but our dilemma does not go away, since the rings in the wood provide information on the age of the tree and the weather in successive years. This evidence can be used to identify the age of other pieces of wood and to date the beams in old buildings. So in burning a log, one is also burning information, just as in burning a book, even though no one may be interested at the time or even later. Still, one hesitates

to regard all wood fires as (destructive) information processing. If it were, then virtually all processes involving change to any physical object would also have to be regarded as being information processing since virtually any physical object might be regarded as evidence, as information, with respect to something.

Chapter 13

Demand

Our interest in information is subordinate to our primary concern with information systems. In this chapter and the next, we examine the demand for and supply of information services through information systems.

In chapter 9 we discussed inquiries, viewing them as motivation for information-seeking behavior even though not all inquiries result in information seeking and even fewer result in the use of formal information systems. We now examine the same activity but from a different perspective. Instead of analyzing the nature of an individual inquiry, we now consider the overall pattern of the sum of all such activities. The seeking, the acquiring, and the supplying of information is best understood as an economic and political activity and will be treated in those terms. If we are to have any serious understanding of the structure and functioning of information services, we need to ask: What determines the level of demand for them? What determines the supply? In this chapter we concentrate on information services provided without direct monetary charges.

We can, more or less in parallel with the stages used to describe the evolution of an individual inquiry, outline a series of stages in the use of an information system:

1. Needs that are not recognized as needs or not recognized as needs for which a specific information system would be useful.

2. Needs that are recognized but nevertheless no action is taken to use an information service in relation to them.

3. Wants, in the sense of conscious desires, to use an information system, whether or not such use is sensible in practice.

4. Unsuccessful attempts to use an information system, as when a search is made but the desired information is not found.

5. Satisfied demand, in the sense that information service perceived as satisfactory by the user resulted from use of the information system.

A variety of terms have been coined in relation to these various sorts of needs and wants (Line 1975; Roberts 1975; T. D. Wilson 1981). For our purposes we shall concentrate on three categories. Two of these are the last two listed above: unsuccessful attempts and attempts that were satisfactory to the user. These two constitute the expressed demand (in an economic sense) with which the provider of an information service is dealing. Demands that might have been expressed but were not constitute the third category and could be designated as latent or potential demand.

In exploring the determinants of demand, we take what is basically an economic and cybernetic approach. By this we mean a process with the following characteristics: individuals have desires that, in their own perceptions, might be satisfied by using a particular information system or at least the probability is high enough to justify an attempt. Individuals weigh the perceived probable price of using the information system against the perceived probable benefit of doing so. Use of the system is likely to follow if the relative price is perceived to be low enough. *Relative* means not only in comparison with the expected benefits of use but also in comparison with known alternatives to that particular information system.

In exploring this approach to demand, we note two paradoxes. First, an economic theory based on price appears inconsistent with the fact that many information services, notably archives, libraries, management information systems, records management services, and museums, are commonly provided for free or with only a nominal monetary charge to the user. Second, if information services are provided for free, then they would appear to lack the responsiveness supposedly necessary for organizations to survive (Pfeffer and Salancik 1978, 43). Since a market economy normally forces responsiveness, there are recurring suggestions that information services traditionally provided without charge should begin to charge in order to become responsive (Ackoff et al. 1976, 41; Getz 1980, 163). Yet information systems commonly exhibit considerable stability and powers of survival, characteristics usually associated with systems that are highly responsive to changing circumstances. The resolution of both paradoxes comes with a reconsideration of the concept of price.

THE REAL PRICE

Economics texts vary in their treatment of the definitions of price. Sometimes price is defined as the monetary exchange value of commodities and services. Sometimes that definition is implicitly assumed. At other times, a more general definition of price is given, and, subsequently, the notion of money as a convenient mode of expression of the price is added as an extension.

Price, measure of the value of a commodity that expresses its worth in exchange for other goods and services. Because it is more convenient to express the relative value of all goods in terms of a common unit of account, one commodity may be selected as the common measure. . . . In modern economies, the national currency serves this function. (*Encyclopaedia Britannica* 1976 VIII: 204)

Adam Smith was emphatic on price being the sum of the disadvantages accruing to the purchaser: "The real price of everything, what everything really costs to the man who wants to acquire it, is the toil and trouble of acquiring it." (Smith 1976, bk. 1, chap. 5, para. 2).

If the real price is distinguished from the monetary expression of price, then we can reappraise the nature of price, the applicability of price mechanisms, and, in particular, any nonmonetary expressions of price, such as effort, and discomfort.

Time: Delay as an Expression of Price

Other things being equal, sooner is better than later for anything one wants to have. There is a distinction to be made between being obliged to spend much time doing something, time that cannot be put to any other good use, and waiting for something and able to put the time to good use, doing other things. In both cases, however, an opportunity cost is implicit: the time and effort could have been spent doing something else. Waiting for information to be provided is an unwelcome delay. An information service in which delays are short is better than one in which they are long, other things being equal. This is true even if one considers only the individual user's time. There may also be consequential costs in delay as can be illustrated by considering the need, for example, to find out which antidote to use after a poison has been absorbed or when data are needed to support a budget request before an imminent budgetary deadline. Best of all is an information service in which information is immediately available, with any necessary tasks of preparation already having been performed by the time a demand for service occurs. One prefers not to have to expend time or to incur delay in getting service:

Waiting time does allocate public services, rationing them, as would money prices, according to the tastes, income and opportunity costs of consumers. Time prices differ from money prices, however, since they appear relatively lower to persons with a lower money value of time. . . . Thus when two individuals who value their time unequally wait in the same queue, they face different prices. (Nicols, Smolensky, and Tidman 1971, 312–23)[1]

Money as an Expression of Price

The use of money as an expression of price needs little comment. One prefers to minimize (ideally to avoid) the expenditure of money to obtain service. Of course, not all money is perceived in the same way; one might view one's employer's money or government funds differently from one's own personal money. A key to the difference lies in the opportunity cost, in the range of alternatives that one could spend that money on.

Effort, Discomfort, and Inconvenience as Price

Among these factors (effort, discomfort, and inconvenience) we include a number of considerations that are even less easy to handle than time and money. However, we are primarily interested in the "real price" rather than whether expressions of price lend themselves to convenient quantitative analysis. Information systems are not always easy or convenient to use. Like elephants, inconveniences can be easier to recognize than to describe. It is a nuisance to have to travel in order to acquire information. Bureaucratic formalities and an unpleasant environment make use of any service less pleasant. These factors can be cultural and interpersonal as well as physiological. One would prefer not to have to put up with inconvenience in order to use an information system. Some other information service or system that was less inconvenient but otherwise comparable would be preferable. Systems are more or less difficult to use.[2]

These aspects of the real price invite several comments. It is clear that there can be nonmonetary elements of price in the toil and trouble of acquiring information. Indeed, the monetary element may be minor or nonexistent (Braunstein 1979). The question arises as to whether some of these aspects of price ought to be considered part of the price at all. For example, delay could be viewed as much an attribute of the service as of the price—a slow service as contrasted with a fast service. From an analytical point of view, there is scope for flexibility here. All of the elements of a cost-benefit relationship are part of the same equation, and it may not matter how one chooses to arrange them. The argument that monetary price is an incomplete expression of price could be countered by the response that, by definition, monetary price is being isolated on one side of the equation and that any aspects not expressed by monetary price can be regarded as attributes of the service (e.g., an inconvenient service). Theoretically, there is a difference between using monetary price as a convenient but incomplete representation of exchange value (in which case something has been lost) and asserting that monetary price is what happens to have been isolated on one side of the equation (in which case nothing has been lost).

Each aspect of a system has some sort of effect in terms of a price mechanism. As the time needed to obtain the service increases, the consumer is more likely to give up. This may involve switching to an alternative source of supply or choosing to forgo satisfying the need. The elasticity of demand (the extent to which demand changes as price changes) is a basic feature of economic behavior. There are limits to the amount of inconvenience people are willing to suffer to satisfy their needs. As with monetary price, the point at which people decide that the amount of inconvenience is too much can be expected to vary from one individual to another and from one situation to another. However, there appears to be no reason to doubt that elasticity of demand exists in relation to information services with respect to the nonmonetary aspects of price as well as with monetary price. The more trouble it is to use an information service, the less one is inclined to use it. Given a choice of services with different degrees of inconvenience, people will tend to choose between them in a rational way.

These different aspects of price are more or less interchangeable. People may be willing to pay to reduce delay. Others may be willing to save money by waiting if, in their personal value system, their money is scarce relative to their time. Similarly, effort and/or discomfort may, for any given situation, be more (or less) preferable to delay or monetary price. Every competent bureaucrat understands that the choice of process can affect the outcome and that a price mechanism can be invoked to discourage demand even without a monetary price; increased delays, more forms to complete, inconveniently located offices, restricted hours of service, redirection from one office to another, and instructions that are difficult to understand are but a few examples. Whether intended or not, these increases in the nonmonetary aspects of price all have a dampening effect on demand just as the imposition of (or an increase in) monetary price does. If there were complete interchangeability between the aspects of price and if there were perfect understanding of what the exchange rates were, then all aspects of price could conveniently be related to money. Such a degree of interchangeability appears to occur only in economic theory.

A Library Example

With this general background, we can use the search for a book in a library as an illustration of the demand mechanism (Buckland 1975). Suppose that the demand for some particular title were to increase. Sooner or later all copies of that title will be in use, and demands for copies will be unsatisfied. From the library's side there are at least five possible courses of action:

1. Acquire additional copies. Assuming no increase in the library's budget, this implies some internal reallocation of resources away from some other part of the library's budget. The price to the users will therefore include an opportunity forgone, a degradation in some other aspect of the library service. There might well be a net improvement in library service overall, especially for users wanting this particular title, but some disbenefit elsewhere in the library service is ordinarily involved, however slight.

2. Increased availability could be achieved by faster turnaround. In other words, the librarian could shorten loan periods and/or confine copies to the reading room, so that they will become available for others sooner. In this case, instead of imposing a price in terms of some reduction in service elsewhere in the library (as when diverting money to buy extra copies), the service is made less convenient in a different way for users of that title. Whether users will accept the increased inconvenience and still use the library's copies or decide that they are unwilling to tolerate the reduced convenience, the library has, in fact, responded to regain earlier, higher levels of immediate availability at the price of reduced length of availability.

3. The library could introduce an optional monetary charge for preferential access to

copies. This would be a commercial response by the library and should be expected to reduce demand, bring in some income to improve the service (e.g., by buying more copies), and might make waiting more tolerable for those who prefer not to pay but realize that they could pay for faster service whenever they valued speed of service highly enough relative to their money.

4. Those who set library policy might adopt different policies for different groups of users as has been traditional in university libraries, thereby allocating inconvenience differentially.

5. The library might decide to do nothing, to adopt no specific action to restore the level of availability, and, thereby, to allow the time aspect of price, delay, to be increased for library users.

It is clear that the librarian has more than one possible response. It is also clear that each different course of action by the library changes the form of but does not remove the real price for the library users. The choice of action or inaction by the librarian implies a decision concerning the preferred mix of elements in the real price for the library's users.

The response of the user to a change in the real price can be expected to be the same as in any other situation of demand for a commodity or service: the customer can accept the price (mainly time and inconvenience in this example), can substitute another source (go to another library, borrow a copy from a friend, buy a copy), or decide to give up, leaving the need unsatisfied. Which choice any individual will make depends on the circumstances: the alternatives known to be available, the importance and urgency of the need, and the various values held by the individual with respect to time, money, effort, discomfort, and inconvenience.

The sum of the customer's decisions determines the level of demand for the title. If the increase in demand is dampened enough, the balance of demand and supply will diminish to where it was originally or lower. We have used a quite specific example, but we believe that the same sort of mechanism applies generally.

THE DOUBLE FEEDBACK LOOP

Of fundamental importance to the understanding of the dynamics of noncommercial information systems is the relative independence of the responsive behavior of the user and that of the provider.[3] We can explain this by building on the example of a library title in increased demand (Buckland 1982).

The librarian can respond by adding copies, reducing loan periods, setting preferential policies, or taking no action. These actions—the last being action by default—constitute adaptive responses (feedback) by the librarian to deal with an unsatisfactory standard of service. The librarian can take these actions more or less independently of the user.

The user can also react more or less independently of the librarian: by coming back later, in which case the demand is not diminished but delayed, or by taking other steps that will have the effect of reducing the level of demand, such as switching to another library, borrowing a friend's copy, buying a copy, using some other book instead, or giving up. This freedom of choice by the user constitutes a second and largely independent feedback mechanism.

This double feedback loop, shown in figure 13.1, is of interest from a cybernetic perspective. These two feedback mechanisms are substantially independent of each other in important ways.[4]

The librarian's action may not depend on response by the user, and the user's response may not depend on response by the librarian. Since library services are normally free, the library's income does not depend directly on the level of demand. Reduced demand therefore does not weaken a public service as it would a commercial business, where a drop in demand would reduce income and profit from sales. Rather, the reverse occurs: a reduced demand for a free service reduces the pressure, leaving existing resources more adequate to cope with the remaining demand. Similarly, serving increased demand would not be as rewarding as it would for a commercial business because it increases workload rather than income or profit.

Note that although the librarian can respond to improve availability, such a response is not to be assumed since, with existing library techniques, evidence about the unsatisfied searches by users commonly does not reach the librarian in a reliable, useful way. However, the user does know reliably whether the book was found. The user's feedback mechanism will be in effect, therefore, whether or not the librarian is responsive. In other words, it is the responsiveness of the users, more than the responsiveness of the librarian, that serves to restore stability to the library service. This helps explain a noteworthy cybernetic aspect of library services: libraries, like other public services, can survive with remarkable stability even in the absence of effective management—survive, that is, not excel.

PRICE, SCARCITY, AND INFORMATION

We now take a closer look at price and scarcity in relation to information.

1. Knowledge can sometimes be communicated indefinitely with little or no effort or expense. Rumors spread like epidemics.

2. Generally, but not always, we want knowledge to be disseminated. We may be glad for others to benefit at little or no disadvantage to ourselves. We might suffer if those with whom we deal are ignorant.

When both of these conditions are met, information (as a means to knowledge) has characteristics of a public good: charging individual fees for it is normally not sensible; shared use of it is mutually beneficial. But these conditions do not always apply.

3. The real price of becoming informed is not always trivial: burdensome access to documents, tedious study, or consultation with others might be needed.

Figure 13.1
Double Feedback Loop

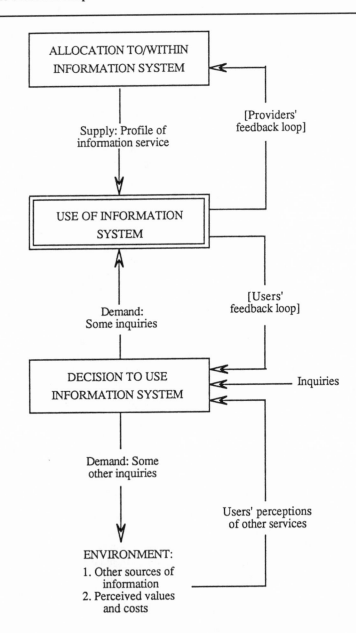

There generally is a price—at least in time and effort—that may have nothing to do with scarcity in the ordinary sense, so condition 1 does not always obtain.

4. A monetary price for access to information arises in another way in relation to the effort and expense of accessing information noted in 3. It may well be possible for someone to reduce the real price of becoming informed by offering—for a fee—a less onerous alternative information service, such as an inexpensive edition of a book, more convenient access to a database, or the same information packaged with helpful supplementary information. The new alternative may cost money, but because it adds value in the form of greater convenience or some similar benefit, a lower real price results, and so the fee may be well worth paying (Taylor 1986).

5. Contrary to condition 2, there may sometimes be an advantage in a competitive situation if others remain ignorant or misinformed. Trade secrets, military intelligence, and advance market information can be beneficial to those privileged to know them. Such knowledge could be well worth keeping secret if you do know and worth paying for if you do not. Such knowledge is a valuable asset, and the expression of the knowledge in the form of information a valuable commodity when all of the following conditions are met: there is a competitive situation, the information is instrumental (useful for some purpose), and the information is scarce in the sense of being restricted.

6. Knowledge is naturally scarce when only few experts have been able and willing to acquire it. Expert information—the expression of expert knowledge—may have a high price because of the effort or expense of acquiring and of sharing it (condition 3) or because the experts may choose to limit availability on economic grounds through restrictive practices such as copyright or professional controls (condition 5).

The motivations can be varied and potentially in conflict: expert knowledge and proprietary information as an asset, the general dissemination of knowledge as a public good, and opportunities to make money through publication and value-added services if access to the information can be restricted.

PATTERNS OF DEMAND

In this section we describe briefly two sorts of regularity in the demand for information services that are not only of research interest but also of great significance for the design and operation of information systems.

Elasticity of Demand

We have noted that we are dealing with a price mechanism, even though it is not usually thought of in terms of a price mechanism and commonly not a commercial situation. A price mechanism means that demand will be more or less elastic, in the sense that the level of demand will be more or less sensitive to changes in the real price.

An information service could be a monopoly, but even with a monopoly, there is elasticity of demand. The degree of elasticity depends on the consumers' ability to reduce, even forgo, consumption of the service. With information services, since we are dealing with open systems, the monopoly is likely to be imperfect or nonexistent. To the extent to which alternatives are available, users can not only reduce or forgo their use of a service, they can also reduce their use of one service by diverting their demands to another. This marketplace situation increases the sensitivity of demand with respect to the real price for any given information service.

It is not easy to assemble and interpret empirical evidence of the elasticity of demand for information services. Nonmonetary aspects of price that are difficult to measure play a large role. The monetary price, where present, is also difficult to interpret because the price is commonly not payable from the personal funds of the user but from other people's funds, such as the user's employer or the user's own customers. Especially common in the use of computerized systems is the use of "funny money," whereby funds are nominally made available to be used for the payment of these charges but may not be used for other purposes such as taking a vacation or buying a good meal. This use of funny money constitutes a form of internal rationing, but it is a lot less than bringing the activity into an open market with free choice.

Yet another difficulty is that, especially with information systems that are not computer based, it is often difficult to know what is actually happening when they are used. What are the visitors actually doing in the library or in the museum? For these and perhaps for other reasons, studies of the dynamics and sensitivity of demand for information services are not well developed. It is easier and commoner to make a survey of the pattern of use at some point in time. In this case, as with a photograph, one may get a view of the situation at a given moment but learn little or nothing of the trends, let alone the underlying dynamics of the situation. This is a serious criticism, since useful, applicable research generally involves trying to answer the question: "What would happen if . . . ?" If it is not known how demand would change if the information service were to be changed, then one does not know much about "What would happen if . . . ?"

As if this were not enough, what is observed and measured of the use of information systems tends to be mere surface phenomena. One might measure how many people looked at the *Mona Lisa* in a year yet not know whether or how any of them were affected by this gazing or how far the same or other people may have been affected in the same way or differently by copies of the *Mona Lisa* elsewhere. One may know how many times a particular document was borrowed but not whether it was actually read, by whom it was read (not necessarily the person who borrowed it), or, if it was read, how much of it was read, whether it was understood, or how, if at all, it changed the beliefs of the reader, let alone what the longer-term intellectual or social consequences were. An excellent illustration of this is the widespread use of citation analysis. There is no doubt that very sophisticated analyses can be done of who cites whom or that the results can be useful and suggestive in a general way for understanding patterns in scholarship. Nevertheless, the lack of understanding of what the act of citing (or not citing) really signifies means that any but the simpler, descriptive conclusions derived from these studies are built on weak foundations (T. A. Brooks 1986, 1987; Buckland 1988b, 193–96; Hertzel 1987; Narin and Moll 1977).

Studies have shown that accessibility is a dominant factor in information gathering behavior. Perceived convenience influences greatly the choice of source of information and amount of use (Allen and Gerstberger 1967; Harris 1966; Rosenberg 1967; E. B. Swanson 1987). The perceived probability that information will be available when sought has also emerged as influential with respect to demand (Buckland 1975). The opening of new, more congenial library buildings is known to increase the use of library services (Holt 1976). A convenient geographical location increases use (Palmer 1981; Zipf 1965). All of these effects are to be expected. Well-planned facilities involve less discomfort; a site that is conveniently located minimizes travel effort; immediate availability saves time and effort.

Unfortunately, these aspects of the real price do not lend themselves to direct quantitative analysis. That fact may lead to their being neglected by researchers eager to quantify but does not make them any less real. For example, the effect of distance has been studied, but the problem is considerably less tractable than might appear at first sight. It is not a matter of distance traveled but more of traveling time, even more, of perceived traveling effort. Further, since more than one task can often be performed on one journey, the effort of making the journey is shared between different goals (e.g., between going to a museum and shopping). Not all modes of traveling are equally congenial, equally attractive to different people, or the same mode at different times, since one can be more or less busy, the weather more or less pleasant, and transportation more or less available. Similarly, the user-friendliness of computer systems is a complex and elusive matter.

As with other human perceptions of value, the appraisal of the price should not be presumed to be linear. To use distance as an example, an increase from 1 meter to 91 meters is much more significant for human behavior than an increase from 101 meters to 191, let alone from 10,001 to 10,091, even though each example involves the same increase in distance in absolute terms: 90 meters. In terms of perceived price and impact on behavior, a geometric progression (e.g., from 1 to 10 meters, from 10 to 100, and from 100 to 1,000) seems more likely to have comparable effects than a linear progression (Brookes 1980).

Distribution of Demand

Quite separate from the elasticity of demand, the use of information services exhibits regularities in the pattern of demand. The distribution of the use of individual items within an information service is likely to be highly skewed (in a statistical sense) in that for any given individual or group of users, a few systems are frequently used, more are sometimes used, and many are rarely used. The same is true of the distribution of demand over individual sources within systems. The details of these distributions provide opportunities for scholarly argument, but the general pattern is well established and appears to be a local manifestation of a pattern that is a common characteristic of human behavior (Hertzel 1987; Zipf 1965).

SUMMARY

The seeking of information, like the seeking of other things, is governed by a price mechanism. The real price includes other components, such as time, effort, and inconvenience, as well as any commercial, monetary price. Does the perceived probable benefit match the perceived probable price? Since information systems are not closed systems, there is generally no monopoly, so the opportunity of substituting alternative sources of information is generally present.

The adaptiveness and therefore the survival of noncommercial information services are aided by a degree of separation between the adaptive response of the users from the adaptive response to the providers. Patterns of demand are characterized by highly skewed distributions.

NOTES

1. For a detailed treatment of time as a cost in the use of library services see Van House (1983a, 1983b).

2. Related issues are discussed in terms of accessibility, e.g., Culnan (1984, 1985).

3. This section is based on insights by Dr. A. Hindle, University of Lancaster, United Kingdom.

4. By double feedback loop we mean two more or less independent feedback loops, each modifying the basic system. This is quite different from a secondary feedback loop (or secondary controller), which modifies the first feedback loop rather than the basic system. If a thermostat is a primary feedback loop controlling a heater, then a secondary feedback loop would modify the thermostat rather than the heater.

Chapter 14

Providing Information

So far we have examined inquiries, information processing, perceiving information, becoming informed, and the demand for information services. We have not paid much attention to what we might have started with: providing information services. What determines the sorts of services provided? This chapter addresses directly one of the six conditions for access to information identified in chapter 8: provision of information service. More generally, we need to ask what sorts of information services are developed and why. Note that we are discussing what is provided, not what is used. One cannot ordinarily make people use particular information services; one can only provide or not provide.

There is, of course, a technical constraint. Not all desirable services or systems are technically feasible. A better technique or an improved technology is, in general terms, one that has constraints that are fewer or preferable, as was discussed in chapter 7. We concern ourselves now with what determines what sorts of services and systems are provided within technical and technological constraints.

The scale and nature of an information service are determined by the allocation of resources to and within the information service. The next question then becomes: How is the allocation of resources to and within the information service determined? The allocating of available resources depends on the values of those doing the allocation, within the constraints imposed by the availability of resources. At the very least, we are concerned with economics, with social values, and with resource allocation.

We start with the case of noncommercial information services, those that are provided with no or only an insignificant direct monetary charge to the user. This is a common pattern, especially with archives, records management, libraries, and museums. We shall consider later the provision of information services on a commercial, quasi-commercial, or partially commercial basis.

NONCOMMERCIAL INFORMATION SERVICES

We take libraries, archives, and public museums as archetypal noncommercial information services. The scale and nature of each archive, library, and museum are determined by the allocation of resources to it and within it. Decisions are made as to what particular services to provide, the extent they are to be provided, and with what priorities. It is essentially a process of allocation of resources. The allocation to the information service determines the overall scale of operations. The allocation within the information service affects the detailed mixture of specific services or functions provided. The mixture of services implies and supports the chosen mission of the service. Charles McCarthy (1873–1921), who allocated resources at the Wisconsin Legislative Reference Library in such a way as to influence what legislation was passed, provides a good illustration (Casey 1981).

The setting of priorities is part of the allocation process, since resources are never sufficient for doing everything one might wish. Also, determining that support of one activity should take priority over support of another is a preferential allocation of resources. As resources, we include anything that could have been used in other ways: money, space, effort, equipment, and labor.

The ability to make and to enforce regulations can be seen as a kind of resource. Like other sorts of resources, regulations can be used as means for achieving ends. To some extent, regulations are substitutable for other resources. For example, the ability to enforce loan periods of limited duration has an effect on the availability of library books comparable (though not identical) to the expenditure of additional money to buy duplicate copies. One may even be able to make a crude estimate of the amount of money saved by specific regulations (Buckland 1975).

We have started by confining attention to the limited but common situation wherein service is not provided on a commercial basis but is free in the sense that it is supported by resources that are not directly derived from the users as users. The support may well be indirectly from the users, however. Corporate information systems may be supported from administrative overhead and so be at the expense of the users' budgets. Users of public libraries, museums, and public archives do, in general, pay for these services but indirectly in their capacity as taxpayers rather than because they are users.

The process of allocation to and within a noncommercial service is a political process. This does not imply that all decisions are made through formal political parties, elections, and the like, though that can happen. Rather, we regard politics as having to do with who gets what, who controls the decisions about who gets what, and how control is exercised in practice.

A dictionary definition of politics is "the process of the formulation and administration of public policy usually by interaction between social groups and political institutions or between political leadership and public opinion" (*Webster's* 1971). Although this appears to refer to the affairs of cities and nations,

Figure 14.1
Noncommercial Allocation of Resources

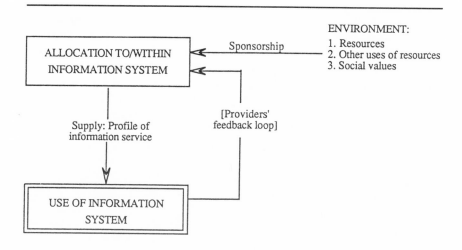

it seems reasonable to follow common practice in extending it to universities, corporations, and other organizations in which resources are allocated.

We should be careful to note the wide range of values that can be involved. For a corporate management information system, the predominant emphasis may be on improved profitability through efficiency and effectiveness. For a library, the primary goal is ordinarily education or recreation, but this has to be interpreted within a context of local values. Knowledge that is seen as a threat to public safety or public morals is not encouraged. Documents that might compromise national security or the careers of individuals are likely to be excluded from or restricted within archive services.

The allocation of resources to and within a noncommercial system is depicted in figure 14.1.

DIFFUSION, SUBVERSION, COMPROMISE

Having defined allocation as a political process, we now examine some of the factors likely to affect the process in practice.

Diffusion and Management

There is a distinction, at least in theory, between those who allocate resources to a service (e.g., a city council, a university president) and the managers (state archivist, chief librarian) responsible for administering the service, who allocate resources within the archive, library, or other information service. In reality, there is usually a significant overlapping of the processes of allocation to and allocation within. The sponsors who allocate resources to the service generally have views as to how these resources should be allocated within the service. Indeed budgetary allocations are commonly made contingent upon prescribed and limited uses of the monies. It is reasonable that the sponsors should have an interest in how the resources will be deployed, since they will want some reassurance that their goals will be honored. Similarly it would be a poor manager who had nothing to say about how big the budget ought to be. In this way the allocation process can be said to have been extended downward.

Noncommercial information services are typically characterized by at least some of the factors associated with human services organizations (Hasenfeld 1983):

• They are labor intensive.
• The organizational structures that prevail are largely hierarchical.
• Services are commonly decentralized geographically for the convenience of users.
• Some degree of division, or rather specialization, of labor is normal. In particular, managers are likely to be dependent on specialist staff for technical advice.
• Precise, adequate, agreed measures of service are lacking.
• The consequences of providing service are unclear.

These factors make for further diffusion of responsibility for allocation among employees, since many of the decisions concerning details are delegated, often to geographically dispersed areas. We take *details* to include individual decisions concerning the choice of data, documents, and objects to be collected, how to represent them, and the detailed deployment of staff time within and between the general areas of helping users directly and of "housekeeping." Although these decisions may individually be small in import, we should not imply or assume that collectively they are unimportant.

Since labor is a major part of the allocatable resources, it follows that anybody with any discretion over the allocation of his or her own time shares in the allocation process.

In these ways, the implementation process is typically widely diffused. Insofar as management includes making decisions that include the deployment of resources and priorities, one could say that management is also diffused. The allocation process can correctly be described as a political and managerial process.

Displacement, Approximation, and Subversion

The diffusion of responsibility for the allocation of resources and priorities makes the allocation process vulnerable to distortion in two sorts of ways.

First, the very diffusion places a strain on the communication of the values and goals motivating those who allocated resources to the service. In the communication and interpretation of these values, some distortion is to be expected.

Second, consciously or unconsciously, different people will tend to bias the selection of values and the choice of means of implementation in accordance with their own preferences. They may feel, quite consciously, that the official intentions are unrealistic and quietly go about interpreting or implementing them in a way that accords more closely to their own sense of values and of the situation, with or without their own self-interest influencing this process. This distortion or adaptation of official intentions may or may not be beneficial from the perspective of those being served (Buckland 1988c, 146–47; Etzioni 1964, 10; Hasenfeld 1983, chap. 4; Levy, Meltsner, and Wildavsky 1974; Meyer 1979; Tompkins and Cheney 1985).

Compromise

We have assumed thus far that there is one set of values and one dominant goal. This is unlikely; an information service will ordinarily serve groups whose interests do not entirely coincide. A corporate management information system designed to suit accountants may not suit planners. A university library service that is ideal for professors may not be what is best for undergraduates. A public library that emphasized service to local historians would not be of most help to local business and industry, though there should be considerable overlap in each of these cases.

There is commonly a further dimension of possible conflict of interest. Information services, especially noncommercial, public services, such as archives, libraries, and museums, commonly help each other across organizational and jurisdictional lines. They benefit from the use of each other's resources, both collections and expertise. Ideally this is a reciprocal and mutually beneficial arrangement. But if borrowing is a benefit, lending is a disbenefit. The collective benefit in cooperative arrangements will be at some price in that resources are diverted from local to collective goals. Such cooperation can be advantageous to all concerned. Nevertheless, an additional tension between collective and local goals is created, and the price of cooperation may be (and at some point should be) perceived locally as being too high. As budgets tighten, collective responsibilities are gradually abandoned in favor of local needs.

Any allocation of resources is necessarily a compromise among services, but it is unlikely to be just any, accidental compromise. Instead, the mixture of services will reflect, albeit imperfectly, the values and preferences of those who have been doing the allocation at all levels.

Disavowal of Values

We have mentioned repeatedly the social values that form the basis for decisions concerning the allocation of resources to and within information services. Resources are not allocated randomly or purposelessly. It is all the more curious, therefore, that in librarianship and perhaps in other information service areas, the role of social values is sometimes denied as unprofessional or not perceived. It is regarded as unprofessional by some who profess a liberal stance that the provider should impose values on the user. This is reflected, for example, in a slogan in librarianship that a librarian should have, in his or her professional capacity, "no politics, no religion, no morals" (Foskett 1962, 3; see also Hennessy 1981; Rogers 1984). It is also sometimes claimed that librarianship has no, or insufficient, "philosophy."

These statements appear to derive from confusion between technique and effects. The techniques of information systems, the technology and skills that are brought to bear in providing an information service, are means of implementation. One might appraise their effectiveness in being instrumental for performing some task. Moral approval or disapproval is meaningful in relation to the choice of tasks for which the techniques are used, not in relation to the effectiveness of the tools and techniques themselves. In this sense the skills and expertise of information service—in archives, management information systems, librarianship, or some other area—can and should be regarded as value-free technique. However, information service is, and must necessarily be, deeply value laden in the sense that the uses of the techniques relate positively or negative to social values. Choices concerning uses are influenced by social values and have to be made on a daily basis as an integral part of managerial decision making. Therefore, the motivating beliefs, concepts, and principles—the social "philosophy"—of those involved in allocation are an inexorable and pervasive feature of information services. To opt out of value-laden decisions is just that: a decision to delegate such decisions to others. As has been said in relation to museums, "A non-political historical museum is self-contradictory" (Hoffman 1973, quoted in Rogalla von Bieberstein 1975, 102).

MISSION, GOAL, OBJECTIVES

The terms for describing what one is seeking to achieve are inconsistently used: *mission, objective, goal, target, aim,* and so on. The best that can be done is to make clear the sense in which one is using each term and not to assume that others will adopt the same definitions. It is usually helpful to distinguish three different but related levels:

Level I: Mission statement. A mission statement is a broad definition of what business the information service is in. What is the sphere of activity of this service? This should be a general, and generally acceptable, definition of the role of the service.

Level II: Goals. In order to articulate day-to-day work with the broad generality of the mission statement, it is usually helpful to spell out a list of sorts of long-term activities, or subordinate purposes, that support the pursuit of the mission. This list of goals should be helpful in perceiving more clearly the best choice of specific tasks in relation to the mission. This list of goals should be comprehensive.

Level III: Objectives (or "performance goals"). Levels I and II are related to the service as a whole and deal with general statements. There remains the question of specific objectives (or "performance goals") for individual units (or individuals) within the service. These are used as guidelines for day-to-day decisions for the use of time and other resources. Negotiation between individual and supervisor of agreed objectives for that individual ordinarily forms the basis of "management by objectives." They can serve as yardsticks with which to review and assess performance and results.

Some aspects of the use of mission, goals, and objectives in relation to information services deserve to be noted. One is that information services commonly serve a larger organization, which supports them (e.g., a corporation, university, city, or state). Social values and social goals are generally difficult to define in practical ways. Hence, public sector institutions such as schools, cities, and universities have difficulty in defining their missions in any other but vague ways. Information services, in turn, can define their mission as being to support the mission of their sponsoring bodies. If anything, this is likely to be even vaguer than the mission of the sponsoring body since the nature of the support also needs to be clarified. It is to be expected, therefore, that the mission of the information service will be at least as difficult to define as the mission of the sponsoring body.

There is an endemic problem, accentuated by the scope for diffusion and subversion, that the lower-level objectives will not be well connected with the mission and goals. This is the more likely since, in practice, people tend to develop formal performance goals rarely and use them even more rarely. The less close the coordination is, the more goal displacement is to be expected. Means become ends.

At any level, there is the likelihood that objectives and goals will be left unrevised as circumstances change. This is not simply a matter of updating written statements, which are often ignored anyway, but, rather, the need to reconsider the continuing appropriateness of the bases for allocation whether they have been written down or not.

Mission statements and, more generally, written plans have an additional role as political tools. The consultative development of a mission statement or a plan provides an opportunity for negotiating a consensus of support or for discovering the lack of one. Once developed, an agreed mission statement or approved plan can be used to deflect criticism of managers into criticism of an approved plan. In the former case the manager is simply the direct object of criticism; in the latter case, the plan, not the manager, is the target, and the critic now appears to be attacking something that has documented formal support. The difference is politically significant for both manager and for the critic. This political advantage of formal plans may help explain a dramatic in-

crease in formal plans in university libraries in the United States since about
1970 (Biddle 1988).

THE GOLDEN RULE AND THE USERS' INFLUENCE

The separation of allocation from use in noncommercial services has been
repeatedly mentioned. The golden rule expresses the situation with respect to
allocation very aptly: "He [or she] who has the gold makes the rule!" However,
this simplistic assertion needs to be qualified in various ways.

The role of the users of sponsored services warrants some comment, since
they can share in the political process directly or indirectly. Particular individual
users may have a formal role in decisions concerning the allocation of resources
to the service. All can be assumed to have at least an indirect role in that their
actions or expressions of opinion are likely to carry some weight with the sponsors
in at least three ways.

First, do the users describe the services as being good or bad? How well do
the services meet their demands? Inasmuch as users have a vested interest in
not having to pay for service, they share the manager's interest in keeping the
sponsors favorably disposed.

Second, are the users voting with their feet? Do they in fact use the service?
In a noncommercial service, a reduction in demand can be advantageous in
operational terms in that it relieves pressure. The service can cope more adequately with the users that remain. However, reduction in demand is dangerous
politically for two reasons: it is usually associated with dissatisfaction among
users, and a service is unlikely to be regarded as having much beneficial effect
if it is hardly used. These contradictory effects help explain the ambivalent
attitude toward improved service (usually meaning increased usage and workload)
among those who provide the service.

Third, it is in the user's best interests to seek to influence the political process.
They can cease to use a service ("exit") or seek to influence it ("voice").[1]
Their involvement or co-optation in the approval of formal plans can be beneficial
to all concerned, not least to the managers. Individual users may be in a position
to influence allocation in some other capacity—as a taxpayer, as a voter, or as
an individual with influence within the sponsoring organization. Users can therefore be influential. This influence arises from their involvement in a political
process rather than directly from their use of the service. The fact that they are
users is likely to add legitimacy to their political statements. The greater the
success the user has in advocating particular preferred priorities in the political
process of allocation, the better the service is likely to be for that particular user.

The involvement of users in the political process of allocation is likely to be
viewed with ambivalence by managers of information services. Conscientious
allocators are likely to be actively interested in users' views and, indeed, solicit
them systematically. At the same time, managers may find, or fear, that users
will usurp the manager's role. Also, of course, users are likely to share in the

decision making if they contribute "gold," a point that brings us to the commercial provision of information services.

COMMERCIAL INFORMATION SERVICE

So far we have viewed the process of allocating resources and priorities to and within information services as being essentially a political process. Resources do not come from users, at least not in their capacity as users but rather from other sources, usually funds assigned from a higher level (e.g., a mayor or a university or corporation president) and, thus, the claims of other users of the resources are considered with respect to the values and goals of those who do the allocating.

We also need to consider information services that are commercial, and we should not ignore mixed strategies, such as the introduction of fees to cover part of the cost of public services and the partial subsidy of the commercial services. No conceptual framework for considering information services could be complete unless it included all of these possibilities.

We are not here concerned with the technical aspects of calculating actual costs and prices. These are treated elsewhere (e.g., Mick 1979; Roberts 1985). Nor need we explore the concepts and rationales associated with the public financing of public services—"merit goods," "public goods," and so on.[2]

Fees for Service

We have been at pains to stress the importance of the "real price," defined by Adam Smith as "the toil and trouble of acquiring" anything. This real price includes not only any monetary price (or fee) but also time, effort, and discomfort. Since monetary price is only part of the real price, we use *fee* to denote monetary price.

To the extent that fees are charged for the use of services, the political process is supplanted by an economic one whereby the allocation of resources to the service comes, at least in part, from the use qua user. We can restate this in terms of our description of noncommercial service by saying that the two independent feedback loops in the double feedback loop characteristic of noncommercial information services begin to lose their independence. The availability of resources for allocation begins to depend on demand, since use is beginning to generate income. This pattern can be shown by modifying figure 14.1 to show the flow of commercially derived income into the resource allocation process. (In figure 14.2, see especially the loop labeled "fees" on the left-hand side.)

More use becomes more income, alias more resources. In fully commercial situations, all resources come from use since fees constitute the only flow of resources into the system, the only source of income.

Income from the use of a particular service is not necessarily used to defray the costs of that particular service since the manager can reallocate resources

Figure 14.2
Allocation of Resources

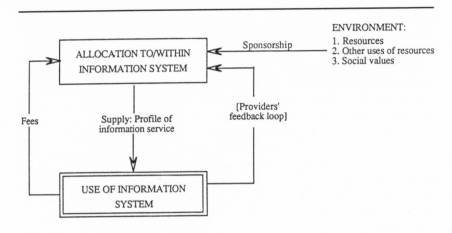

internally in ways that do not entirely coincide with the distribution of demand; a shopkeeper may subsidize a loss leader to stimulate business. However, such reallocation is conditional upon having a spare margin of resources, a margin of profit, or a margin from noncommercial sources.

Pursuing this theoretical analysis further, we consider the point of pure competition. Each specific service would then have to be priced at the very margin of profitability. If it were set higher, business would be lost to competitors; if lower, bankruptcy would follow. In this situation, no margin would remain for internal allocation, and so the allocation of resources internally also becomes determined, in detail, by demand for each particular service. In a cybernetic sense, the system has lost its autonomy by becoming controlled in detail by market forces, by the users who have economic power. Those without economic power will have ceased to be users.

Moving away from pure competition through scarcity in supply to a monopoly leads, in a commercial context, to the ability to increase fees relative to costs. Users will increasingly refuse to pay, preferring to forgo the service, but up to that point the provider has a degree of independence to raise fees above costs.

The degree of autonomy of the provider of the service is indicated by the relationship between the fee (the price charged) and the cost (the monetary cost of providing the service).

Moving away from dependence on users' fees as noncommercial sources of income are developed is reflected in the ability to reduce fees below costs— even to providing services at no monetary charge. Indeed, inducements to use the service could be provided. This would be rational if one wanted more use than would otherwise occur and represents a very high level of independence from users.

INTERPLAY OF POLITICAL AND ECONOMIC ASPECTS

Our use of the terms *autonomy* and *independence* should be viewed cautiously. Resources to provide service must come from somewhere; one cannot provide much service if one has neither fees nor sponsor. We referred above to economic independence from the user. However, reducing economic dependence on the user only increases dependence on wherever else the resources do come from. The dependence remains, but its nature shifts from being economic (dependence on commercial service) to being political (dependence on whoever is willing to assign resources without commercial return). The information service that provides service for free can therefore disregard demand and the level of use just so long as the political origin of its resources remains sufficiently supportive.

A shift between commercial and noncommercial provision is a transition from one sort of dependence to another. The need in a commercial situation to promote one's services persuasively among actual and potential users becomes instead a need in a political situation to promote, to market, one's service among actual and potential sponsors. Both sorts of persuasion may be difficult in practice, and the intensity of need for it can be expected to vary from one situation to another. Shifting from fees to sponsorship, or vice versa, does nothing to remove the need for marketing; it only changes the target.

For a political source of resources to remain supportive, two conditions are required: the source must continue to have resources to allocate, and the information service (or other claimant) must remain competitively congruent with the social values of the source.

Let us consider some possible perceptions on the part of sponsors who allocate resources to an information service.

They may perceive a lack of effectiveness. Do the actual or intended users complain that the service is unsuitable or irrelevant to their needs or that some other alternative would be more satisfactory? If so, then the resources are likely to be differently allocated in the future. In other words, the service may not be perceived as being suitable for the sorts of demands placed on it. It does not have the right kind of capability.

Sponsors may perceive that the good being done by the service is no longer sufficiently valuable in terms of the sponsor's social values to warrant continued support, especially if the overall amount of resources to be allocated is perceived as insufficient for the demands. How do the benefits from supporting the information service (museum, library, records management service, or online data base) compare with alternative uses of those resources (higher salaries, more parking, reduced air pollution, or increased research)? In other words, the information service may be perceived as satisfactory but not competitively valuable. The beneficial effects appear insufficient.

A sponsor may perceive inadequate performance. The service may be suitable, but those who are currently providing it appear to be incompetent or lazy. If so, those supplying the resources may bring pressure to change or improve the management of the service or, if practicable, shift support to an alternative service. In other words, the information service could be suitable and even valuable but unsatisfactory in other ways.

The sponsors may regard the information service as satisfactory, competitive, and well managed and still decide to reduce or terminate sponsorship. This is likely to occur if the users would continue to use the service even if fees were introduced. This would be the case if demand were inelastic and if any secondary consequences of introducing fees ("externalities") were not regarded by the sponsors as harmful. That both conditions would be met is, in general, improbable. Demand is not usually inelastic, and the poor are typically affected more than the rich. However, some mitigating arrangements might be regarded as feasible, such as waiving museum entrance fees one day a week or subsidized service for targeted groups, such as students. This sort of approach has great attraction for sponsors since it holds out the prospect of being able to achieve one's social goals at reduced cost, conserving resources for other purposes. In other words, a mixed strategy emerges, involving only such sponsorship as is really necessary.

It is not difficult to see what, in theory, the manager needs to do. Those in a position to allocate resources are more likely to continue to do so if:

1. They perceive the service to be good. That is, they perceive the service as being capable of satisfying a demand. Is evidence of such satisfaction being passed on, directly or indirectly, to the sponsors? Are complaints adequately resolved?

2. They perceive the service to be beneficial in the sense of implementing the values of the sponsors. Are the managers looking beyond the daily routines and the techniques of provision in order to note and, more important, to draw the sponsors' attention to the beneficial effects of what is being done? The fact that identifying, let alone quantifying, these beneficial effects may be difficult is inconvenient and, in an important sense, irrelevant, since difficulty in assessment does nothing to reduce the need for assessment.

3. The manager and staff appear to be competent, diligent, and effective. Are the difficulties, initiatives, and successes being made known to the sponsors?

Given the structure and functioning or sponsored services, the manager who fails to attend to the persuasion of those who allocate resources cannot be regarded as having accepted the full range of responsibilities inherent in the role of manager.

SUMMARY

The profile of information service in any given situation is the result of the detailed allocation of resources to and within the service. In a noncommercial situation, resources come from sponsors, not from users (at least not directly from users). In a commercial situation, usage, not sponsorship, generates resources. An information service is therefore always dependent on some combination of sponsors and users' fees.

Information services are labor intensive and tend to have the characteristics of human services generally: unclear goals, uncertain effects, and diffused responsibility.

NOTES

1. On this and on the interrelatedness of economic and political processes see Hirschman (1970).

2. Material on information services as public goods can be found in and through Schwuchow (1973) and Van House (1983a).

Relationships

Chapter 15

Connections and Coherence

THE BASIC STRUCTURE

Having examined both concepts and processes, we now need to ask how these various elements are related to each other.

Becoming informed can involve a variety of different sorts of human behavior: economic, political, and cognitive. Observation, communication, and, especially, retrieval include intellectual, cultural, social, and engineering activities, so no simple model would be able to reflect reality in any helpful way. In the more complex cases, all of the different processes described in part III are involved. Now, in the three chapters of part IV, we look at how they are related. In this chapter we examine how cognitive, economic, political, and managerial aspects are related.

The goal is to be able to describe complex information systems, not just simple ones. Accordingly, we regard the description and explanation of the provision and use of retrieval-based information systems designed to increase individuals' knowledge, provided partly but not only on a noncommercial basis, as the definitive challenge. If that can be achieved, then the description and explanation of all simpler cases of information systems will, we hope, also have been achieved, implicitly or explicitly.

A model based on three connected systems appears to constitute an efficient representation of the actual complexity. These three connected systems have the following characteristics:

1. They are different from each other in their nature.

2. They are connected with each other but only to a very limited extent.

3. Each is dominated as much or more by interaction with its external environment as it is by its relationships with the other two systems.

Provision: A Political and Managerial System

The allocation of resources to and with an information service has been discussed in detail in chapter 14. The process can be briefly summarized, starting with sponsored (noncommercial) provision. The external environment—some social, civic, or corporate situation—possesses resources, some of which are allocated for the support of an information system. In this environment, other possible uses are competing for these resources.

Social values guide the allocation process. In a corporate environment, one would refer to the corporate culture. There is, of course, variation among individuals and groups, from one time to another, and from one place to another in these social values. Consensus is likely to emerge but is also likely to change. There are also changes in who gets to do the allocating of the resources. Resources may be more or less plentiful. Other needs may be more or less pressing. The balance of influence in political processes will change as power structures evolve. Nevertheless, the combination of these factors dominates the allocation of resources between the information system and alternative uses and, internally, within the information system, constrained by the techniques and technology in use.

The allocation of resources to and within the information system determines in detail the profile of the service provided:

In a corporate database system:
- What data are collected.
- How frequently the data are updated.
- How many people can access the service simultaneously.
- The distribution of response times.
- The quality and quantity of user assistance.
- What hours of service are provided.
- The security and reliability of the system.
- How easy it is to use.

In a library:
- How many of what sorts of titles are acquired.
- How many of what sorts of titles are discarded.
- Regulations of access and use: shelf access, duplication, borrowing.
- The availability of space for users.
- Arrangement of books on the shelves.
- Catalogs and retrieval services.
- Readers' advisory and reference services.

These aspects of service are not independent of one another.

Figure 15.1
Provision: A Political and Managerial System

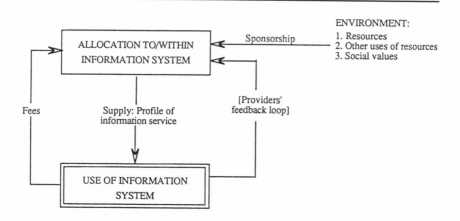

Perceptions of quality of service by those who allocate, including information system staff, provide an element of feedback that can be expected to influence future (re)allocations of resources and thereby modify the profile of service. However, this feedback has tended historically to be rather weak, mainly because of the difficulties associated with knowing about what is actually happening when the system is used and about unexpressed demand.

It is important to remember that the quality of a service is perceived and judged in terms of the values derived from the environment. The goodness of a system is ordinarily conceived in terms of both the use (hence the benefits of use) and the nature (or quality) of the system. In other words, resources may be reallocated away from even an excellent system if little or no use is being made of it or away from a heavily used system that is perceived as having little relevance to the mission and values of the sponsoring body. To the extent that provision is commercial, resources are allocated to, and to some extent within, the information service as a result of fees associated with use.

This political and managerial system, which determines the scale and profile of the provision of service, is shown in figure 15.1. It is the same as in figure 14.2.

Information through Retrieval: A Cognitive System

In chapter 9 we considered inquiries as the driving force behind the use of information systems. Inquiries, we argued, derive from distressing ignorance, which we attributed to the combination of particular states of personal knowledge (notably gaps and incongruencies) and personal values that make important and, therefore, distressing, particular portions of our ignorance or uncertainty.

Figure 15.2
Information through Retrieval: A Cognitive System

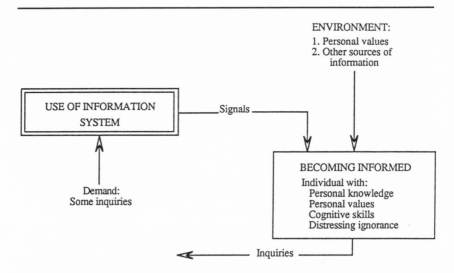

Inquiries motivate observation and communication. In some cases, they lead
to the use of retrieval-based information systems, and, by a combination of
collected sources of information-as-thing and retrieval processes that are rooted
in logic, language, information processing, and technology, a set of signals is
retrieved.

If informative objects, events, or signs are perceived by the user, then a
learning process takes place—a process of becoming informed and of changing
what the individual knows. This is a cognitive process, dependent on the individual's prior personal knowledge and cognitive skills.

Here, again, the external environment dominates. The environment is the
dominant source of personal values, cognitive skills, and factors that spark the
desire to use formal and informal information systems. This cognitive system is
summarized in figure 15.2, an expansion of figure 11.1.

Deciding to Use an Information Service:
An Economic System

The mere fact that distressing ignorance has stimulated an inquiry in somebody's mind does not mean that any action will in fact be taken to resolve the
inquiry, even less that any particular information system will be used to reduce
the distress. There is a decision process whereby the perceived probable benefit
of using any given information system is compared with the perceived probable
cost. The benefit derives from the personal values of the individual and the
perceived chances of successful reduction of the distress through use of the

information system. The cost—the "real price"—has elements of time, effort, discomfort, and, sometimes, money. Therefore, a significant factor in the decision whether to use an information system is the perceived value of the service from the perspective of the potential user. The benefits and costs of previous experiences in using the service are likely to influence the potential user's perceptions heavily. Use of any given system, or particular functions within it, for an inquiry is likely only if it seems worthwhile. More formally, all of three conditions would need to be met:

1. The perceived probable benefit exceeds the perceived probable cost.
2. Alternative sources of information are perceived as less attractive in terms of probable cost and benefit.
3. The individual has not decided to discontinue, temporarily or permanently, the attempt to resolve the distressing ignorance, as is liable to happen at any time.

Here again the external environment dominates because there are usually many alternative sources of information: people, publications, other information systems. Most people, most of the time, resolve their inquiries without resource to formal information systems. In that sense, using an information system is an unusual, atypical activity. The challenge for all parties is to determine what sorts of inquiries each information system is most appropriate for. Anyone eager to increase the use of an information system would be well advised to reduce the perceived costs and to publicize probable benefits.

We describe this process as being economic even though the commercial element is often absent and summarize it in figure 15.3, which is the user feedback loop described in chapter 13 as one part of the double feedback loop shown in figure 13.1

How Are the Three Systems Connected?

The one and only element that connects all three systems is the act of using the information system. In the cognitive system, using the information service generates the set of perceived signals that lead to the user becoming informed. In the political and managerial system of provision, use of the information system generates income from any fees and justifies the allocation of resources in a sponsored system. Perceptions of use constitute feedback to those who allocate. In the economic system, the experience of using the information system provides part of the basis for the user's future decisions whether or not to use the service. The other parts are the potential user's assessment of the alternative sources of information and of the importance (and urgency) of the inquiry itself.

The other, separate interaction of two of the systems (the cognitive system and the economic system) is the decision point at which it is decided whether an inquiry will be brought to the information system or whether it will be taken

Figure 15.3
Use: An Economic System

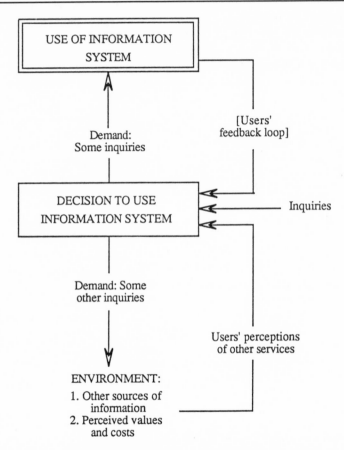

to some other source of information in the external environment. The importance of this decision point in determining demand can hardly be exaggerated.

The relationships between these three different systems can be shown by superimposing figures 15.1, 15.2, and 15.3, which represent the three systems. This is done in figure 15.4.

Figure 15.4 shows the domination of each system and, therefore, of the whole, by the external environment, which determines the resources for provision of service, the values and preferences of providers and users, most of the knowledge and causes of distress of the users, and alternative sources of information. The dominating role of the external environment is easily overlooked or underestimated when attention is concentrated on the technical aspects of information systems. (For a similar model, see Van House 1986.)

Figure 15.4
An Information System as Three Connected Systems

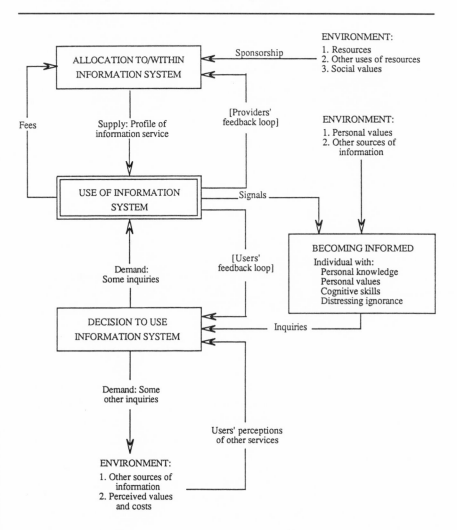

LESS COMPLEX SITUATIONS

Commercial Provision

In an entirely sponsored, noncommercial situation, the feedback in the form of resources derived from fees for use (labeled "Fees" in figures 15.1 and 15.4) would be inactive. In the provision of an information service entirely on a commercial basis, the flow of fees would be the sole source of resources. However, the flow of resources labeled "Sponsorship" would be inactive. Whenever the provision of an information system is mixed, partly commercial and partly sponsored, both the "Fees" and the "Sponsored" flows would be active. The relative amounts in each flow would reflect the balance between commercial and noncommercial support. In practice, given the economic, social, and fiscal policies of government agencies, entirely commercial provision without any trace of sponsorship (i.e., subsidy) is unlikely.

Communication

So far we have concentrated on the provision and use of retrieval-based information systems. What of communication that does not involve collection, storage, and retrieval but is, more simply, communication, whether provided commercially or not?

The diagrams in this chapter show cognitive, political, and economic relationships; they do not depict the technology underlying the provision. Hence, provision of information that is simpler only with respect to technology, such as not involving collection, storage, arrangement, and retrieval, would not necessarily appear any differently in these diagrams. Assuming that the receiver has an option to choose whether to receive the information, the relationship described as figure 15.4 would appear to remain sufficient for communications systems as well.

If communications are received that one cannot ignore, as in the case of an unexpected fire alarm or compulsory education, then the economic decision making by the receiver ("user") is inactive or, as with a summons from the police or other messages one dare not ignore, ineffectual.

Observation

Following the terminology of chapter 10, we use *observation* to denote perceiving information when intentional communication is absent. In terms of the relationships outlined, including figure 15.4, mere observation would be characterized by the cognitive and economic systems without the political and managerial system.

Involuntary observation, as when one unintentionally notices something, would, in addition, be characterized by the absence of inquiries and of the economic decision system, the lower part of figure 15.4. In this minimal case, there is only the signal being received by the "user" as shown as figure 11.1 and as part of the cognitive system in figure 15.2

COHERENT, CONSISTENT, OPTIMAL

In previous chapters we have made frequent references to the detailed allocation of resources and to the profile of service provided. It is clear that individual patterns of service can vary greatly. Showing how the different parts are related provides a basis for asking more difficult questions: What would be the best blend of services for a given situation? What internal deployment of resources would be most effective? How should an information system be tuned for its mission? What sorts of internal budget allocations would avoid inconsistencies?

The lack of a single, unifying measure of effectiveness for the evaluation of information systems makes it difficult to relate the parts to the whole. The challenge for the information system manager is to make decisions that are consistent and coherent in relation to each other and to the goals sought, even though the individual decisions may be concerned with disparate matters.

Any given deployment of resources may be inconsistent with or not well suited to the stated mission and goals of the system. If so, then the continued validity of the mission and goals, as well as the deployment, ought to be reviewed to see if they are still what is wanted. If the mission and goals are still valid, inconsistency commonly arises when insufficient attention or underinvestment in one part of the system has a disproportionate effect on the system as a whole.

One could imagine a reliable, detailed corporate database that is avoided and underutilized because it is difficult to use, because inadequate support and training are provided for users, or because it is accessible from too narrow a range of workstations.

A museum might have fine collections, but its role in support of research would be undermined if the materials are not properly cataloged. Its educational role could be seriously diminished if the museum had inconvenient hours and location, if there were insufficient space for exhibiting its materials, or if the exhibits could be seen but the labels and explanations were nonexistent or deficient.[1]

An archive might acquire large collections of material, but little can be made of it unless it has been processed for use and registers and indexes prepared.

A library might buy many titles, but the utility of the library would be diminished if the titles were poorly selected or the books were allowed to remain effectively unavailable because of delays in cataloging or excessively long loan periods.

What characterizes each of these situations is a lack of coherence in the sense of the parts holding together in a meaningful way. In other words one might say that the internal allocation of resources, the profile of service, in these cases was not optimal. Each aspect of an information system is more or less affected by each of the others. Poor performance in one aspect can usually be improved by an internal reallocation of resources to it away from other aspects or by additional new resources.

The problem of optimal coherence, of providing a well-balanced service, is made more difficult by the lack of any single measure of performance.

Scale, Scope, and Completeness

Economies of scale occur when increased activity results in a lower cost per unit of activity. Typically economies of scale result when large-scale operation permits the use of specialized staff or equipment. Apparent economies of scale in information systems need careful examination, especially when localized technology of paper, microfilm, or other physical objects is involved. Achieving a larger scale of operation is likely to involve geographical consolidation, which is likely to affect the price or effort of access for would-be users. Consolidating collections of objects or documents into large central archives, libraries, or museums is advantageous for those located where the consolidated collection is; the collection is conveniently nearby and contains a great variety of evidence. But centralization has disadvantages for everyone located elsewhere in terms of the choice available locally and the cost of access to the central collection. Any increase in users' effort or cost can be expected to have a secondary effect in reducing usage and thereby the benefits derived from the system. Some activities in the use of information systems, notably those involving queuing, are characterized by economies of scale, but other activities, such as searching and retrieving, are more likely in practice to involve diseconomies of scale.

Economies of scope occur when it is more economical to perform two or more activities together than separately. Economies of scope are likely in information systems because it is a characteristic of information that it can be shared and reused indefinitely in different ways. The same data can be published in a book and also made available in an online database.

Related to issues of scope and scale is the question of the completeness of information systems. It is a marked characteristic of the use of information that, like much other human behavior, it is highly skewed. In other words, for any individual or homogeneous group, a few sources are very often used, some more are frequently used, more are used only sometimes, and most sources are rarely used. This pattern means that a few judiciously selected items can satisfy a significant proportion of demand, but that as a collection is expanded to include progressively less often used material, the benefits derived from each additionally acquired source are fewer. A pattern of diminishing returns obtains; each additional benefit is progressively more expensive to achieve.

Optimal Size

Assuming that inconsistencies could be resolved and that an information system were optimally tuned for achieving its mission and goals, how large should it be? Could a database, library, or museum be too big?

For any information system at any given budget level, it is entirely possible that too large a portion of the resources are being allocated to the collection of informative material and not enough to other aspects of access, such as indicative access (arrangement, cataloging, indexing) or cognitive access (explaining, helping users). We noted some examples of such inconsistencies. Hence, for any given budget level, expansion of the collection could be excessive. More generally, any one aspect of an information system could be disproportionately provided in relation to other parts.

Assuming that adjustments have been made to resolve inconsistencies and that an optimal internal allocation of resources has been achieved, then, in the last resort, bigger is better. With increasing size, some restructuring of the system is to be expected. Diminishing returns are to be expected as the benefits of marginal improvements become progressively smaller. Nevertheless, every additional informative object added and every additional means of access to the collection increases the capability of the service and thereby improves it. Bigger is better when information systems are viewed in isolation.

In a noncommercial service, the limit to optimal size is imposed from outside by the sponsors. Those who allocate resources to the information system can be expected to be sympathetic to continued expansion and improvement. The problem lies elsewhere. They have other agendas. The city needs roads and police as well as a museum. The university needs professors and students as well as library service. The corporation needs sales more than a corporate management information system if it is to avoid bankruptcy. At some point a judgment is made by the sponsors as to what can be afforded.

Similarly with commercial information systems, the constraint comes from outside. Users have other uses for their money and usually alternative sources of information. Fee income is finite and can support only a limited size of information system in any given circumstances.

Searches as Determinants of Information System Design

We have looked at inquiries as the driving force behind the use of information systems. We now extend that discussion by considering searches—the expression of inquiries in a form that an information system can handle—as a factor in the design of information systems.[2]

One variation among searches is the relationship between two goals: finding a specific document—some particular information-as-thing—and/or acquiring some particular knowledge or, more precisely, information-as-knowledge.

Where the emphasis is on identifying and obtaining one or more specific documents, the information system needs to emphasize contextual attributes such as author, title, date, or identifying numbers of documents. Representations of what the document is "about"—indexes and classifications of subject access— serve a minor, auxiliary role. Reliable document delivery is at a premium because requests are specific and, by implication, the substitution of other, alternative titles is unlikely to be appropriate. There is need for a staff knowledgeable about how the information system works but less need for staff to know about the information stored.

Staff who know about what information is available through the system, as well as about how the system works, become more important when searches are for knowledge, for some information-as-knowledge. In this case, the contextual descriptions become secondary. It is the contents of the document that matters most. The delivery of some suitable document is needed rather than any particular document. Browsing among representations of the documents (indexes, summaries, data dictionaries) and among the documents themselves becomes more important.

Any search is likely to be some combination of a search for a document and a search for knowledge. There is great variation in the emphasis placed on each and on the narrowness with which each is defined. Similarly, searches vary greatly in importance and urgency. Since each of these aspects of search calls for a particular emphasis in information system design, the optimal design will depend on the pattern of searches to be supported. Just as one can hardly design equipment unless the design requirements are known, so information systems are unlikely to be cost-effective unless the characteristics of the people to be served are known in terms that can be related to the decisions that the designer and manager can make.

SUMMARY

The processes examined in part III combine to provide the structure of information systems. They form three systems: a political and managerial system determines the provision of information systems; the process of becoming informed, a cognitive system, which may involve observation, communication, and/or retrieval, affects what one learns from an information system; and an economic system determines the level and pattern of use of an information system. These three systems are only loosely connected to each other, but each is deeply rooted in its environment. In simpler cases of information system, such as communication without retrieval, not all of these processes are involved.

Economies of scope are likely in information systems. Achieving economies of scale may be difficult. The skewed nature of the use of information systems accentuates patterns of diminishing returns. Achieving an optimal internal allocation of resources is likely to be difficult. In terms of an information system itself, bigger is generally better. The constraints on optimal size derive from alternative uses of resources in the environment outside the information system. In any complex system, effort is needed to ensure that the parts are coherently related and that the internal allocation of resources is suited to the particular situation.

NOTES

1. The variation is substantial, as some examples from Austria and Germany show. There was no labeling at all in the Goethe Haus, Frankfurt, in 1988; minimal and largely

irrelevant labeling unless one also buys a guidebook in the Mozart "Figaro" Haus, Vienna, in 1989; substantial labeling but likely to be understood only by those already knowledgeable in the Sturm and Drang exhibit, Goethe Museum, Frankfurt, in 1988; and detailed, intelligible, and multilingual labels in the Freud Museum, Vienna, in 1989.

2. For a more detailed treatment of searches in relation to library design, see Buckland (1979). For a discussion of internal consistency and optimal size of libraries, see Buckland and Hindle (1976).

Chapter 16

Expertise and Artificial Intelligence

In chapter 8, the conditions for successful access to information were summarized. Since then, we have reviewed the various processes involved and now can take a closer look at the conditions for successful access to information. We do so by considering the expertise required of the user of information systems and how, in principle, artificial intelligence might be useful in supplementing the expertise of the individual in the use of information systems.[1]

Users of information systems face a variety of tasks involved in using the system, expressing inquiries, retrieving suitable documents, and understanding what has been retrieved. In these tasks, the user encounters difficulties in understanding the system, determining what to do next, how and when to do it, and understanding the results. The options may not be self-evident and are likely to be numerous, difficult to compare, unfamiliar, and/or ill defined. We use the term *task complexity* to denote this range of difficulties.[2] We use the term *expertise* to denote the user's ability to deal with this complexity.

There is a large and rapidly increasing literature on how artificial intelligence might be used to develop more "intelligent" information systems (*Advances* 1985; Brooks 1987; Brooks, Daniels, and Belkin 1986; Davies 1986; Florian 1990; Geghard 1985; Morris and Neill 1988; Sharma 1987; Smith 1987; Sparck Jones 1983; Vickery and Brooks 1987; Walker 1981). Of special interest have been expert systems that use rules of inference representing how human experts operate in order to determine automatically what course of action should be taken in any given situation. Dreyfus and Dreyfus (1986) point out that expert systems can be expected to work only in limited, structured applications and that, in practice, expert systems tend to achieve only at modest levels of competence since, among humans, it is beginners rather than experts who use rules. Nevertheless, expert systems, like linear programming and queuing theory, constitute a powerful tool. But there can be a temptation to concentrate more on applying the tool than on the nature of the problem or on alternatives.

We are not concerned here with the technical aspects of artificial intelligence or expert systems. Rather, we seek to examine in more general terms what in theory the potential role of artificial intelligence might be in information systems.

COPING WITH COMPLEXITY

Four different approaches are possible when the complexity of a task strains or exceeds one's expertise, as can be illustrated by reference to the task of shifting gears when driving an automobile:

1. *Education.* The user can increase his or her expertise. A novice driver could read a teach-yourself-to-drive manual.

2. *Advice.* The system may be capable of offering helpful information. A tachometer does nothing to reduce the complexity of shifting gears, but the indication of engine speed can help one judge better when to operate the gas pedal and the clutch. Advice increases the user's understanding of the system and how it works, so that the user can know better what the options are and how the system works. In large measure, this can be viewed as "revealing the structure." This approach has been referred to as developing the user's conceptual model of the system (e.g., Duncan and McAleese 1987). The complexity of the task is unchanged, but one has a better understanding of what needs to be done.

3. *Simplification.* If the complexity facing the user could be reduced, the user's expertise would become more adequate relative to the task. The system itself could be simplified. Perhaps an intermediary, either a human or an artificial "front-end," could make the task simpler for the user even though the system itself may remain just as complex. The novice driver could use only one gear, change to an electric motor that has only one gear, or hire a chauffeur.

4. *Delegation.* If some of the complexity could be moved inside the system, the user's role in coping with complexity would be eased and any given level of user expertise would become more adequate. With automatic transmission, the complexity of shifting gears is still present, but the burden of dealing with it has been removed from the (human) driver to the (artificial) automatic trans-mission system. If artificial intelligence is viewed as "the science of making machines do things that would require intelligence if done by men" (Minsky 1963, 406), then an automobile automatic transmission is a good example of artificial intelligence. To the extent that a system itself can infer reliably what the user wants done, tasks and their associated complexity can be delegated to the system itself. This reduction in the task complexity facing the user constitutes a reduction in the user's need for expertise. But this delegation depends critically on the system's ability to predict what the user wants done. The system has to make assumptions, be told, or be able to learn about users' needs and preferences. In other words, the system needs to have an adaptive cognitive model of the user.

We can sort these four approaches to making the user's expertise sufficient for the complexity of the task in two ways: Two of them (1 and 2) are concerned with improving the user's expertise—the user's ability to cope with task complexity. The other two (three and four) seek to reduce the user's need to cope with task complexity, thereby making the user's existing expertise more adequate relative to the task. In two cases (1 and 3) the change is introduced from the environment in the form of more education for the user (1) or simplification imposed on the system (3). In both cases, the role of the system is a passive one. In the other two cases, the system adopts an active role, either by providing helpful information to the user (2) or by itself taking responsibility for dealing with some of the task complexity (4). (This interpretation depends on where the system boundaries are drawn. By definition, we regard an intermediary, the chauffeur, as being outside the information system.) This analysis is summarized as a two-by-two contingency table in table 16.1.

Because the feasibility and cost-effectiveness of adopting each of these four approaches are likely to vary greatly from one situation to another, selecting a cost-effective solution depends on careful comparison of these quite different strategies.

VARIETIES OF TASK COMPLEXITY

We use the term *complexity* to denote whatever difficulties the user may face, but in reality there are distinct types of difficulty or dimensions of complexity (Campbell 1988). For example, in information retrieval systems, a distinction can be made between difficulties arising from the subject matter of the inquiry and those arising from the retrieval system itself (Culnan 1984, 1985).

Ingwersen (1984) proposed four categories of user expertise in relation to online bibliographic retrieval systems:

1. The elite, who have expertise in using the information retrieval system and also good knowledge of the subject area.

2. The intermediary, who has expertise in using the system but lacks appropriate subject expertise.

3. The end user, who has expertise in the subject but not in the system; and

4. The layman, who has expertise in neither the system nor the subject matter.

These four categories can also be expressed as the four possible combinations of high and low values for each of the two dimensions of expertise in using the retrieval system and expertise in the subject area of the inquiry. Considering the two kinds of expertise as a continuous variable would provide a more generalized categorization. In effect, one would represent each user's expertise as a point in two-dimensional space (figure 16.1). A person with medium competence in using the system and a medium knowledge of the subject area would be positioned in the middle.

Increasing the user's subject expertise would move the user's position in this

Table 16.1
Different Approaches to Task Complexity

	INCREASE EXPERTISE	REDUCE THE NEED FOR EXPERTISE
CHANGE FROM ENVIRONMENT	1. User education	3. Simplify task Use intermediary
CHANGE FROM WITHIN SYSTEM	2. Make the system offer advice	4. Delegate tasks to the system

Figure 16.1
Expertise in Two Dimensions

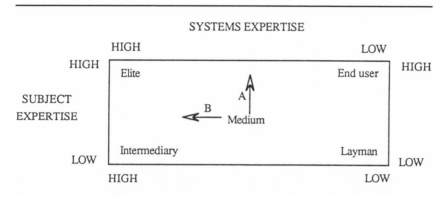

space upward along the arrow marked A. Increasing the user's expertise with the system would move the user's position to the left along the arrow marked B. The ideal might seem to be always in the top left-hand "elite," corner but this is unlikely, expensive in effort, and generally unnecessary. One's position in such a space would vary from system to system and from one inquiry to another, depending on the subject. Inquiries and systems vary in the amount of complexity involved and, therefore, in the expertise required.

The expert's paradox is that greater subject expertise both increases and decreases information-seeking success. The greater the subject expertise, the greater the probability of finding information (pertinent material) and the lower the probability that it would be informative (novel to the searcher) (Christozov 1990).

More complex models could be developed. For example, quite apart from the "language" of the retrieval system (index vocabulary, classification scheme), there is also the language of the document retrieved (English, German, Spanish, etc.). This could be treated as another dimension.

This discussion has been stated in simple and general terms but does provide a conceptual framework for the systematic identification of options and trade-offs with respect to the feasibility and the effectiveness of increasing subject expertise (moving the user upward) compared with greater systems expertise (moving the user to the left). For any given system, the answers are likely to vary by field of discourse, by type of inquiry, and by user. They are likely to vary by type of information system or interface. What are the implications of the desirability of increasing each type of expertise for the design of information systems and especially their interfaces? The less user friendly the system is, the more difficult the task of using it and, therefore, the greater the need for the user to be a subject expert and, more especially, to be expert with the system. The more user friendly the system is, the less the need is. Hence the effort involved in moving the user to the left in this two-dimensional expertise space could be seen as an indication of user friendliness.

How far could the user's need for expertise to deal with the complexity of the system be reduced? How far can the task complexity facing the user be reduced by lessening the complexity and/or delegating from the user to the system? How costly are the deleterious consequences of any given level of task complexity? The real challenge is to determine the optimal combination of education, advice, simplification, and delegation in any given situation.

EXAMPLES

We now examine more closely the types of tactics that might be adopted in the use of artificial intelligence in information systems, while noting that to evaluate possible uses of artificial intelligence in providing information systems, it is necessary also to consider alternative solutions outside the system, such as an increase in the user's education (category 1) and simplifying or mediating the system (category 3). The tactics that involve the use of artificial intelligence inside an information system fall into the two active categories noted above: advice (2), augmenting the user's expertise; and delegation (4), reducing the user's need for expertise by moving responsibility for coping with task complexity into the system.

The more the system can assume about the user, the more reliably it can infer what the best next step would be. This is reflected in interfaces that default to what is inferred to be the preferred next step. This is true whether tactics of advice or tactics of delegation are attempted. The difference between the two tactics can be illustrated by a hypothetical example.

Example 1: A Difficult Text

A user of an information system who has retrieved a document that he or she does not understand is unlikely to become informed. This problem is likely to occur whenever someone asks a technical question outside his or her areas of expertise. With considerable simplification, the situation can be represented symbolically in terms of the relationships between two scales: the difficulty (complexity) of the text and the expertise (knowledge) of the user. Doubtless these are complex multidimensional domains in reality, but the mismatch is represented symbolically as if one-dimensional in figure 16.2 for the sake of explanation.

What needs to happen for this mismatch to be resolved? Solutions from outside the system include persuading the user to acquire more education (1) concerning the subject of the document or to search for a simpler text (3). For the information system to play an active role in enabling the user to become informed requires some combination of the tactics of advice (2) and delegation (4). Tactics of advice might include online access to general and specialized dictionaries, encyclopedias, grammars, and textbooks as needed to supply the additional background knowledge. Any such improvement in the user's expertise would lead

Figure 16.2
User's Expertise (C) and Difficulty of a Text (D)

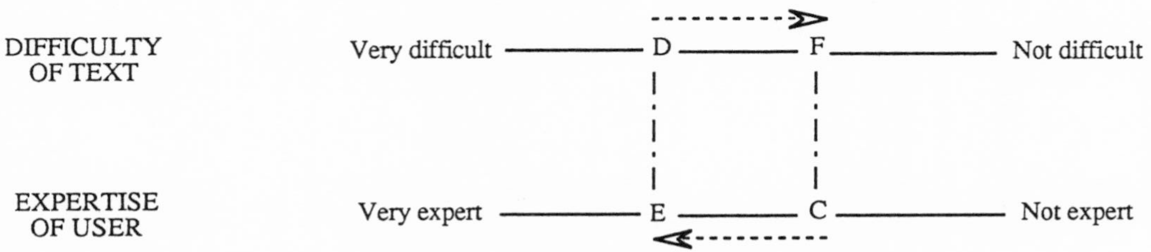

DIFFICULTY
OF TEXT

Very difficult —————— D ——— F —————— Not difficult

EXPERTISE
OF USER

Very expert —————— E ——— C —————— Not expert

to a move in the position of the user from C, denoting the initial state of knowledge, toward E, denoting a state of knowledge matching the difficulty of the text (D). The distance from C to E denotes the needed increase in the user's expertise.

Tactics of delegation would be concerned not with increasing the user's expertise but with reducing the difficulty of the text by providing an explanation and/or by substituting a less difficult text (F), thereby matching the user's level of expertise. There is, however, an important constraint: simplification necessarily involves some loss of information, and the text needs to remain detailed enough to answer the original inquiry.

It is clear that not all cases are the same. The difficulty may lie in the vocabulary, the concepts, or the use of a foreign language. Selection of the appropriate course of action would require the system to make (or be told) the correct assumption concerning the user. The sum of the system's assumptions concerning the user has been called the system's cognitive model (Duncan and McAleese 1987).

Cognitive Models and Conceptual Models

The custom of using *conceptual model* to denote the user's assumptions concerning the system and *cognitive model* to denote the system's assumptions concerning the user has disadvantages. The meanings of the two terms are not obvious or self-explanatory. Insofar as *conceptual* ordinarily relates to understanding and *cognitive* ordinarily relates to learning, the usage is not entirely correct. For an intelligent system to be effective, it needs to be able to make assumptions not only about what the user knows but also about how the user learns. Nontrivial knowledge of a system on the part of a user includes assumptions about how the system adapts to (infers from) different situations. In effect, the system's assumptions about the user and the user's assumptions about the system both contain conceptual as well as cognitive elements (cf. Hollnagel 1987). The two sorts of tactics noted above can be further illustrated by another example.

Example 2: Initial Search Command in Information Retrieval

Information retrieval depends on the matching of the representation of an inquiry (the search command) and the representation of what is retrievable in the system (Belkin and Croft 1987). Various problems arise in the matching— for example, with homographs (e.g., Lafayette, California; Lafayette, Indiana; Lafayette, Marquis de) and with synonyms and different but related terms (e.g., AI; artificial intelligence; expert system; intelligent interface).

Tactics of advice include revealing the structure, enabling the user to examine and become familiar with the indexing terms used and with their interrelationships. With tactics of delegation, the system would make inferences about what the user wanted and act accordingly. Synonyms and related terms would be invoked automatically, and homographs (e.g., places named for the marquis de Lafayette) would be selectively discarded on the basis of the inferences that the system draws from its assumptions concerning the user. However, as one begins to explore actual or hypothetical cases, the difference between these two tactics tends to become increasingly blurred. Tactic 1 (revealing the structure) has two components. The first component is the capability of revealing the structure, for example, segments of indexes and useful "help" screens. Every system is programmed to have more or less of this capability, but even copious provision of this capability does not in itself imply the provision of an intelligent system. The revealing of the structure could be extensive but entirely passive, available only as invoked by the user. Such a situation does not require any of the knowledge bases or rules of inference characteristic of an expert system.

The other component is knowing when to reveal which part of the structure. A system would become intelligent when the revealing of the structure is programmed to be situational, that is, the system itself infers what particular part of the system would most usefully be revealed and decides when, without being intentionally invoked by the user, to supply information likely to be helpful concerning the system. In other words, the system decides when and how to try to improve the user's understanding of the system. Unprompted, situational "help" screens are a good example. The more intelligent the system is, the more different situations it can identify as a basis for selecting a part of the system to reveal.

An actively helpful system is one that presumes to propose or perform what it infers needs to be done next; however, the degree of "intelligence" involved can vary greatly. A relatively unintelligent system might, in any situation determined to be problematic (e.g., retrieval of zero or an excessive number of items), return the user to an initial menu to start again. A more intelligent system would draw inferences from the situation to select which next action to perform or to propose. Computer-assisted instruction systems vary greatly from simple menus to promptings based on conclusions drawn from the user's input. The more different situations a system can distinguish as the basis for selecting some alternative next action, the more intelligent we should be inclined to consider it to be.

A PRAGMATIC MEASURE OF SYSTEM INTELLIGENCE

In both the tactics of advising and the tactics of delegation, the intelligence of the system lies in its ability to discriminate between a variety of situations in order to determine what action would be appropriate. The ability to choose outcomes situationally can be illustrated by imagining an information system that died whenever it encountered an unusual situation. A system that returned the user to the main menu to start again whenever an unusual situation was encountered would be less inconvenient but could hardly be described as helpful or intelligent.

This formulation suggests that the intelligence of a system could be indicated pragmatically by the number of different, situation-related responses it can reliably provide. On this basis, when comparing expert systems in any given situation, the system that can identify the most different situations with any given level of reliability would be regarded as the most intelligent, and for any given number of recognized situations, the system that discriminated most reliably would be the most intelligent.

Two conclusions follow from this view of system intelligence. First, it is not at all clear that a system following the tactics of advice is inherently any less intelligent than a system using tactics of delegation, programmed to determine the next step to be taken. Rather, both sorts of systems could be more or less intelligent. Second, in this context, intelligence has to do with the diagnosing and drawing of inferences from assumptions and situations. In the case of information systems, assumptions and situations have two components: the characteristics of the system, including the database, and the need and expertise of the user. Unless the user, for whom the system has been developed, is to be ignored, diagnosis of the situation depends, for both the system and the user, on the ability to judge both the system's situation and the user's. This is particularly relevant when the searching has been delegated by the end user to an intermediary.

COMPUTER ASSISTED AND COMPUTER DELEGATED

It is tempting to assume that the truly intelligent systems are those in which decision making has been delegated to the computer and that computer assisted systems—those using tactics of advice—are either not intelligent or in some sense less intelligent. These assumptions are erroneous, as two examples show.

Example 3: Record Consolidation

A noteworthy example of a successful application of artificial intelligence in libraries is the use of automated procedures to compare similar bibliographic records in order to decide which pairs of records are (a) records that are variant descriptions of the same edition and so should be merged ("consolidated") and (b) records that, although similar, relate to different editions and so should not be merged. Erroneous merging has more serious consequences than failing to merge. Decision rules operating on weighted comparison of several different attributes of records have been in operational use for some years (Coyle and Gallagher-Brown 1985). Not only does such a system infer which records should be merged, but, in practice, on grounds of economy, the inferences of the system are accepted as decisions without individual review by expert catalogers.

It is reasonable to assume that performance would be improved, in terms of the proportion of decisions made correctly, if the system's inferences, or at least some of them, were reviewed by human experts. Suppose that the arrangements were changed so that each of the system's inferences was to be reviewed by a human expert. The situation would then have changed from a computer-delegated expert system to a computer-assisted expert system, but the change has involved no change in the expert system itself, only in the subsequent use of its inferences. We conclude that although a computer-delegated system implies some degree of system intelligence, the degree is independent of the degree of delegation. In other words the distinction between computer assisted and computer delegated should not be confused with differences in system intelligence. Other things being equal, computer-assisted systems involve more total intelligence because the user's expertise is invoked in addition.

THE USER'S PERSPECTIVE

For information system designers, the prospect of building intelligent systems to which decisions can be delegated is an attractive challenge. For the user, the perspective is less simple. As in example 3, a preference for computer-delegated over computer-assisted systems may be a matter of economy rather than effectiveness. Administrators may prefer delegated over assisted solutions in order to reduce labor costs so long as the penalties for error do not outweigh the labor savings.

Unless one presumes the user to be dangerously lacking in expertise, it is inherently unlikely that adding the expertise of the user to the expertise of an intelligent system would not increase the quality of the outcome.

Three considerations argue in favor of computer-assisted over computer-delegated systems.

First, as a general principle, the one thing better than being able to delegate is not needing to delegate. Likewise the one thing better than receiving advice is not needing advice. The first consideration argues in favor of advice rather than delegation, the second argues for improving the user's expertise in order to diminish the need for any kind of help.

Second, an intelligent system that tried to outguess the user as to what is needed and how the user might behave (as in probabilistic retrieval systems [Bookstein 1984]) would seem to work best with a user who is static rather than capable of learning and adapting. An intelligent, adaptive user can be expected to adapt to the system and to try to predict the system's future actions. At least in theory, a highly adaptive system and a highly adaptive user could combine to create a situation so dynamic as to be frustrating and even unstable (''hunting''). Dynamic user behavior would argue for computer-assisted rather than computer-delegated processes.

Third, delegation, with computers as with people, invites the possibilities of undesirable decisions by the person or machine to whom or which the decision has been delegated. The more those decisions are subject to verification and approval, the more reliable the decisions are likely to be and the more the relationship changes from delegation to advisory. A patient in a hospital would presumably prefer intelligent medical systems to be no more than advisory to the doctors.

SUMMARY

Exploration of the relationships between user expertise, task complexity, and the scope for the use of artificial intelligence leads to six conclusions.

First, the expertise of the user needs to match the task complexity. When expertise is insufficient, two sorts of solutions derived from the environment may be possible: increasing the user's expertise through education and simplifying (or mediating) the system. Also two sorts of solutions can be built into the system using intelligent techniques: system-generated guidance for the user (tactics of advice) and moving some of the complexity inside the system (tactics of delegation).

Second, the feasibility and cost-effectiveness of different solutions are likely to vary greatly according to the circumstances.

Third, a pragmatic measure of a system's intelligence is the number of situation-related outcomes the system can reliably distinguish. Other things being equal, system intelligence can be assessed by two criteria: the number of different situations the system can identify and the reliability with which they are identified.

Fourth, the distinction between computer-delegated and computer-assisted systems is logically separate from the degree of intelligence of a system.

Fifth, a computer-delegated system may be more economical than a comparable computer-assisted one, but for all levels of system intelligence, a computer-assisted approach is likely to be more effective because the intelligence of the system and the intelligence of the user ought to augment each other.

Sixth, the distinction between the assumptions made by the system concerning the user and the user's assumptions concerning the system are both important. Calling the former a cognitive model and the latter a conceptual model is potentially misleading. Insofar as *conceptual* denotes knowledge and *cognitive* denotes learning, both the system's model of the user and the user's model of the system, if well developed, will include both conceptual and cognitive elements.

NOTES

1. This chapter benefited substantially from the collaboration of Doris Florian, Forschungsgesellschaft Joanneum GesmbH, Graz, Austria, during 1989.

2. For a general review of task complexity, see Campbell (1988). For task complexity in information systems, see Culnan (1984, 1985).

Chapter 17

Social Context

Knowledge is instrumental. It improves one's ability to achieve what one wants and to avoid what one does not want. The role of knowledge and, therefore, of information and information systems in society is a topic of great importance but too vast to be addressed here. Instead we limit our comments to a brief review of selected aspects of the relationships between information systems and their social context.

Information and information systems are deeply rooted in their social environment. Hirschheim (1985, 3) states that "information systems are not technical systems but social systems and must be developed within a social and organizational context." Beliefs, values, alternative sources of information, and the resources with which to provide information all derive from the external environment.

VALUES AND MOTIVATIONS

Motivations of the User

Everyone is massively ignorant, and much ignorance is not, in itself, cause for concern. One can lead a happy, productive life without knowing the birthdates of the children of King George III. But sometimes, in some situations, particular bits of ignorance can be distressing. Distressing ignorance generates inquiries. But "distressing" is meaningful only in relation to some personal sense of value or preference. These personal values and preferences are largely derived from the individual's social environment.

Having an inquiry does not, in and of itself, mean that any information system will be used. Action and choice of where to seek for information will depend in part on the options known to be available and in part on the individual's perceptions of the probability of success and on the real price.

Motivations of the Provider

Noncommercial provision of information sources is of particular interest because it provides empirical evidence of the values and social goals of individuals and groups providing information and of perceptions of the cost-effectiveness of information systems. A few examples will illustrate this point.

- Many organizations, although motivated to minimize their operating costs, choose to invest in the provision of a newsletter, distributed unsolicited and without charge.
- The mechanisms behind the sponsorship of noncommercial information systems are necessarily political though the motivations may not be obvious, noticed, or agreed upon.
- Governments, although under pressure to reduce taxes, choose to invest in the provision of information services, not only within their own territories but also in other countries. In addition to the obvious forms of press releases, speeches, and diplomatic initiatives, some countries invest significantly in the provision of information services as an arm of foreign policy. (Stephens 1955; Hausrath 1981)

In commercial provision of information systems, a motivation is to make money, but there can be other motivations. Newspapers are commonly founded to exert political and social influence. Commercial provision, charging fees, may reluctantly be seen as the only viable means. Often where the motivation is not primarily financial, a mixed strategy of fees and sponsorship is attempted if sponsors can be found and if the dependence on the sponsor is tolerable.

Organizational Technology

No information system is likely to become, or to remain, operational unless there is an adequate political and economic structure of governance, authority, resource allocation, control, and accountability. This structure has simply been assumed in previous chapters but deserves some additional comment since failure to develop satisfactory governance and administrative arrangements can have serious consequences.

Administrative and governance structures are situational. They need to be compatible with the corporate culture of the larger organization or community in which the information system operates.

Administrative and governance structures should, in a sense, be the last aspect to be considered in the design of information systems. This assertion implies no lack of respect for the importance of administrative arrangements but is a tactical consideration. Different organizational structures lend themselves to different sorts of activities. In this the manner of organizing, the organizational technology, shares the attributes of any other technology. Each technology, each organizational approach, offers different constraints in terms of activities for which it is suited. Given the importance of compatibility between activities and administrative structure, to start by assuming any given organizational structure is to begin by imposing on the information systems the constraints and limitations of that organizational structure. It would, in theory, be far better to defer administrative considerations and to concentrate initially on the needs of users and the potential of available information technology. Then political and economic realities need to be considered and the constraints that they bring imposed. Ideals may well have to be compromised, but by the tactic of deferring consideration of administrative solutions, one may hope to achieve a better, less inhibited result. Such advice is idealistic in that those involved in the design usually have a major vested interest not only in specific future designs but also in present and in future organizational structures.

Detailed discussion of the design and use of organizational structures is outside our scope, and reference should be made to general texts on management and organizational behavior (e.g., Daft, 1988; Koontz, O'Donnell, and Weihrich 1984). Basic guidelines are those for any activity within organizations: responsibility should be matched by adequate authority and resources; authority should be matched by accountability; accountability is ineffective without the dissemination of information and mechanisms for changing decisions; any organizational structure needs to be compatible with and acceptable to the parent organization or broader social context; and technical standards should be respected to ensure flexibility and adaptability.

INFORMATION HANDLING, ORGANIZATIONS, AND POWER

The traditional approach to the design of information services is to design capabilities to support the organization for which it is intended. However, if one takes a longer view, the evidence indicates that the reverse process is also in effect: the structure of organizations tends to adapt to, and to follow, changes in information handling capabilities.[1]

Communications and Delegation: An Inverse Relationship

The evolution of military strategic communications provides a clear illustration of the effect of communications on power structure. The duke of Marlborough, Prince Eugene of Savoy, and other generals before the nineteenth century could, and did, march off and conduct brilliant military campaigns. Lord Nelson and other admirals could sail their fleets away and demonstrate their tactical and strategical skills. It could not be otherwise because checking with London, Paris, Vienna, or wherever else might take weeks using the telecommunications technologies of horse, stagecoach, and sailing ship. A message could take a month crossing the Atlantic one way. Not only the battle but the campaign might be over by the time new instructions could arrive from headquarters. Warfare was largely a summer activity; the summer would be over.

In 1789, for example, there was an incident at Nootka Sound, off Vancouver Island, involving Spanish and British ships. It would have taken several weeks before the news could have reached London or Madrid. There was no transcontinental railroad, no Panama canal, no AT&T. In those days, there was, of necessity, substantial delegation of decision making to the commander on the spot.

In 1794, however, the French Revolutionary government hired a communications consultant, Claude Chappe, to find some faster means to deliver messages than a courier on horseback or a sailing ship. Chappe recommended mechanical flag waving: semaphores on hilltops in line of sight. At its best, his semaphore system could be used to send a fifty-character message from Toulon (a Mediterranean naval base) to Paris (425 miles) in one hour. Horseback couriers took three to four days.[2] Variants of this system—the "visual" telegraph—were adopted in other countries but were superseded around 1850 by the electrical or field telegraph, whereby electrical pulses were sent along wires. What really impressed contemporaries was the use of field telegraph in the Franco-Prussian War of 1870–1871, when the Prussians used it with great effect to coordinate and control their armed forces, using railroads to transport them.

In World War II, the battle of Stalingrad is a poignant example of the effects of improved information technology on decision making. The German Sixth Army was deep in Soviet territory in an exposed position, encircled by Soviet troops and far from effective German support. Winter weather had set in, and supplies were very low. It was not a good place to be, but Hitler had ordered the army to stay there and fight. A century earlier, a general would have sized up the situation, realized that an immediate breakout was the only tenable option, and acted accordingly. By now, however, improved information technology enabled radio contact with the Army High Command to be maintained even though the Sixth Army was surrounded, so the general, Von Seydlitz, sent a desperate radio message: "The Army is faced with a clear either-or: Breakthrough to the south-west . . . or annihilation within a few days." Radio enabled the Army High Command to send instructions to stay put. The army did stay. Fewer than 6,000 out of more than 200,000 soldiers survived.

What had happened to the delegation of decision making to the commander on the spot that was so evident in earlier centuries? It seems unlikely that the great generals and admirals of the past could achieve now what they did in the eighteenth century and before. They probably would not be allowed to. Improved telecommunications now enable headquarters to control distant operations tightly. Delegation is now only at the discretion of the central authority. The success of U.S. World War II naval operations in the Pacific Ocean against the Japanese has been attributed in part to greater delegation of decision making by the U.S. headquarters than was allowed by the Japanese (Karig and Purdon 1947, 246–50). Some balance is clearly needed between the unfortunate battle of New Orleans, fought on January 8, 1815, by commanders unaware that a peace treaty had been signed in Europe two weeks earlier, and modern complaints from commanding officers of oversupervision (Kelly 1978).

These examples of military strategic communications reveal more than a trend of diminishing decision making by local commanders. They provide a basis for additional conclusions. The diminution of delegated authority exactly parallels and follows improvements in communications between the local commander and the central headquarters. There is an inverse relationship between communications and the delegation of decision making: the worse the communications, the greater the delegation of decision making; the better the communications, the less the delegation of decision making. Yet technology provides no more than tools, so it is unreasonable to ascribe changed patterns of activity only or directly to the development of better tools. There must be human values at work motivating changed behavior. The explanation is not simply that communications technology has improved but also that central authorities prefer to exercise greater control. Improvements in information technology have made it more feasible for the central authority to exercise its preference for retaining control. Given the choice, control will tend to be retained. Given the preference of central authority to retain control to the extent feasible, the delegation of decision making can, in general, be regarded as caused by (and as an adaptive response to) inadequate communications capabilities. A corollary is that technical improvements in communications can be expected to lead to reduced delegation.

Span of Control

The inverse relationship between communications and delegation can be generalized further when spans of control are considered. If the task to be supervised is very simple and the situation is stable, comparatively little instruction, consultation, and supervisorial decision making is needed. It is not difficult to imagine the direct and effective supervision of many workers in such a situation, a relatively flat hierarchy. In 1914, for example, at the Ford plant assembly line, there was only one foreman to fifty-eight workers. In this case, it could be argued that the line itself was providing some of the supervision (Tompkins and Cheney 1985, 182). In contrast, if the tasks are complex, the roles varied, the situation changeable, and extensive liaison or consultation is needed, then fewer individuals can be effectively supervised directly. Anyone who attempted to supervise fifty-eight individuals in such circumstances would suffer from information overload and would either fail to supervise effectively or would be obliged to delegate some of the supervision, probably by diverting resources to an intermediate level of assistant supervisors. Hence there would be a taller hierarchy, an organization with more delegation of decision making and more levels of hierarchy.

Since the process of supervision is in large measure a role based on handling information (learning, consulting, deciding, negotiating, informing), it would be reasonable to regard this as another manifestation of the inverse relationship between communication and delegation of decision making. In the case of supervision, however, there is more involved than merely communicating information since information not only needs to be communicated, it also needs to be analyzed, thought about, and acted upon. The two cases are not the same, but since both have to do with information handling, both can be regarded as examples of the more general proposition that delegation increases with information handling difficulties: the more effectively information is handled, the less the delegation, the flatter the organizational hierarchy, and the greater the centralization of control.

Individuals cannot cope with unlimited complexity, and organizational structures can be viewed as means of easing information handling (Beniger 1990). Organizational structures can be expected to vary because, as mechanisms for coordination and information handling, they should be and generally are adapted to the circumstances of the group of individuals constituting the organization. In terms of contingency theories of organizational structure, an organization is likely to be decentralized when matters requiring decisions are so turbulent or complex that high-level managers are too far removed from the details to make informed decisions (McPhee 1985; Pfeffer and Leblebici 1977; Tushman and Nadler 1978).

In this context, degrees of turbulence and complexity need to be considered relative to the information handling capability of the organization. The consequences of any given level of turbulence and complexity could reasonably be expected to be different for otherwise comparable organizations that had different information handling capabilities. An organization with sophisticated information handling capabilities would operate with less decentralization than could one with a more primitive information handling capability or might handle more work through its greater effectiveness (Foster and Flynn 1985). In this sense, the requirement for decentralization is inversely related to information handling capability for any given level of turbulence and complexity. It follows that information handling capability should be seen as a defining variable in organizational structure and in the distribution of power within that structure.

There are different approaches to improving information handling capability: greater coordination and hierarchy are one approach; improvements in information systems are another.

Delegation as the Granting of Power

Markus, in her *Systems in Organizations* (1984), reviews some of these issues and describes two relevant case studies. In a firm with three divisions, the corporate headquarters sought to introduce a new accounting system that would enable it to know much more about what was going on in the divisions and would also take over some of the role of the divisional accountants. Implementation ran into significant resistance at the divisional level where autonomy would be reduced. In another case a new planning and decision system for keeping track of the location of equipment was developed for a branch of the U.S. military. Junior officers were given online terminals with access to more information and found that they could handle requests routinely without reference to senior officers. This may seem to be greater delegation since the decision making has apparently moved to a lower level in the hierarchy, but the reverse was the case. By making the senior officers redundant, the new information system was enabling the elimination of a whole level of hierarchy in the decision making. The new information system undermined the traditional authority structure and the power of the senior officers, who vigorously protested, claimed that the data in the new system were not accurate, and successfully insisted that it be redesigned to prevent junior officers from acting in ways that circumvented the established, formal channels.

Why, in both cases, would new information systems be opposed when they appeared more efficient and reduced the need for delegation? It is *because* they reduced the need for delegation.

Delegation is the granting of autonomy, or independence. Independence is an aspect of power, since power has to do with the ability to make decisions. Delegation is therefore a granting of power. It is liable to be done reluctantly, out of necessity, since for organizational leaders it is a reasonable goal to want to minimize dependence on others. Remove the necessity, and delegation will ordinarily be retracted by any top management interested in maintaining control and flexibility as a means to survival and success. For similar reasons, people are reluctant to give up independence and power that has been delegated to them. If top management introduces new information systems that allow more centralized decision making or bypasses a middle level, one can expect resistance, much as one would expect resistance to a structural reorganization that eliminated a middle level.

Information Handling and Complexity of Organization

Much of the discussion has focused on the particular case of strategic military communications wherein distant decentralized operations are unavoidable and improvements in information handling (primarily telecommunications) clearly affected the manner in which they are managed. In other, nonmilitary activities, operations that were extended in terms of geographical distance or complexity tended not to be undertaken until sufficient means for information handling had been developed. Traditionally business firms were single-unit enterprises; an individual or a small number of owners operated a shop, factory, or service from a single office. Ordinarily this type of firm would handle a single function, deal with a single product line, and operate in a single geographical area. Market and price mechanisms affected coordination. In contrast, modern enterprises commonly operate many units, at different locations, often conducting multiple economic activities, and offering diverse goods and services. Improved information handling procedures constitute an important element in making complex modern enterprises feasible.[3] Information systems are ordinarily regarded as supporting an organization's effectiveness.[4]

Decentralization is commonly regarded as beneficial. Here we are concerned only with the delegation of decision making, which is only one of the several aspects of decentralization (Kochen and Deutsch 1980). In particular, one can have deconcentration, where work is decentralized but decision making is not, or one can have spurious delegation of decision making, where the authority to make decisions is delegated but is so subject to centralized monitoring and correction as to constitute little effective delegation of power. A cat that plays with a captured mouse may allow the mouse to decide which way to run, but the cat has no intention of allowing the mouse to go more than a few inches. The mouse has little effective autonomy.[5]

Those in control of an organization will tend, out of concern for survival and success, to delegate that control reluctantly and only as necessary. One example of such necessity is when geographical considerations so strain communications that the distribution of some decision-making authority to those on the spot is necessary. Another example is when the complexity of supervision becomes so great that some assistance (delegation of the supervision) is needed. In both cases, the common cause of delegation is difficulty in handling information. In both cases, as information handling becomes easier, for whatever reason, one can expect to see a retraction of that delegation, probably opposed by those to whom it had been delegated. These relationships can be summarized as a series of propositions:

1. The centralization of decision making is directly related to the effectiveness of information handling.
2. The greater the difficulties of information handling, the more layers of hierarchy there are.
3. More generally, the delegation of decision making is inversely related to the effectiveness of information handling.
4. Technical improvements in information handling will tend to result in centralization of power.

And, as corollaries:

5. The effective centralization of power is indicative of effective information handling.
6. Therefore, more effective centralization can be viewed as a measure of technical improvement in information systems.

Certainly no implication is intended that the centralization of decision making necessarily results in better (or worse) decisions. The example of the battle of Stalingrad shows that central decision making can be unfortunate. Nor is it argued that information systems should not be designed to support decentralized organizations. Clearly it would be risky to design information systems to a pattern that differs from that of the organization for which it is intended. However, since the control and, hence, the survival of organizations depend profoundly on receiving and reacting to information, it is only to be expected that, in the long term, more effective communication and handling of information can be expected to lead to a simplification of the organization, greater centralization, and larger organizations.

More generally our understanding of information systems will remain significantly incomplete unless the relationship between information systems and organizations is included as a significant aspect of the study of information systems (Dery 1986).

CHANGE IN INFORMATION SYSTEMS

The allocation and reallocation of resources and improvements in technology have been mentioned several times as leading to changes in information systems. We now take a look at long-term change. There has been a long tradition of fantasy about future information systems—whether of a world brain, a procognitive system, or a Memex. Given the extent to which the provision and use of libraries are influenced by the social environment and given possibilities for the use of new information technology, the issue is not whether there will be change but what will be the nature of it. If we are to make any claim to understand the nature of information systems, then we ought to have some ideas about how they might change.[6]

In considering forecasts of future information systems, we need to ask some questions:

1. How complete is the forecast in its own terms? Consistent, unambiguous representation (e.g., indexing and abstracting) is more feasible in some fields of discourse than in others, in the hard sciences than in the soft sciences, in descriptions of the physical world than of intellectual and social worlds, so powerful future information systems seem more plausible for some topics than for others.

2. Is the forecast incomplete, covering only one aspect of the area being forecasted? Are we considering improvements in communications or in retrieval? In projecting what may happen, an author will tend to focus, consciously or otherwise, on one aspect that has interesting possibilities and to extrapolate its development. This is standard technique in science fiction writing. It can be used in reverse—to project anachronisms into the past for humorous effect, as in Mark Twain's *A Connecticut Yankee in King Arthur's Court*. In this case of projecting backward into the past, the incongruity is obvious. With projections into the future, selective and uneven extrapolation can be difficult to detect.

3. How complete is the extrapolation in terms of its effect? The computer and associated technologies are usually seen as a means of easing access to recorded knowledge. But we can also see that computers are aggravating the problem by enabling a great increase in the quantity of recorded knowledge through word processing, teleconferencing, and the recording and accumulation of vast stores of data.

4. What could change? Modern information technology has already resulted in dramatic changes in information systems. But consider, for example, copyright, public access to government records, education for information professions, selection and censorship of information, and improved subject access. Each of these is a thoroughly contemporary issue, yet each was being actively discussed a century ago in surprisingly contemporary terms and probably will be discussed a century hence. It is clear that not all aspects of information systems change rapidly.

Three Sorts of Change

The stark contrast in degrees of change in technological and social aspects of change in information systems suggests three categories with respect to change: information-related values, information technology, and information studies.

1. Information-related values include social values as they influence information policies and professional concerns of information specialists. These values determine the mission of information systems and information specialists' attitudes toward users. The concern here is with values that underlie day-to-day priorities and decisions, not with the practical techniques used to implement those decisions. Information-related values appear to have changed rather little since the 1880s in the United States. Consideration of selection and censorship (both book burning and book buying) helps clarify the issues. The specific items that a publisher, librarian, or museum curator is willing or allowed to make available clearly change with time. Similar issues arise in corporate and government information policies from the conflicting principles of freedom of access to information and rights to personal privacy. Where the line is drawn between acceptable and unacceptable to the provider or to the community will vary as society's standards and social, political, and religious values change. Yet there will always be a line drawn somewhere, and the arguments concerning where the line should be appear to vary little over time.

Information policies are not universal or unchanging. What would be acceptable in San Francisco today may not be acceptable in Tehran or Beijing. What is acceptable in Massachusetts now might not have been acceptable in colonial times—and vice versa. Although there can be change over time in a given place, such changes are based on cultural forces rather than the passage of time.

2. Information technology is concerned with the handling of physical things: paper, cardboard, microform, and magnetic, optical, or other recording media. Technology is of particular significance because information systems are concerned with recorded knowledge. Ideas and assertions are represented in texts and images but only through text-bearing and image-bearing objects, such as books made of paper, sound recordings on magnetic tape, numbers on cathode ray screens, and so on. These are the principal text-bearing objects. Carbon paper, microfilm, and typewriter were all available a century ago. The telephone,

teletype, punch cards, television, and electronic computers have added to the options. It cannot be known what technology will be available a hundred years from now, but the trend is clear: additional media for bearing text, more powerful technologies for handling text, and, unlike the social values associated with information, a clear line of progress with time. We can be confident that the technological tools available for information systems will be very much improved in the future.

3. A third aspect of information systems is different in kind from social values and from information technology: our understanding of information systems. (This book is intended to be about the understanding of information systems rather than information technology or social values concerning information.) We use the term *information studies* to designate this third category, which draws heavily on engineering, several sorts of social sciences, and the humanities insofar as information, knowledge, and belief are rooted in culture, broadly defined. Central concerns include:

- The role of information and of information systems in society.
- The needs, information-gathering behavior, and institutional contexts of groups to be served: students, researchers, children, managers, the aged, and so on.
- The theory and practice of information retrieval, including the broad areas of the description and representation of the contents of pieces of recorded knowledge: indexing, cataloging, classification, abstracting, and bibliography.
- The managerial, political, and technological means most likely to be useful in developing and providing good information systems (cf. Wilson 1986).

There has been some progress in information studies in the past century but not very much. Because the central issues—information retrieval theory and information gathering behavior—are, or should be, rooted in truly obscure aspects of human behavior, progress in understanding them will be slow and difficult. Scholarly explanation will tend to lag behind the intuitive understanding of those intimately involved in the activities. So, unlike information technology, we cannot claim that there has been much progress. Nor can we assume that there is likely to be much in the foreseeable future. Much of the progress of the last century in these areas has been the refinement of earlier progress (e.g., indexing principles) or concerned with relative superficial symptoms of deeper phenomena (e.g., statistical study of information system use).

INFORMATION PROFESSIONALS

So far we have paid little direct attention to the people involved in providing information, except for some discussion of the important influence of the personal values of individuals engaged in the provision of information services.

Information professionals are embedded in both the provision of information systems and their societal environment, and so it is only to be expected that they should be subject to the realities and ambiguities of both spheres concerning their roles, tasks, and qualifications. One ambiguity concerns their role. If information is power, should information professionals be regarded as power brokers dealing with information-as-knowledge and information-as-process? Or are they technicians retained to perform purely physical tasks handling information-as-thing to support the agendas of others? Another ambiguity concerns their tasks. There is a duality between viewing information professionals as being concerned with knowledge and culture on the one hand and physical objects on the other. That they may be concerned with both simultaneously may explain some of the ambiguity in the status of information professionals: an individual who fosters knowledge, power, and culture can reasonably be viewed differently from one who merely transmits, stores, and retrieves physical objects.

Variations in the way the roles and tasks of information professionals are viewed can only compound disagreement over the proper education and training of information professionals. Power brokers need to understand power, politics, management, and "real worlds." Those transmitting knowledge and culture need a deep appreciation of the knowledge and culture with which they are concerned. On this basis, the curator of an art museum should be well grounded in the art history of the periods and schools covered. Those concerned with the logistics of physical objects that others regard as information-as-thing need quite different management and engineering skills.

As if this were not complicated enough, further confusion arises because much of what is referred to as the information industry, the information sector, information systems, and even information science has little to do in any direct sense, with knowledge, culture, or power. Rather, most of these areas are concerned with the design, improvement, and marketing of information technology or with purely procedural aspects of information processing.

SUMMARY

In this chapter we have looked more closely at information and information systems in their social context. The values and motivations that drive inquiries and the provision and use of information systems derive from the social environment. In noncommercial provision, the allocation of resources depends on the motivations of those who allocate resources to or within information systems.

The managerial organizational structure of an information system is important for its effectiveness, but care should be taken not to let that structure constrain the design of the information systems more than is necessary.

Because organizations depend on handling information, the information handling capability of an organization is a defining variable in the distribution of power in organizations. The degree of delegation of decision making increases and the breadth of spans of control decreases with difficulties in information handling. Improvements in information systems tend to reverse these effects and to result in more centralized control.

The duality of knowledge on the one hand and physical objects on the other as the realm of information professionals may explain some of the ambiguity in their status: an individual who promotes knowledge, culture, and power can reasonably be viewed differently from one who merely stores physical objects.

NOTES

1. This section is based on M. K. Buckland, "Information Handling, Organizational Structure, and Power," *Journal of the American Society for Information Science* 40 (1989): 329–33.

2. For material on the history of telecommunications see *Encyclopaedia Britannica*, 11th ed. (1911), v. 25, s.v. "Signal," 70–73; *Encyclopaedia Britannica*, 15th ed. (1977), v. 18, s.v. "Telegraph," 66–78; and J. H. Morrison, *Wave to Whisper: British Military Communications in Halifax and the Empire, 1790–1880*, History and Archaeology, 64 (Quebec: Canadian Government Publishing Centre, 1982).

3. For a broad historical background, see A. D. Chandler, *The Visible Hand: The Managerial Revolution in American Business* (Cambridge: Harvard University Press, 1977). For more explicit analysis of the role of information handling in society, see J. R. Beniger, *The Control Revolution: Technological and Economic Origins of the Information Society* (Cambridge: Harvard University Press, 1986).

4. For a view of organization as information systems, see Knight and McDaniel (1979).

5. For a concise review of relevant literature, see M. L. Markus, *Systems in Organizations: Bugs + Features* (Boston: Pitman, 1984), 51–54. For a more general review, see *Organizational Communication: Traditional Themes and New Directions*, ed. R. D. McPhee and P. K. Tompkins, Sage Annual Reviews of Communications Research, 13 (Beverly Hills, Calif.: Sage Publications, 1985).

6. This section is based on M. K. Buckland, "Education for Librarianship in the Next Century," *Library Trends* 34 (1986): 777–87. The help of John L. Ober is gratefully acknowledged.

Part **V**

Conclusion

Chapter 18

Summary and Retrospect

SUMMARY

Our intention has been to provide a general introduction to information systems, their nature, and how they relate to their contexts. Examining information systems has required us to consider information and knowledge. We have used three of the numerous meanings of the word *information*: (1) information-as-process, the process of becoming informed; (2) information-as-knowledge, that knowledge which is imparted by information-as-process; and (3) information-as-thing, the attributive use of *information* to denote things regarded as informative. Of these, information-as-thing is of special interest because information systems deal directly with information only as information-as-thing: data, documents, signals (chapter 1).

Theory is the description of the nature of something, a view of it. Information and information systems involve a rich mix of technique, technology, social sciences, and culture. Therefore, a rigorous, formal approach to theory, as if for a formal, exact science, seems unlikely to represent much of the reality of information and information systems (chapter 2). The nature of systems and some examples of information systems were summarized (chapter 3).

Knowledge is a matter of belief. Recorded knowledge is information-as-thing. Information-as-knowledge is the knowledge imparted as a result of information-as-process (chapter 4).

Information-as-thing denotes any thing regarded as informative, as evidence. This definition leads to a very broad view of information, including objects and events, as well as data and documents. Whether something is information is a matter of opinion and, perhaps, of consensus (chapter 5). Information-as-thing is of special interest for us because information systems deal directly with information only in this sense. Information systems and knowledge-based systems deal not with knowledge but with representations of knowledge. The use of retrieval systems is necessarily a historical activity (chapter 6).

What information systems do is determined in part by the characteristics of the information-as-thing and in part by the constraints of the information technologies used (chapters 6 and 7).

Access can be regarded as a unifying concept for the whole field. Six aspects of access are: identification of sources; availability of sources; price to the user; cost to the provider; understanding; and acceptability. An information system that supplies information-as-thing must meet the first four aspects of access adequately. For an information system to inform, the last two aspects also become important (chapter 8).

Everyone is massively ignorant. Sometimes we wish to do something about some detail of our ignorance or uncertainty by informing ourselves and an inquiry results, providing motivation to use an information system. Inquiries have to be expressed in a form suited to the information system (chapter 9). Thought alone can sometimes resolve ignorance, but we are primarily interested in the perceiving of pertinent information, pertinent evidence, by observing, by receiving communications, by retrieving information-as-thing. Retrieval presupposes the collecting of information. Collecting presupposes the creation of information. Retrieval includes three different activities: physically retrieving something, locating something to be retrieved, and identifying something to be located (chapter 10).

To have been informed is to know something. Becoming informed means a change in what one knows. Physically receiving text or other information-as-thing does not ensure that the recipient becomes informed. Understanding and belief are necessary ingredients (chapter 11).

When considering information and information processing, we need to include all possible transformations between intangible ideas and physical representations: thinking, perceiving, expressing, and information processing. ''Information processing'' normally means automatic data processing, but for a general discussion of information systems, a broader view is needed. *Deriving* information would be more apt than *processing* information. Of central importance is the creation of representations of inquiries and of information (chapter 12).

Distressing ignorance provides the motivation to use information systems. There is, however, always some price for using information systems, composed of time, effort, inconvenience, and, sometimes, money. The expressed demand is governed by a price mechanism: does the perceived probable benefit match the perceived probable price and, even if it does, would some other course of action be preferable? Supply may adapt to demand: demand will adapt to supply (chapter 13).

The provision of information systems is determined, in detail, by the allocation of resources to and within specific systems. In commercial systems, the resources come from fees. In noncommercial systems the resources come from sponsors, a political process influenced by all who participate in allocation decisions (chapter 14).

The complex web of relationships in the provision and use of an information system can be viewed as three loosely coupled systems: provision is a political and managerial system, becoming informed is a cognitive process, and demand results from an economic system. These three systems are linked through the use of the information system. Each system is as dominated by the external environment as by the other two systems. A major challenge to information system managers is to achieve the optimal blend of components and optimal size of system (chapter 15).

Use of information and information systems involves tasks that may be beyond a user's expertise. If so, there are different types of remedy: increase the user's expertise through education; provide advice as needed; simplify the system; use an intermediary; and use artificial intelligence to enable the information system to take over tasks from the user (chapter 16).

Information and information systems are rooted in their social environment. the motivations to use and the motivations to provide information arise from social values. Information systems are designed to serve organizations and societies. They also influence the distribution of knowledge and, thereby, the distribution of power and resources (chapter 17).

SOME PROBLEMS RECONSIDERED

In the first chapter we identified some problems and paradoxes associated with information and information systems. These have been addressed, more or less, in succeeding chapters and can be revisited here.

1. *Do information systems really handle information?* Some theorists have dismissed the notion of information being "stuff." Rather, information is something intangible—either knowledge imparted (information-as-knowledge) or the process of becoming informed (information-as-process). However, things regarded as being informative are generally referred to attributively as "information," despite what purists may wish. To say that a document "contains" information is convenient but metaphorical; the document may have meaningful marks, but the meaning is something attributed to the marks and is not a physical property of the marks. The meaning of marks can change even if the marks do not. Every information system built, or ever likely to be built, deals directly with neither information-as-knowledge nor information-as-process but with physical matter—information-as-thing—such as printed books, digital codes, and other physical images and objects. Just as a film of an event is not really the event itself, so a book or database "of knowledge" is not really knowledge but a representation of knowledge. The distinction is important.

The term *information system* is commonly used to denote a system that delivers information, but delivering information is not in itself sufficient for becoming informed.

2. *What is and what is not information?* We found it convenient to approach the question of what is and what is not information pragmatically. Information, in the sense of information-as-thing, is anything by or on account of which people are informed. People are, in practice, informed by the perceiving of a very wide range of things: data, texts, objects (including other people), and events. Some of these lend themselves to being stored and retrieved more easily than others, but in all cases it is possible, at least in theory, to derive representations of them that can be used in lieu of the original. Nevertheless, whether something is informative depends on whether it is regarded as informative. It would therefore be rash to assert of anything that it could not in any circumstances be information.

Information-as-process is situational. Therefore, evidence involved in information-as-process is so situationally. Beyond this, whether it is sensible to describe something as information is a matter of opinion, judgment, and consensus. Everyone may agree that some things, notably data in databases and books in libraries, can reasonably be referred to as information. The probability of their actually being information is, by consensus, high. Of other things there may well be general doubt as to whether anyone will, or should, be informed by them.

3. *Is information a commodity?* Knowledge can be beneficial in a variety of ways, so useful knowledge and, therefore, information-as-knowledge and information-as-thing can be well worth paying for and worth sharing with others. There is always some real price in effort, time, inconvenience, and/or money in becoming informed, though it may sometimes be insignificant. Much of the time we are content to communicate information to others since we do not want them to be ignorant. When we want others to know or, at least, have no objection to their knowing and when the price of their becoming informed is trivial, knowledge can be disseminated very easily. Rumors spread like epidemics. But these circumstances do not always obtain. The real price of becoming informed may be significant. Access to information may depend on the actions of others, such as information professionals, who expect reward for their efforts. In a sponsored information system, the sponsors (university, city, corporation) pay the archivist, librarian, or information systems manager. In a commercial service, the user will be charged. Opportunities arise for a specialized service to provide a value-added service, meaning an alternative information service that is advantageous enough to the user to be worth paying for.

There is a motivation not to share knowledge if there is a competitive situation, if the knowledge is instrumental for some purpose, and if the knowledge or recorded knowledge is restricted. In such cases (for example, industrial secrets or military intelligence), information would be a valuable asset whether sold or kept secret.

4. *Is old information processed into new?* In most processing, ingredients are

transformed into something new, but in information processing, the new is produced but the ingredients are not transformed. Our explanation is that:

1. Knowledge is intangible.
2. Being information-as-thing is not an inherent physical property but a quality perceived in or attributed to physical entities, with more or less consensus.
3. Perceptions and attributed qualities can be extended and multiplied indefinitely without consuming the objects in which they have been perceived. Physical properties cannot be replicated in this way.
4. The term *information processing* is unsatisfactory. It is not that old information is processed into new but rather that new information is derived from the old.
5. The processing of physical media can indeed change them; books can be burned and disks erased.

5. *How should retrieval systems be evaluated?* The problem of the evaluation of retrieval systems is associated with the difficulties in defining the term *relevance*. It is important to distinguish three different processes: the representation of an inquiry in the terms of the system; the retrieval process itself, which depends more or less on representations of what is retrievable; and the use made of what has been retrieved.

A retrieval system can retrieve stored items only in terms of the attributes used as a basis for retrieval—whether the physical attributes, such as words in the text, or descriptions of the items or of what it is about. To the extent to which items consistent with the specification of the inquiry as formulated are yielded, the retrieval system can be said to be responsive. Whether a retrieved item is found by the receiver to have utility depends not only on the retrieval system but also on the human being who examines it. "Value is not inherent in, nor is it carried by, an information message. Consequently a message has value only in context. It is given value by its users" (Taylor 1986, 203).

There are, therefore, two different bases for evaluation: Evaluation in the narrow sense of an evaluation of the retrieval system itself is a matter of responsiveness, of ability to yield consistently items that fit the descriptions expressed in formulated inquiries. Evaluation in the wider sense has to do with the utility of the items that have been retrieved and examined. This differs from the narrower sense in two ways: it is not an evaluation of the retrieval system but of the combination of retrieval system and its users, and it is concerned with human values from which alone utility and beneficial effects derive. It is therefore different in scope and different in kind.

6. *Is there an optimal size for an information system?* Is a bigger information system (database, archive, library, museum) always better? Could it be too big? There may be some imbalances and inconsistencies in the profile of an information system that cause it to be less than optimal. Possibly more resources need to be allocated to collecting material. More likely, an information system would best be improved by attention to other aspects, such as assisting would-

be users. But when all such internal adjustments have been made and other things being equal, the larger the collection is, the more informative it will be. Expansion may become decreasingly economical, but viewing the information system in isolation, bigger is better.

The limit to the optimal size of information systems comes not from inside the system but from the outside environment. In cities, parks are desirable, and, other things being equal, bigger parks are better than small ones. But a city that was entirely parkland would not be a city. Similarly with noncommercial information systems, it is not that bigger is not better but that there is a law of diminishing returns, and there are other needs to be met. At some point the sponsors providing the resources reach the point where the claims of other, rival uses of resources should form a limit to continued expansion of the information system. In commercial information systems, fee income can support only a limited size in any given circumstances.

7. *How do information services survive?* Noncommercial information services, notably libraries and museums, present a paradox. In systems theory, survival depends on adaptability, and adaptability depends, in turn, on feedback from the environment. Libraries and museums appear to be, and to a significant extent are, weak in feedback. What is known about the nature, activities, and success of their visitors is limited. Nevertheless, they show considerable powers not only of survival but also stability.

A large part of the explanation is that there are two largely independent flows of feedback. In addition to the sometimes rather weak feedback in terms of what the providers of the service know, the users have a sense of their own satisfaction with what is provided and adapt accordingly in ways that tend to compensate for any weaknesses in the ability of the service to adapt to change. If demand becomes excessive, the quality of service deteriorates, and demand, being elastic and based on a price mechanism, diminishes. If demand is low relative to provision, then service will tend to be good, and demand is likely to increase. It is as much a question of survival through demand adapting to supply than of supply adapting to demand. Hence survival depends not only on an organization's responsiveness to the environment but also on mechanisms whereby the environment adapts to the organization. In this way, even relatively unadaptive organizations can survive.

8. *What is information system goodness?* How does one know whether one information system is better than another or that it is improving or degenerating? Can there be a single measure of information system goodness? If so, what is it? If not, why not?

Complex things of personal interest—automobiles, potential spouses, information systems—typically have numerous good and less good features. One can always concoct a single measure of goodness built up of the sum of sundry weighted measures of this and that. The problem is in the lack of credibility that such a measure would have.

An approach that can be very helpful in this context was developed by Orr

(1973), who points out that there is a fundamental ambiguity in discussions of goodness of service because there are two quite different sorts of goodness: how good is it?—a measure of quality—and, what good does it do?—a measure of value.

A highly sophisticated service capable of providing rapid and reliable information on some topic would have to be regarded as a good service, a service of high quality. In practice, this means that it is good because it has a substantial capability for delivering certain sorts of information. But even the best service capability is of little value if nobody is interested. There cannot be much by way of beneficial effects if it is not used.

Unfortunately, both quality and value are difficult to measure operationally. In practice, one tends to fall back on indirect, surrogate measures. If the resources allocated to the service are large, then the service ought to be good. If the service is heavily utilized, there is an implication both that the service is good and that it is beneficial. One would expect the value of a service to be reflected in the resources allocated to it. These relationships are shown as the dashed lines in figure 18.1.

Other things being equal, one would expect the allocation of more resources to the service to result in better capability—that is, better quality of service. Improved capability, to the extent that it is appropriate to the demand, should lead to increased utilization. Assuming that the capability is related to an accepted mission, then more utilization ought to mean increased beneficial effects. A perception of greater beneficial effects (i.e., value) is likely to result in the allocation of increased resources.

As Orr pointed out, good management is reflected in tight connections at each point: the greater the increase in capability for any given increase in resources; the greater the increase in utilization for any given increase in capability; and so on.

IDEALS

An Ideal Information System

Francis Bacon (1561–1626) was a statesman and lawyer who wrote thoughtfully about knowledge. He is known for his comment that since ignorance reduces ability to achieve, "knowledge is power."[1] Bacon's aphorism is commonly misquoted as "Information is power," which is not the same. However, if knowledge is power, then recorded knowledge (information-as-thing) is a potential source of knowledge and so of power.

In a drama performed in 1594, whose authorship has been attributed to Bacon, the Prince of Purple is advised by six Counsellors. The Second Counsellor urges support for research and depicts an ideal information support system, using assumptions resembling those we have adopted here. It was assumed that objects

Figure 18.1
Information System Goodness

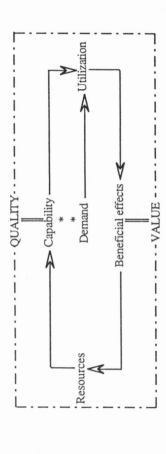

═══ denotes the practical interpretations that quality means capability and value means beneficial effects.

──── denotes assumed causal relationship.

* * signifies the need for capability to be related to demand.

─ ∙ ─ denotes surrogate measures. The allocation of resources implies a perception quality and value; utilization also implies a perception of quality and value.

Based on Orr (1973).

and experiments as well as documents were informative. This ideal system had four parts:

First, the collecting of a most perfect and general library, wherein whatsoever the wit of man had heretofore committed to books of worth . . . may be made contributory to your wisdom. Next, a spacious, wonderful garden, wherein whatsoever plant the sun of divers climate, or the earth out of divers moulds, either wild or by the culture of man brought forth, may be . . . set and cherished. This garden to be built about with rooms to stable in all rare beasts and to cage in all rare birds; with two lakes adjoining, the one of fresh water the other of salt, for like variety of fishes. And so you may have . . . a model of the universal nature made private. The third, a goodly, huge cabinet [museum], wherein whatsoever the hand of man, by exquisite art or engine, hath made rare in stuff, form, or motion, whatsoever singularity chance, and the shuffle of things hath produced, what-soever Nature has wrought in things that want life and may be kept, shall be sorted and included. The fourth such a still-house [laboratory], so furnished with mills, instruments, furnaces, and vessels as may be a palace fit for a philosopher's stone. (*Gesta Grayorum*, 1968, 47–48; also quoted in Impey and MacGregor 1985, 1)

Goals

The conceptual framework and assumptions underlying any given information system should rest on two foundations: the role of the information system is to facilitate access to information, and the purpose of the information system is to support the purpose of the institution or group served.

The first statement stimulates us to ask how *facilitate*, *access*, and *information* should be interpreted and how the role of this particular information system is related to the roles of others. Hitherto, the dominant interpretation has been the judicious assembling of local collections as the only effective means of providing convenient physical access to items, augmented by retrieval tools and advice. Contemporary changes in the technology underlying access to information in-dicate a need to reconsider how information services are provided as well as changes in relationships between systems and between local and remote collec-tions. The second general statement suggests that what should be done is unique to each specific context.

Any examination of the foundations of information systems must meet three conditions:

First, we need to distinguish between means and ends. The purposes of, and justification for, an information service should not be confused with the tech-niques and technologies adopted as means for providing service, even though the availability of techniques and technologies determines our options.

Second, we need to consider not only what is good and what is not so good, but also different sorts of goodness: "How good is it?" addresses means. "What good does it do?" asks about ends. "How well is it done?" has to do with efficiency and cost-effectiveness.

Finally, we need to be able to describe the nature of our concerns, or more concisely, we need adequate *theory*. We need a better understanding of information and information systems.

NOTE

1. In "De Haeresibus" ("Concerning heresies") in his *Meditationes sacrae* (1597), Bacon observed parenthetically "Nam et ipsa scientia potestas est" ("For knowledge itself is power") (*Works* 1859, 7: 241, 253). Later, in his *Novum Organum*, book 1, part 2, aphorism 3, he explained, "Scientia et potentia humana in idem coincidunt, quia ignoratio causae destituit effectum" (*Works* 1858, 1: 157), which has been translated as "Human knowledge and human power meet in one; for where the cause is not known the effect cannot be produced" (*Works* 1875, new ed., 4: 47).

References

Ackoff, R. L., et al. 1976. *The SCATT Report: Designing a National Scientific and Technological Communication System*. Philadelphia: University of Pennsylvania Press.

Advances in Intelligent Retrieval. Informatics 8. 1985. London: Aslib.

ALA World Encyclopedia of Library and Information Sciences. 1986. 2d ed. Chicago: American Library Association.

Allen, T. J., and P. G. Gerstberger. 1967. *Criteria for Selection of an Information Source*. Cambridge, Mass.: MIT, Sloane School of Management. (PB 176 899)

American Library Association. Committee on Freedom and Equality of Access to Information. 1986. *Freedom and Equality of Access to Information* ("Lacy Report"). Chicago: American Library Association.

Aristotle. 1955. *The Ethics of Aristotle: The Nichomachean Ethics Translated*. Harmondsworth, U.K.: Penguin.

Bacon, F. 1857–1874. *The Works*. Ed. J. Spedding, R. L. Ellis, and D. D. Heath. London: Longman Green. New ed., 1875–1879.

Barber, L. 1980. *The Heyday of Natural History, 1820–1870*. Garden City, N.Y.: Doubleday.

Bar-Hillel, Y. 1964. *Language and Information*. London: Addison-Wesley.

Barnes, M., ed. 1981. *Information in Society* [Leeds, England]: Leeds Polytechnic, Department of Librarianship.

Bearman, D. 1989. "Archives and Manuscript Control with Bibliographic Utilities." *American Archivist* 52:26–39.

Belkin, N. J., and W. B. Croft. 1987. "Retrieval Techniques." *Annual Review of Information Science and Technology* 22: 109–45.

Belkin, N. J., and S. E. Robertson. 1976. "Information Science and the Phenomena of Information." *Journal of the American Society for Information Science* 27: 197–204.

Belkin, N. J., R. N. Oddy, and H. M. Brooks. 1982. "ASK for Information Retrieval: Part I. Background and Theory." *Journal of Documentation* 38: 261–71.

Benedon, W. 1969. *Records Management*. New York: Prentice-Hall.

Beniger, J. R. 1986. *The Control Revolution: Technological and Economic Origins of the Information Society.* Cambridge: Harvard University Press.

Beniger, J. R. 1990. "Conceptualizing Information Technology as Organization and Vice Versa." In *Organizations and Communications Technology*, ed. J. Fulk and C. Steinfield, 29–45. Newbury Park, Calif.: Sage Publications.

Bergen, D. 1984. *Issues of Access in the New Information Age.* [Kingston, R.I.: Graduate School of Library and Information Studies]. (ERIC Report ED 271 119)

Biddle, S. 1988. "The Planning Function in the Management of University Libraries: Survey, Analysis, Conclusions, and Recommendations." DLIS dissertation. University of California at Berkeley.

Blair, D. C. 1984. "The Data-Document Distinction in Information Retrieval." *Communications of the Association for Computing Machinery* 27: 369–74.

Blair, D. C. 1990. *Language and Representation in Information Retrieval.* Amsterdam: Elsevier Science.

Blake, F. M., and E. L. Perlmutter. 1974. "Libraries in the Market Place." *Library Journal*, January 15: 108–11.

Blouin, F. X. 1986. "The Relevance of Archival Theory and Practice for Library Education: An Argument for a Broader Vision." *Journal of Library Administration* 7: 155–66.

Bookstein, A. 1984. "Probability and Fuzzy-Set Applications to Information Retrieval." *Annual Review of Information Science and Technology* 20: 117–51.

Boyce, B. R., and D. H. Kraft. 1985. "Principles and Theories in Information Science." *Annual Review of Information Science and Technology* 20: 153–78.

Braman, S. 1989. "Defining Information." *Telecommunications Policy* 3: 233–42.

Braunstein, Y. M. 1979. "Costs and Benefits of Library Information: The User Point of View." *Library Trends* 28: 79–87.

Briet, S. 1951. *Qu'est-ce que la documentation?* Paris: Editions Documentaires Industrielles et Techniques.

Brookes, B. C. 1974. "Robert Fairthorne and the Scope of Information Science." *Journal of Documentation* 30: 139–52.

Brookes, B. C. 1979. "Theoretical Informatics in Stage II Mechanization of IR Processes." In International Federation for Documentation. *Theoretical Problems of Informatics: New Trends in Informatics and Its Terminology*, 10–18. Moscow: VINITI. (FID 568)

Brookes, B. C. 1980. "The Foundations of Information Science. Part III. Quantitative Aspects: Objective Maps and Subjective Landscapes." *Journal of Information Science* 2: 269–75.

Brooks, H. M. 1987. "Expert Systems and Intelligent Information Retrieval." *Information Processing and Management* 23: 367–82.

Brooks, H. M., P. J. Daniels, and N. J. Belkin. 1986. "Research on Information Interaction and Intelligent Information Provision Mechanisms." *Journal of Information Science* 12: 37–44.

Brooks, T. A. 1986. "Private Acts and Public Motivations: An Investigation of Citer Motivations." *Journal of the American Society for Information Science* 36: 223–29.

Brooks, T. A. 1987. "Evidence of Complex Citer Motivations." *Journal of the American Society for Information Science* 37: 34–36.

Buckland, M. K. 1975. *Book Availability and the Library User.* New York: Pergamon.

Buckland, M. K. 1979. "Types of Search and the Allocation of Library Resources." *Journal of the American Society for Information Science* 30: 143–47.

Buckland, M. K. 1982. "Structure and Dynamics of Library Service." In R. Trappl et al., eds., *Progress in Cybernetics and Systems Research* 9:147–51. Washington, D.C.: Hemisphere Publishing Corp.

Buckland, M. K. 1983. "Relatedness, Relevance, and Responsiveness in Retrieval Systems." *Information Processing and Management* 18: 237–41.

Buckland, M. K. 1986. "Education for Librarianship in the Next Century." *Library Trends* 34: 777–87.

Buckland, M. K. 1987. "Combining Electronic Mail with Information Retrieval in a Library Context." *Information Technology and Libraries* 6: 266–71.

Buckland, M. K. 1988a. "Bibliography, Library Records, and the Redefinition of the Library Catalog." *Library Resources and Technical Services* 33:299–311.

Buckland, M. K. 1988b. "Library Materials: Paper, Microform, Database." *College and Research Libraries* 49: 117–22.

Buckland, M. K. 1988c. *Library Services in Theory and Context.* 2d ed. New York: Pergamon.

Buckland, M. K. 1989a. "Foundations of Academic Librarianship." *College and Research Libraries* 50: 389–96.

Buckland, M. K. 1989b. "The Roles of Collections and the Scope of Collection Development." *Journal of Documentation* 45: 213–26.

Buckland, M. K., and A. Hindle. 1976. "Acquisitions, Growth, and Performance Control through Systems Analysis." In *Farewell to Alexandria: Solutions to Space, Growth, and Performance Problems in Libraries*, ed. D. Gore, 44–61. Westport, Conn.: Greenwood Press.

Buckland, M. K., and C. A. Lynch. 1987. "The Linked Systems Protocol and the Future of Bibliographic Networks and Systems." *Information Technology and Libraries* 6: 83–88.

Buckland, M. K., and C. A. Lynch. 1988. "National and International Implications of the Linked Systems Protocol for Online Bibliographic Systems." *Cataloging and Classification Quarterly* 8: 15–33.

Bunge, M. 1967. *Scientific Research I: The Search for System.* Berlin: Springer.

Buzzard, J. H. et al. 1976. *Phipson on Evidence.* 12th ed. Common Law Library, 10. London: Sweet & Maxwell.

Campbell, D. J. 1988. "Task Complexity: A Review and Analysis." *Academy of Management Review* 13: 40–52.

Casey, M. 1981. *Charles McCarthy: Librarianship and Reform.* Chicago: American Library Association.

Chambers's Twentieth Century Dictionary. 1959. New ed. Edinburgh: Chambers.

Chan, L. M. 1981. *Cataloging and Classification: An Introduction.* New York: McGraw-Hill.

Chandler, A. D. 1977. *The Visible Hand: The Managerial Revolution in American Business.* Cambridge: Harvard University Press.

Christozov, D. G. 1990. Personal communication.

Clarke, D. S. 1987. *Principles of Semiotic.* London: Routledge & Kegan Paul.

Codrington, K. De B. 1944. "Museums and the Provision of Information." *British Society for International Bibliography, Proceedings* 6: 46–54.

Cooper, M. D. 1984. "Economies of Scale in Large Academic Libraries." *Library and Information Science Research* 6: 321–33.

Cooper, W. S. 1978. *Foundations of Logico-Logistics*. Dordrecht, Netherlands: Reidel.

Coyle, K., and L. Gallagher-Brown. 1985. "Record Matching: An Expert Algorithm." In *Proceedings of the 48th ASIS Meeting, October 1985, Las Vegas*, 77–80. Medford, N.J.: Learned Information.

Crowley, T., and T. Childers. 1971. *Information Services in Public Libraries: Two Studies*. Metuchen, N.J.: Scarecrow Press.

Culnan, M. J. 1984. "The Dimensions of Accessibility to Online Information: Implications for Implementing Office Information Systems." *ACM Transactions on Office Information Systems* 2: 141–50.

Culnan, M. J. 1985. "The Dimensions of Perceived Accessibility to Information." *Journal of the American Society for Information Science* 36: 302–8.

Daft, R. L. 1988. *Management*. Chicago: Dryden.

Daft, R. L., R. H. Lengel, and L. K. Trevino. 1987. "Message Equivocality, Media Selection, and Manager Performance: Implications for Information Systems." *MIS Quarterly* 11: 355–66.

Daniels, M. F., and T. Walch. 1984. *A Modern Archives Reader: Basic Readings on Archival Theory and Practice*. Washington, D.C.: National Archives and Records Service.

Davies, R., ed. 1986. *Intelligent Information Systems: Progress and Prospects*. Chichester, U.K.: Ellis Horwood.

Davis, G. B., and M. H. Olson. 1985. *Management Information Systems: Conceptual Foundations, Structure, and Development*. 2d ed. New York: McGraw-Hill.

Debons, A., E. Horne, and S. Cronenweth. 1988. *Information Science: An Integrated View*. Boston: G. K. Hall.

Dervin, B., and M. Nilan. 1986. "Information Needs and Users." *Annual Review of Information Science and Technology* 21: 3–33.

Dery, D. 1986. "Knowledge and Organizations." *Policy Studies Review* 6: 14–25.

Dictionary of Computing. 1986. 2d ed. Oxford: Oxford University Press.

Dreyfus, H. L., and S. E. Dreyfus. 1986. *Mind over Machine: The Power of Human Intuition and Expertise in the Era of the Computer*. New York: Free Press.

Duncan, E., and R. McAleese. 1987. "Intelligent Access to Databases Using a Thesaurus in Graphical Form." In *Online Information 87: Proceedings of the 11th International Online Information Meeting, London, 1987*, 377–87. Medford, N.J.: Learned Information.

Duranti, L. 1989. The Odyssey of Records Management. *ARMA Quarterly* 23, no. 3 (July): 3–11, and no. 4 (October): 3–11.

Eco, U. 1976. *A Theory of Semiotics*. Bloomington: Indiana University Press.

Encyclopaedia Britannica. 11th ed. 1910–1911; 15th ed. 1977.

Encyclopedia of Library and Information Science. 1968– . New York: Marcel Dekker.

Etzioni, A. 1964. *Modern Organizations*. Englewood Cliffs, N.J.: Prentice-Hall.

Euster, J. R. 1986. "Changing Views on Library Collections." *Library Issues* 6: 1–2.

Fairthorne, R. A. 1954. "The Theory of Communication." *Aslib Proceedings* 6: 255–67. Reprinted in Fairthorne, R. A. 1961. *Towards Information Retrieval*, 64–79. London: Butterworths.

Fairthorne, R. A. 1961. *Towards Information Retrieval*. London: Butterworths.

Fairthorne, R. A. 1967. "The Morphology of 'Information Flow.' " *Journal of the Association for Computing Machinery* 14: 710–19.

Festinger, L. 1957. *A Theory of Cognitive Dissonance*. Stanford: Stanford University Press.

Fine, S. F. 1986. "Technological Innovation, Diffusion and Resistance: An Historical Perspective." *Journal of Library Administration* 7: 83–108.

Florian, D. 1990. "Information retrieval Systeme: Eine systematische Analyze der Probleme und Prioritäten für zukunftsweisende Lösungskonzepte: Von Expertise bis Artificial Intelligence." Dissertation Dr. techn. Wiss. Technische Universität, Graz.

Forrester, T., ed. 1985. *The Information Technology Revolution*. Oxford: Blackwells.

Foskett, D. J. 1962. *The Creed of a Librarian—No Politics, No Religion, No Morals*. Reference, Special and Information Section, Northwestern Group, Occasional papers 3. London: Library Association.

Foster, L. W., and D. M. Flynn. 1985. "Management Information Technology: Its Effects on Organization and Function." *MIS Quarterly* 8: 229–35.

Fox, C. J. 1983. *Information and Misinformation: An Investigation of the Notions of Information and Misinformation, Informing and Misinforming*. Westport, Conn.: Greenwood.

Fugman, R. 1985. "The Five-Axiom Theory of Indexing and Information Supply." *Journal of the American Society for Information Science* 36: 116–29.

Gebhardt, F. 1985. "Querverbindungen zwischen Information Retrieval and Experten Systemen." *Nachrichten für Dokumentation* 36: 255–63.

Gesta Grayorum. 1968. Edited by D. Bland. Liverpool: Liverpool University Press.

Getz, M. 1980. *Public Libraries: An Economic View*. Baltimore: Johns Hopkins Press.

Göth, G. 1861. *Das Joanneum in Gratz*. Graz, Austria: Leykam.

Greenwald, A. G., and D. L. Ronis. 1978. "Twenty Years of Cognitive Dissonance: Case Study of the Evolution of a Theory." *Psychological Review* 85: 53–57.

Hafter, R. 1979. "Types of Search by Type of Library." *Information Processing and Management* 15: 261–64.

Hagler, R., and P. Simmons. 1982. *The Bibliographic Record and Information Technology*. Chicago: American Library Association.

Harris, I. W. 1966. "The Influence of Perceived Accessibility on Academic Library Use." Ph.D. diss., Rutgers University. (University Microfilms 67–5262.)

Hasenfeld, Y. 1983. *Human Service Organizations*. Englewood Cliffs, N.J.: Prentice-Hall.

Hausrath, D. C. 1981. "United States International Communication Agency." In *Encyclopedia of Library and Information Science*, 32: 70–112. New York: Marcel Dekker.

Heilprin, L. 1974. "Operational Definitions." In NATO Advanced Study Institute in Information Science, Champion, 1972, *Information Science: Search for Identity*. Ed. A. Debons. New York: Marcel Dekker.

Heilprin, L. B. 1989. "Foundations of Information Science Reexamined." *Annual Review of Information Science and Technology* 24: 343–72.

Hennessy, J. A. 1981. "Myths and Alibis: Political Information in Libraries." *Assistant Librarian* 74: 126–28.

Hertzel, D. H. 1987. "Bibliometrics, History of the Development of Ideas." In *Encyclopedia of Library and Information Science* 42: 144–214. New York: Marcel Dekker.

Hirsch, E. D. 1987. *Cultural Literacy: What Every American Needs to Know*. Boston: Houghton Mifflin.

Hirschheim, R. A. 1985. *Office Automation: A Social and Organizational Perspective.* Chichester, U.K.: Wiley.

Hirschman, A. O. 1970. *Exit, Voice, and Loyalty: Responses to Decline in Firms, Organizations, and States.* Cambridge: Harvard University Press.

Hoffmann, H. 1973. "Ein unpolitische Historisches Museum wäre ein Selbstwiderspruch." *Frankfurter Rundschau,* June 30, viii.

Hollnagel, E. 1987. "Cognitive Models, Cognitive Tasks, and Information Retrieval." In *Knowledge Engineering: Expert Systems and Information Retrieval,* ed. I. Wormell, 34–52. London: Taylor Graham.

Holt, R. M., ed. 1976. *An Architectural Strategy for Change: Remodelling and Expanding for Contemporary Library Needs. Proceedings of the Library Architecture Preconference Institute, New York, 4–6, July 1974.* Chicago: American Library Association.

Horton, F. W. 1979. *Information Resources Management.* Cleveland: Association for Systems Management.

Houser, L., and A. M. Schrader. 1978. *The Search for a Scientific Profession: Library Science Education in the U.S. and Canada.* Metuchen, N.J. Scarecrow Press.

Hutchins, W. J. 1975. *Languages of Indexing and Classification: A Linguistic Study of Structures and Functions.* Stevenage, England: Peter Peregrinus.

Hyman, R. J. 1982. *Shelf Access in Libraries.* Chicago: American Library Association.

Impey, O., and A. MacGregor, eds. 1985. *The Origins of Museums: The Cabinets of Curiosities in Sixteenth- and Seventeenth-Century Europe.* Oxford: Clarendon Press.

Ingwersen, P. 1984. "A Cognitive View of Three Selected Online Search Facilities." *Online Review* 8:465–92.

International Federation of Library Associations. 1963. *International Conference on Cataloging Principles, Paris, 1961.* London: Organizing Committee of the International Conference on Cataloguing Principles.

Jahoda, G. 1977. *The Process of Answering Reference Questions: A Test of a Descriptive Model.* Tallahassee: Florida State University, School of Library Science.

Jenkinson, H. 1948. *The English Archivist: A New Profession.* London: H. K. Lewis.

Johnson, W. E. 1932. "Protection and Profits through Photography." *Bankers Magazine* 123: 537–40.

Kantor, P. B. 1976. "Availability Analysis." *Journal of the American Society for Information Science* 27:311–19.

Karig, W., and E. Purdon. 1947. *Battle Report: Pacific War: Middle Phase.* New York: Rinehart.

Kelly, J. F. 1978. "Command Authority and Professionalism." *United States Naval Institute: Proceedings* 104, no. 8 (August): 26–32.

Kesner, R. M. 1988. *Information Systems: A Strategic Approach to Planning and Implementation.* Chicago: American Library Association.

Kilgour, F. G. 1978. "The Impact of Technology on Libraries." In *The Information Society: Issues and Answers,* ed. E. J. Josey, 12–19. Phoenix: Oryx Press. Reprinted in Kilgour, F. G. 1984. *Collected Papers of Frederick G. Kilgour: OCLC Years,* 393–97. Dublin, Ohio: OCLC.

Kilgour, F. G. 1985. *Beyond Bibliography.* London: British Library.

Knight, K. E., and R. R. McDaniel, 1979. *Organizations: An Information Systems Perspective.* Belmont, Calif.: Wadsworth.

Kochen, M., and K. W. Deutsch. 1980. *Decentralization: Sketches toward a Rational Theory.* Cambridge, Mass.: Gunn & Hain.

Koontz, H., C. O'Donnell, and H. Weihrich. 1984. *Management.* 8th ed. New York: McGraw-Hill.

Laisiepen, K., E. Lutterbeck, and K.-H. Meyer-Uhlenried. 1980. *Grundlagen der praktischen Information und Dokumentation: Eine Einführung.* 2. Aufl. München: Saur.

Lancaster, F. W. 1977. *The Measurement and Evaluation of Library Services.* Washington, D.C.: Information Resources Press.

Lawrence, G. S. 1981. "A Cost Model for Storage and Weeding Problems." *College and Research Libraries* 42:139–47.

Levy, F., A. J. Meltsner, and A. Wildavsky. 1974. *Urban Outcomes: Schools, Streets, and Libraries.* Berkeley: University of California Press.

Lexikon des Bibliothekswesens. Herausg. von H. Kunze und G. Rückl. 2. Aufl. Leipzig: VEB Bibliographisches Institut.

Library Trends. 1986. Issue on Privacy, Secrecy, and National Information Policy. 35, no. 1:3–183.

Light, R. B., D. A. Roberts, and J. D. Stewart, eds. 1986. *Museum Documentation Systems: Developments and Applications.* London: Butterworths.

Line, M. B. 1975. "Draft Definitions: Information and Library Needs, Wants, Demands, and Users." *Aslib Proceedings* 26:87.

Longley, D., and M. Shain. 1989. *Van Nostrand Reinhold Dictionary of Information Technology.* 3d ed. New York: Van Nostrand Reinhold.

Lynch, C. A., and C. M. Preston. 1990. "Internet Access to Information Resources." *Annual Review of Information Science and Technology* 25:263–312.

Lytle, R. H. 1986. "Information Resource Management: 1981–1986. *Annual Review of Information Science and Technology* 21:309–36.

McDonald, J. A. 1987. "Academic Library Effectiveness: An Organizational Perspective." Ph.D. dissertation, Drexel University. (University Microfilms 8806515)

Machlup, F. 1980. *Knowledge and Knowledge Production.* Princeton, N.J.: Princeton University Press.

Machlup, F. 1983. "Semantic Quirks in Studies of Information." In *The Study of Information: Interdisciplinary Messages*, ed. F. Machlup and U. Mansfield, 641–71. New York: Wiley.

Machlup, F., and U. Mansfield, eds. 1983. *The Study of Information: Interdisciplinary Voices.* New York: Wiley.

McPhee, R. D. 1985. "Formal Structure and Organizational Communication." In *Organizational Communication: Traditional Themes and New Directions*, ed. R. D. McPhee and P. K. Tompkins, 149–77. Sage Annual Reviews of Communications Research, 13. Beverly Hills, Calif.: Sage Publications.

McPhee, R. D., and P. K. Tompkins, eds. 1985. *Organizational Communication: Traditional Themes and New Directions.* Sage Annual Reviews of Communications Research, 13. Beverly Hills, Calif.: Sage Publications.

Maedke, W. O., M. F. Robek, and G. F. Brown 1981. *Information and Records Management.* 2d ed. Encino, Calif.: Glencoe.

Markey, K. 1981. "Levels of Question Formulation in Negotiation of Information Need during the Online Presearch Interview: A Proposed Model." *Information Processing and Management* 17:212–25.

Markey, K. 1984. "Interindexer Consistency Tests: A Literature Review and Report of a Test of Consistency in Indexing Visual Materials." *Library and Information Science Research* 6:155–77.

Markus, M. L. 1984. *Systems in Organizations: Bugs + Features.* Boston: Pitman.

Maroevic, I. 1983. "The Museum Item—Source and Carrier of Information." *Informatologia Yugoslavica* 15:237–48.

Maroevic, I. 1986. "Museum Object as a Link between Museology and Fundamental Scientific Discipline." *Informatologica Yugoslavica* 18:27–33.

Meadows, A. J., et al. 1987. *Dictionary of Computing and New Information Technology.* 3d ed. London: Koogan Page.

Medawar, P. B. 1967. *The Art of the Soluble.* London: Methuen.

Meijer, J. G. 1982. *Librarianship: A Definition.* Occasional Paper 155. Urbana: University of Illinois, Graduate School of Library and Information Science.

Meyer, K. E. 1979. *The Art Museum: Power, Money, Ethics.* New York: William Morrow.

Mick, C. K. 1979. "Cost Analysis of Information Systems and Services." *Annual Review of Information Science and Technology* 14:37–64.

Mills, J. F., and J. M. Mansfield. 1979. *The Genuine Article.* London: British Broadcasting Corporation.

Minsky, M. 1963. "Steps toward Artificial Intelligence." In *Computers and Thought*, ed. E. A. Feigenbaum and J. Feldman, 406–50. New York: McGraw-Hill.

Mintzberg, H. 1990. "The Manager's Job: Folklore and Fact." *Harvard Business Review* 68:163–76.

Mooers, C. 1951. "Information Retrieval Viewed as Temporal Signalling." In *International Congress of Mathematicians. Cambridge, Mass., 1950. Proceedings*, 1:572–73. Providence, R.I.: American Mathematical Society.

Morris, A., and M. O. Neill. 1988. "Information Professionals: Roles in the Design and Development of Expert Systems." *Information Processing and Management* 24:173–81.

Morrison, J. H. 1982. *Wave to Whisper: British Military Communications in Halifax and the Empire, 1790–1880.* History and Archaeology, 64. Quebec: Canadian Government Publishing Centre.

Narin, F., and J. K. Moll. 1977. "Bibliometrics." *Annual Review of Information Science and Technology* 12:35–58.

Nass, C., and L. Mason. 1990. "On the Study of Technology and Task: A Variable-Based Approach." In *Organizations and Communication Technology*, ed. J. Fulk and C. Steinfield, 46–67. Newbury Park, Calif.: Sage Publications.

NATO Advanced Study Institute in Information Science, Aberystwyth, 1974. 1975. *Perspectives in Information Science*, ed. A. Debons and W. J. Cameron. Leyden, Netherlands: Noordhoff.

NATO Advanced Study Institute in Information Science, Champion, 1972. 1974. *Information Science: Search for Identity*, ed. A. Debons. New York: Marcel Dekker.

NATO Advanced Study Institute in Information Science, Crete, 1978. 1983. *Information Science in Action: Systems Design.* ed. A. Debons and A. G. Larson. Boston: Martinus Nijhoff.

Neff, R. K. 1985. "Merging Libraries and Computer Centers: Manifest Destiny or Manifestly Deranged." *EDUCOM Bulletin* 20:8–12, 16.

Neill, S. D. 1987. "The Dilemma of the Subjective in Information Organization and Retrieval." *Journal of Documentation* 43: 193–211.

Nicols, D., E. Smolensky, and T. N. Tidman. 1971. "Discrimination by Waiting Time in Merit Goods." *American Economic Review* 61:312–23.

Oddy, R. N. et al., eds. 1981. *Information Retrieval Research*. London: Butterworths.

Orna, E., and C. Pettit. 1980. *Information Handling Systems in Museums*. New York: Saur.

Orr, R. M. 1973. "Measuring the Goodness of Library Services: A General Framework for Considering Quantitative Measures." *Journal of Documentation* 29:315–32.

Otlet, P. 1934. *Traité de documentation*. Brussels: Editiones Mundaneum. Repr. 1989: Liège: Centre de Lecture Publique de la Communauté Française.

Ottaway, B. S., ed. 1983. *Archaeology, Dendrochronology, and the Radiocarbon Calibrating Curve*. Edinburgh: Edinburgh University, Department of Archaeology.

Otten, K. W. 1975. "Information and Communication: A Conceptual Model as Framework for Development of Theories of Information." In NATO Advanced Study Institute on Perspectives in Information Science, Aberystwyth, 1973. 1975. *Proceedings. Perspectives in Information Science*, ed. A. Debons and W. J. Cameron, 127–48. Leyden, Netherlands: Noordhoff.

Oxford English Dictionary. 1989. 2d ed. Oxford: Clarendon Press.

Palmer, E. S. 1981. "The Effect of Distance on Public Library Use: A Literature Survey." *Library Research* 3:315–54.

Pao, M. L., and D. B. Worthen. 1989. "Retrieval Effectiveness by Semantic and Citation Searching." *Journal of the American Society for Information Science* 40:226–35.

Pederson, A., ed. 1987. *Keeping Archives*. Sydney: Australian Society of Archivists.

Pemberton, J. M., and A. Prentice. 1990. *Information Science: The Interdisciplinary Context*. New York: Neal-Schuman.

Pfeffer, J., and H. Leblebici. 1977. "Information Technology and Organizational Structure." *Pacific Sociological Review* 20:241–61.

Pfeffer, J., and G. R. Salancik. 1978. *The External Control of Organizations*. New York: Harper & Row.

Pieptea, D., and E. Anderson. 1987. "Price and Value of Decision Support Systems." *MIS Quarterly* 11:514–28.

Pollard, A.F.C. 1944. *British Society for International Bibliography Proceedings* 6:54.

Pratt, A. D. 1982. *The Information of the Image*. Norwood, N.J.: Ablex.

Price, P. P., ed. 1982. *International Book and Library Activities: The History of a U.S. Foreign Policy*. Metuchen, N.J.: Scarecrow Press.

Quint, B. 1987. "Journal Article Coverage in Online Library Catalogs: Next Stage for Online Databases? *Online* 11:87–90.

Ravetz, J. R. 1971. *Scientific Knowledge and Its Social Problems*. Oxford: Oxford University Press.

Reingold, H. 1985. *Tools for Thought: The People and Ideas behind the Next Computer Revolution*. New York: Simon & Schuster.

Ricks, B. R., and K. F. Gow. 1984. *Information Resource Management*. Cincinnati: South-Western Publishing.

Roberts, N. 1975. "Draft Definitions: Information and Library Needs, Wants, Demands and Users: A Comment." *Aslib Proceedings* 27:308–13.

Roberts, S. A. 1985. *Cost Management of Library and Information Services*. London: Butterworths.

Rogalla von Bieberstein, J. 1975. *Archiv, Bibliothek und Museum als Dokumentationsbereiche: Einheit und gegenseitige Abgrenzung.* Pullach bei München: Verlag Dokumentation.

Rogers, A. R. 1984. "An Introduction to the Philosophies of Librarianship." In *The Library in Society*, ed. A. R. Rogers, 17–32. Littleton, Colo.: Libraries Unlimited.

Rosenberg, V. 1967. "Factors Affecting the Preferences of Industrial Personnel for Information Gathering Methods." *Information Storage and Retrieval* 3:119–27.

Rowley, J. E. 1987. *Organizing Knowledge: An Introduction to Information Retrieval.* Aldershot, England: Gower.

Russell, B. 1948. *Human Knowledge: Its Scope and Limits.* New York: Simon & Schuster.

Sadie. S., ed. 1980. *The New Grove Dictionary of Music and Musicians.* London: Macmillan.

Sagredo, F., and J. M. Izquierdo. 1983. *Concepción lógico-lingüístico de la Documentación.* Madrid: Ibercom—Red Comnet de la Unesco.

Salmon, S. R. 1975. *Library Automation Systems.* New York: Dekker.

Salton, G., and M. J. McGill. 1983. *Introduction to Modern Information Retrieval.* New York: McGraw-Hill.

Schlebecker, J. T. 1977. "The Use of Objects in Historical Research." *Agricultural History* 51:200–208.

Schön, D. A. 1983. *The Reflective Practitioner: How Professionals Think in Action.* New York: Basic Books.

Schrader, A. 1984. "In Search of a Name: Information Science and Its Conceptual Antecedents." *Library and Information Science Research* 6:227–71.

Schreiner, K. 1985. *Fundamentals of Museology: On the Theory and Methodology of Collecting, Preserving, Decoding, and Utilizing Musealia.* Waren, GDR: n.p.

Schrettinger, M. 1829. *Versuch eines vollständigen Lehrbuchs des Bibliothekswissenschaft oder Anleitung zur vollkommenen Geschäftsführing eines Bibliothekars.* Munich: Lindauer.

Schuller, A. L. 1982. *Erzherzog Johann . . . und was von ihm blieb . . .* Graz, Austria: Kulturreferat der Steiermärkischen Landesregierung.

Schwuchow, W. 1973. "Fundamental Aspects of the Financing of Information Centres." *Information Storage and Retrieval* 9:569–75.

Seals, R. A. 1986. "Academic Branch Libraries." *Advances in Librarianship* 14:175–209.

Sebeok, T. A., ed. 1986. *Encyclopedic Dictionary of Semiotics.* Berlin: Mouton de Gruyter.

Sharma, R. S. 1987. "Some Thoughts on Intelligence in Information Retrieval." In *National Computer Conference, 1987*, 601–7. AFIPS Conference Proceedings, 56. Reston, Va.: AFIPS Press.

Shaw, W., and P. B. Culkin. 1987. "Systems That Inform: Emerging Trends in Library Automation and Network Development." *Annual Review of Information Science and Technology* 22:265–92.

Shera, J. H. 1972. *The Foundations of Education for Librarianship.* New York: Becker and Hayes.

Shera, J. H. 1983. "Librarianship and Information Science." In *The Study of Information: Interdisciplinary Messages*, ed. F. Machlup and U. Mansfield, 379–88. New York: Wiley.

Sherman, D. J. 1989. *Worthy Monuments: Art Museums and the Politics of Culture in Nineteenth-Century France*. Cambridge: Harvard University Press.

Smith, A. 1976. *An Inquiry into the Nature and Causes of the Wealth of Nations*. Oxford: Clarendon Press.

Smith, L. 1987. "Artificial Intelligence." *Annual Review of Information Science and Technology* 22:41–77.

Smith, M. D. 1986. *Information and Records Management*. New York: Quorum.

Sparck Jones, K., ed. 1981. *Information Retrieval Experiment*. London: Butterworths.

Sparck Jones, K. 1983. "Intelligent Retrieval." In *Informatics 7: Intelligent Information Retrieval*, ed. K. Jones, 136–42. London: Aslib.

Sprague, R. H., and B. C. McNurlin, eds. 1986. *Information Systems Management in Practice*. Englewood Cliffs, N.J.: Prentice Hall.

Stephens, O. 1955. *Facts to a Candid World: America's Overseas Information Program*. Stanford: Stanford University Press.

Swanson, D. R. 1988. "Information Retrieval and the Future of an Illusion." *Journal of the American Society for Information Science* 39:92–98.

Swanson, E. B. 1987. "Information Channel Disposition and Use." *Decision Sciences* 18:131–45.

Swigger, B. K. 1985. "Questions in Library and Information Science." *Library and Information Science Research* 7:369–83.

Taylor, R. S. 1986. *Value-Added Processes in Information Systems*. Norwood, N.J.: Ablex.

Tompkins, P. K., and G. Cheney. 1985. "Communications and Unobtrusive Control in Contemporary Organizations." In *Organizational Communication: The Traditional Themes and New Directions*, ed. R. D. McPhee and P. K. Tompkins, 179–210. Sage Annual Reviews of Communications Research, 13. Beverly Hills, Calif.: Sage Publications.

Toulmin, S. 1972. *Human Understanding*. Oxford: Clarendon Press.

Tushman, M., and D. Nadler. 1978. "Information Processing as an Integrating Concept in Organizational Design." *Academy of Management Review* 3:613–24.

U.S. Congress. Office of Technology Assessment. 1986. *Intellectual Property Rights in the Age of Electronics and Information*. OTA-CIT–302. Washington, D.C.: U.S. Government Printing Office.

Van House, N. 1983a. *Public Library User Fees: The Use and Finance of Public Libraries*. Westport, Conn.: Greenwood.

Van House, N. 1983b. "Time Allocation Theory of Public Library Use." *Library and Information Science Research* 5:365–84.

Van House, N. 1986. "Public Library Effectiveness: Theory, Measures, and Determinants." *Library and Information Research* 8:261–83.

van Rijsbergen, C. R. 1979. *Information Retrieval*. 2d ed. London: Butterworths.

Vervest, P. 1985. *Electronic Mail and Message Handling*. Westport, Conn.: Quorum Books.

Vickery, A., and H. Brooks. 1987. "Expert Systems and Their Application in LIS." *Online Review* 11:149–65.

Vickery, B. C., and A. Vickery. 1987. *Information Science in Theory and Practice*. London: Butterworths.

Walker, D. E. 1981. "The Organization and the Use of Information Science, Computational Linguistics and Artificial Intelligence.'' *Journal of the American Society for Information Science* 32:347–63.

Waples, D., et al. 1940. *What Reading Does to People*. Chicago: University of Chicago Press.

Washburn, W. E. 1964. ''Manuscripts and Manufacts.'' *American Archivist* 27:245–50.

Webster's Third New International Dictionary of the English Language Unabridged. 1971. Springfield, Mass.: Merriam.

Wellisch, H. 1972. ''From Information Science to Informatics.'' *Journal of Librarianship* 4:157–87.

Wersig, G. 1979. ''The Problematic Situation as a Basic Concept of Information Science in the Framework of the Social Sciences: A Reply to Belkin.'' In International Federation for Documentation, *Theoretical Problems of Informatics: New Trends in Informatics and its Terminology*, 48–57. FID 568. Moscow: VINITI.

Wersig, G. 1980. ''Informationstätigkeit.'' In *Grundlagen der praktischen Information und Dokumentation: Eine Einführung*, K. Laisiepen et al., 2. Aufl. 161–92. Munich: Saur.

Wersig, G., and U. Neveling. 1975. ''The Phenomena of Interest to Information Science.'' *Information Scientist* 9:127–40.

Wiener, N. 1961. *Cybernetics: or, Control and Communication and Control in the Animal and the Machine*. 2d ed. Cambridge: MIT Press.

Wigmore, J. H. 1983. *Evidence in Trials at Common Law*. Vol. 1, rev. P. Tillers. Boston: Little, Brown.

Wilson, P. G. 1968. *Two Kinds of Power: An Essay on Bibliographical Control*. Berkeley: University of California Press.

Wilson, P. G. 1973. ''Situational Relevance.'' *Information Processing and Management* 9:457–71.

Wilson, P. G. 1977. *Public Knowledge, Private Ignorance: Toward a Library and Information Policy*. Westport, Conn.: Greenwood.

Wilson, P. G. 1983. *Second-hand Knowledge: An Inquiry into Cognitive Authority*. Westport, Conn.: Greenwood Press.

Wilson, P. G. 1986. ''Bibliographical R&D.'' In *The Study of Information: Interdisciplinary Messages*, ed. F. Machlup and U. Mansfield, 389–97. New York: Wiley.

Wilson, T. D. 1981. ''On User Studies and Information Needs.'' *Journal of Documentation* 37:3–15.

Winter, M. F. 1988. *The Culture and Control of Expertise: Toward a Sociological Understanding of Librarianship*. Westport, Conn.: Greenwood Press.

Wormell, I., ed. 1987. *Knowledge Engineering: Expert Systems and Information Retrieval*. London: Taylor Graham.

Wright, D. W. 1983. ''Idealized Structures in Museums of General Technology.'' *Museums Journal* 83:111–19.

Wright, H. C. 1988. *Jesse Shera, Librarianship, and Information Science*. Provo, Utah: Brigham Young University, School of Library and Information Sciences.

Wynar, B. S. 1985. *Introduction to Cataloging and Classification*. 7th ed. Ed. A. Taylor. Littleton, Colo.: Libraries Unlimited.

Yokoi, T. 1989. ''Giving Priority to 'Information-oriented Technology' over 'Computer-oriented Technology.' '' *New Generation Computing* 6:359–60.

Zhang Yuexiao. 1988. ''Definitions and Sciences of Information.'' *Information Processing and Management* 24:479–91.

Zipf, G. K. 1965. *Human Behavior and the Principle of Least Effort*. New York: Hafner.

Index

About the Author

MICHAEL BUCKLAND is Professor, School of Library and Information Science, University of California, Berkeley. He is the author of *Library Services in Theory and Context*.